Architecture and
the Arts and Crafts Movement
in Boston

ARCHITECTURE·AND THE·ARTS·AND·CRAFTS MOVEMENT·IN·BOSTON

Harvard's H. Langford Warren

MAUREEN MEISTER

University Press of New England

Hanover and London

For David, Peter, and Stephen:
builders all

University Press of New England,

37 Lafayette St., Lebanon, NH 03766

© 2003 by Maureen Meister

Printed in the United States of America

5 4 3 2 1

Library of Congress Cataloging-in-Publication Data

Meister, Maureen.
  Architecture and the Arts and Crafts movement in Boston : Harvard's H.
Langford Warren / Maureen Meister.—1st ed.
     p. cm.
Includes bibliographical references and index.
  ISBN 1-58465-351-5 (cloth : alk. paper)
  1. Warren, Herbert Langford, 1857-1917. 2.
Architects—Massachusetts—Biography. 3. College
teachers—Massachusetts—Biography 4. Arts and Crafts
movement—Massachusetts—Boston—History—20th century. I. Title.
NA737.W35M45 2003
  720'.92—dc22   2003015320

Photographs without credits are by the author.

Contents

Illustrations

Preface

Over the course of the past twenty years, I have taken pleasure in the quiet Yankee sort of beauty that characterizes many of the houses and public buildings in the town where I live: Winchester, Massachusetts, a suburb northwest of Boston. And for just about as long a time, I have puzzled over these buildings, investigating who designed them and establishing when they were erected and by whom. In the past few years, I have come to realize that many of the architects who enriched this small town with their work were connected in some way with Herbert Langford Warren, the architect whose career is the subject of this book.

Most important, Warren's junior partner, Frank Patterson Smith, lived in Winchester from 1895 until his death in 1943. Warren and Smith designed the Church of the Epiphany, begun in 1904, the Winchester Country Club, 1916, and a number of elegant houses. The church is Gothic Revival, inspired by English sources, while the country club is a reconstructed and expanded early-nineteenth-century farmhouse and barn.

Warren's colleagues and collaborators in his other endeavors also left their mark on Winchester. Warren was the founder of the architecture program at Harvard, and his first instructor of design, George F. Newton, contributed at least three significant buildings to Winchester's town center. Newton designed two English Gothic churches, the Winchester Unitarian Church, 1898, and the First Baptist Church, 1928, as well as the Wadleigh Grammar School, 1900, now demolished. Frederick Law Olmsted, Jr., hired by Warren to establish Harvard's landscape architecture program, worked with Warren and Smith in the planning and development of Winchester's Myopia Hill, beginning in 1901, and the

Olmsted firm worked independently on additional projects in the community. Then there was the man whom Warren hired to teach life drawing, Hermann Dudley Murphy. A successful artist, Murphy built a large home and studio on Highland Avenue, called Carrig-Rohane, where he not only painted but also established a nationally recognized picture frame-carving shop.

In addition to his professional practice and his work at Harvard, Warren was a founder and long-term president of the Society of Arts and Crafts, Boston. In this capacity, he collaborated with a number of leading Boston architects during the first two decades of the twentieth century. One of them was R. Clipston Sturgis, who succeeded Warren as president of the Society. Sturgis, too, was engaged to work in Winchester; he was architect of the Georgian Revival junior high school that the town built from 1931 to 1932.

Over time I've come to understand that these men were more than mere acquaintances, more than colleagues. Rather they shared a mission. Along with a number of other Boston architects, they were advocates for a certain type of design, a design that distinguishes much of the best work of the early twentieth century in the city and its environs. Furthermore, these men received commissions for major projects throughout New England and across the United States. What they promoted was an architecture that was grounded in an Arts and Crafts philosophy, a philosophy that they developed and refined to mesh with the region's tastes and traditions.

Thus I began my study with a narrow focus—on my town and on Warren—as I sought to make sense of the streetscapes where I live. While my exploration has gone far beyond the borders of Winchester, I have retained the focus on Warren, with the belief that his views provide a basis for understanding how Arts and Crafts ideas were applied to architecture in the Boston area. It is my hope that the outcome of this investigation will help us better understand the many handsome buildings from the turn of the last century that are to be found in the New England region and elsewhere in the United States, wherever the men in this circle of Boston architects were given an opportunity to see their vision take form.

Of all the people I wish to thank for their assistance with this book, I first want to acknowledge the generous descendants of Warren and Smith. Indeed, were it not for the early interest of Richard Smith Joslin of Cambridge, Massachusetts, a grandson of Frank Patterson Smith, the book would not have been written. Dick located the records and photographs that had been retained by a member of his family from the firm of Warren and Smith and has given me complete access to them. I have been equally fortunate in receiving ongoing assistance from one of Warren's descendants, Elizabeth Warren Stoutamire of Tallahassee, Florida, who inherited journals, letters, photographs, and works of art that had belonged to her grandfather. Another family member, Langford Warren of Kittery Point, Maine, also has contributed to this project by sharing a sketchbook with me.

When I considered how the subject of my research might become a topic of a doctoral dissertation, I was greatly encouraged by my conversations with the late William H. Jordy of Brown University. When I embarked on writing the dissertation that is the basis for this book, much real labor, time, and direction were contributed by Dietrich Neumann and Kermit S. Champa, both of Brown, and James F. O'Gorman of Wellesley College.

My colleagues have helped and cheered me along in a variety of ways. I would like to extend special thanks to Daniel Abramson, Tufts University; Beverly K. Brandt, Arizona State University; Thomas C. Hubka, University of Wisconsin-Milwaukee; Francis R. Kowsky, Buffalo State College; and Jeffrey Karl Ochsner, University of Washington.

In June of 2002, it was my privilege to present a paper on Warren as part of a conference titled "Sources and Inspiration: Boston as a Beacon for the American Arts and Crafts Movement." Sponsored by New York University's School of Continuing and Professional Studies, this treat for Arts and Crafts enthusiasts was a major endeavor that was organized by Lisa Koenigsberg and Bruce Smith.

For their insights and their time, I wish to thank Susan K. Anderson, Edward R. Bosley, Lorna Condon, Mary Daniels, Lance Kasparian, Roger G. Reed, Peter Shaver, Lars Wiberg, Charles Will, and Sally Zimmerman. Also to be thanked are the talented staffs of the Boston Public Library, Brookline Preservation Commission, Cambridge Historical Commission, Harvard University Archives, the Loeb Library at Harvard University, the Historical Society of Saratoga Springs, the Society for the Preservation of New England Antiquities, and the Winchester Public Library. Home owners, ministers, and other stewards of buildings that I have examined have been supportive and gracious in opening their doors to me.

In working with the University Press of New England, I have been tremendously grateful for the confidence and the organizational talent of Phyllis Deutsch, executive editor.

Finally I offer my thanks to my husband, David Feigenbaum, who has patiently responded to my requests for help with more than one computer, who has assisted with my photographic needs, and who has expressed continued faith in the value of my work.

M.M.

Architecture and
the Arts and Crafts Movement
in Boston

FIG. 1. Herbert Langford Warren (1857–1917). *Courtesy of Elizabeth Warren Stoutamire, Talla-hassee, Florida.*

INTRODUCTION

W HEN BOSTON ARCHITECT Herbert Langford Warren died in
1917, his colleague Ralph Adams Cram wrote in the *Boston Tran-script* that of the hundreds of architects in the city, few had not en-countered Warren at one point or another.[1] Warren had been well known
among architects, both in New England and nationally (fig. 1). At the
time of his death, he was dean of the School of Architecture at Harvard,
having taught there continuously since offering the first course in ar-chitecture in 1893, and he was president of the Society of Arts and
Crafts, Boston, having been a founder and leader of that organization
since its inception in 1897. He also served as the first president of the
National League of Handicraft Societies.

Through his work at Harvard and in the Arts and Crafts movement,
Warren played an influential role in articulating and promoting a partic-ular aesthetic—an aesthetic that was adopted by a generation of archi-tects who were working in Boston for clients across the country. These
architects built English Gothic churches and Colonial Revival town halls
and school buildings, now a century old, located throughout New En-gland and beyond. Guiding their aesthetic vision was an attachment to
the past that characterized Brahmin Boston and a broader Yankee pop-ulation.

The courses that Warren taught at Harvard reflected this reverence.
Students were exposed to major European monuments from antiquity
and forward through time, ultimately coming to understand how various
architectural traditions culminated in the buildings of England. Warren's
architectural history courses affirmed the view that English culture was
the basis of American culture, which he defined in terms of political and

social traditions. In the architectural design courses at Harvard, Warren and his colleagues presented this heritage to their students as a rationale for encouraging them to revive and reinterpret English and Anglo-American models.

Another characteristic of the aesthetic promoted by Warren and his circle was its attachment to the concept of "restraint," a quality that was generally attributed to the region's Puritan founders. When applied to architecture, "restraint" meant a rejection of the lavish ornamentation that was a hallmark of the designs fostered by the Ecole des Beaux-Arts in Paris. "Restraint" also meant a rejection of the more original styles such as Art Nouveau that were emerging at the turn of the twentieth century.

Warren and his architect-colleagues encouraged a close collaboration with craftsmen in order to enhance their buildings. Several of the architects, including Warren, had trained in the offices of Henry Hobson Richardson, who had worked with favorite artists and craftsmen in an incipient Arts and Crafts spirit. The young architects appreciated the beauty of handcrafted ornament, advocated by John Ruskin, William Morris, and later leaders in the English Arts and Crafts movement. Artisans were identified and trained so that they could provide the architects with tile, iron, and carved wood and stone. To promote craft production further, Warren and several fellow professionals played a significant part in establishing the Society of Arts and Crafts, which became one of the country's leading Arts and Crafts organizations. The architects who took leading roles in the Society, including Warren, Cram, and Alexander Wadsworth Longfellow, Jr., promoted a look that was commonly accepted and adopted by other Boston architects, including many who were not members. Some of the more successful firms, such as Cram's and Longfellow's, as well as Shepley, Rutan, and Coolidge, carried the Boston aesthetic and its distinctive Arts and Crafts outlook to the Midwest and the West Coast, to Florida and Texas. Typically the architects were hired for academic, civic, and religious commissions.

The building designs by the men in this circle represent an important contribution to the development of American Arts and Crafts architecture—a complement to the much better-known work of protomodern designers such as Frank Lloyd Wright or Greene and Greene. In fact, Arts and Crafts architecture in North America was extremely diverse and included relatively conservative responses to the ideas of Morris and other reformers. Warren's own buildings, integrally allied with his Arts and Crafts activities, illustrate this more conservative branch of Arts and Crafts architecture from the turn of the last century.

As it happens, the period when Warren was active professionally, from 1885 to 1917, corresponds to a period that is commonly treated as a chapter in the national story of American architecture. These years were defined by a new intensity of academic study by architects who turned to an ever expanding range of historical models for inspiration. Architects from the early to mid-nineteenth century already had applied themselves to working with forms derived from Greek, Roman, and Gothic monuments. During the middle of the century, architects began focusing on Renaissance Italy and Baroque France. By the last decades of the nineteenth century, the entire sweep of Western architectural history was contributing to the designs that American architects were producing. They turned to ancient, medieval, and Renaissance sources, from Italy, Germany, France, and England. An interest in the Arab world also emerged, while Japan was another locale that sometimes captured the imagination of designers. Modern historians who have considered America's stylistically varied architecture of the late nineteenth and early twentieth centuries have identified its "creative eclecticism" or "academic eclecticism," labels that have gained wide acceptance.[2]

The decades surrounding the turn of the twentieth century saw new building types emerge as well as new building materials. Most important was the development of the skyscraper, long identified with Chicago architects such as William Le Baron Jenney, designer of the Home Insurance Building, 1884–1885, but also embraced by builders and architects in New York City. Ernest Flagg's Singer Building, erected in New York City from 1906 to 1908, and Cass Gilbert's Woolworth Building, also in New York City, 1911–1913, were major monuments of the period. The train station, which emerged as another new building type during the nineteenth century, was built on a far grander scale in the early twentieth century. Especially notable were New York's Pennsylvania Station by McKim, Mead, and White, from 1902 to 1910, and Grand Central Terminal by Warren and Wetmore, from 1903 to 1913. In Boston, South Station was erected in 1899, designed by Shepley, Rutan, and Coolidge. The most important new building materials were steel and concrete. Dreams of structures that were taller and vaster in scale now became possible.

As the wealth of the upper and upper-middle classes grew, there were other developments in architecture, developments that were less grandiose yet noteworthy all the same. Suburbs grew. The period saw a proliferation of suburban houses, municipal and religious buildings. In some of the more exclusive communities, country clubs were organized and built. College and university campuses also benefited from the largesse of the newly wealthy. Houses, churches, college buildings—virtually all were designed for the ages, girded by the optimism of the Progressive Era. The buildings of the period were enhanced by expensive materials worked by a labor force of skilled tradesmen who produced an overall quality of construction that has never been matched to the same extent in this country.

Boston continued to be dominated socially, if not politically, by its Brahmin population. While the old families, English in their ancestry, eventually lost control of the city government to the Irish community, they still held their own in the city's cultural sphere. From Beacon Hill the Brahmin families moved into the Back Bay, where they erected the first Museum of Fine Arts building, designed by Sturgis and Brigham, from 1870 to 1879. Brahmin families constructed Trinity Church across the way on Copley Square, 1872–1877, by H. H. Richardson, followed by the Boston Public Library, across from Trinity, by McKim, Mead, and White, from 1888 to 1895. An inbred, stable population, this community also supported Harvard College, across the Charles River in Cambridge, in a relationship that dated to the seventeenth century.

Harvard in the 1870s had embarked upon a bold new direction. In 1869 an innovative young Charles W. Eliot became president, and through the rest of the century and into the next, he broadened the college's offerings, expanded its graduate programs, and transformed Harvard into a nationally recognized university. In 1871, Charles Herbert Moore started teaching art. Three years later, Charles Eliot Norton began teaching art history as a professor of fine arts, the first such appointment in the United States. Norton and Moore became vocal crusaders for a greater interest in aesthetics at Harvard, in Boston, and more broadly in American life.

Thus when Warren was asked to establish an architecture program at Harvard in 1893, he faced an institutional environment that was conservative in culture yet welcoming and supportive for a young man with ambition. The new architecture program at Harvard would not be important for being the first such program in the country. That distinction belonged to the Massachusetts Institute of Technology, which admitted its first architecture students in 1868. Instead the Harvard program became distinctive because of its association with the fine-arts courses taught by Norton and Moore. Both professors were close friends with Ruskin, and Warren was suitably sympathetic to a perspective that extolled the quality of the art of preindustrial times. When Warren took a leading role in establishing the Society of Arts and Crafts, Boston, he reinforced and extended the Ruskinian orientation of Harvard's architectural program. The new program soon became influential because of Harvard's role within Boston's elite. The program also benefited from President Eliot's success and Harvard's growing prominence in the United States. Warren, dynamic and outgoing, was able to advance his views and his program on a national level.

Warren's interests in architecture and design were very much a part of national trends, while they also reflected the particular interests of the Arts and Crafts movement that took root in Boston. Consistent with other American architects of the period, Warren was eclectic in drawing on historical models. But his preference for English and Anglo-American sources—not, for example, Rhineland castles or French châteaux—meant that he endorsed a narrower range of stylistic choices than was to be found more generally at the time. Warren's approach, shared by many architects in his circle, was supported by an Arts and Crafts ideology, expressed first in England, favoring allusions to sources that affirmed one's own cultural heritage.

The building types that Warren preferred were, by and large, antiurban, also reflecting an Arts and Crafts outlook. Small-town churches and suburban houses appealed to him. He was not interested in designs for skyscrapers, commercial buildings, or industrial buildings, and the Harvard students' assignments generally reflected his orientation. A dislike of commercial and industrial buildings was shared by a few of his architect-colleagues, most notably Cram. This sensibility was extreme, however, even in Warren's circle. On the other hand, skyscrapers were widely viewed negatively in the Boston community: between the 1890s and early 1900s, Boston and then Massachusetts passed a series of laws restricting the heights of new buildings.

As for new building materials, Warren distanced himself from the outlook of English Arts and Crafts theorists who identified iron and steel as destructive to modern society. Like most architects of the day, Warren welcomed the opportunity to explore new materials and methods of construction. He incorporated steel and concrete in his own projects, and he saw that Harvard students were trained to work with them.

Most important, like so many of his American colleagues of the period, Warren advocated building with fine materials and craftsmanship. But typically architects of the period sought out artisans in an independent way, while Warren and his architect-colleagues in Boston created an institutionalized approach to promote ongoing collaborative relationships between architects and skilled craftsmen. Fostering this formal collaboration between architect and craftsman became Warren's cause, complementing his work at Harvard and his private practice. Arguably the central figure in the Boston Arts and Crafts movement, Warren articulated an ideology that formed the basis for a distinctive academic approach to design that characterized the buildings that he and many of his fellow Boston architects erected from the 1890s through the teens and into the 1920s.

~ONE~

EARLY YEARS
(1857–1885)

REVERENCE FOR ENGLISH HISTORY and traditions was widely held in Boston at the turn of the twentieth century. Yankees, whose forebears had settled in the region during the colonial period, generally thought of English culture as the foundation of American culture. This was a view that was especially dear to Herbert Langford Warren, for his father was American and his mother was English. His father, Samuel Mills Warren (1822–1908), descended from what Herbert described as "an old Massachusetts family."[1] His family traced its origins to a Warren who had settled in the town of Weymouth by 1638.[2] The family's heritage was a point of pride, as were similar lineages to an entire generation of Yankees by the late nineteenth century, especially in and around Boston, when waves of immigrants were coming into the city. Samuel Mills Warren was a successful entrepreneur, having established a partnership with his brothers in a tar roofing business. While maintaining his interest in the company, he embraced the Swedenborgian faith and became a missionary in England, serving in Manchester and then London.

Soon after arriving in Manchester, he met Sarah Anne Broadfield (1827–1878), whom he married in 1855.[3] The Broadfields, of Bridgnorth, Shropshire, were people of comfortable means, who had made their money transporting cotton to cottage weavers.[4] Both the Warren and Broadfield families enjoyed the benefits of enterprise and seem to have instilled in Herbert a belief in the virtue of financial success. As an adult later, he would promote such an outlook while actively rejecting more socialistic concerns for the Society of Arts and Crafts, Boston.

Samuel Mills Warren's commitment to the Swedenborgian religion also shaped Herbert's views. Throughout his life, Herbert was a practicing Swedenborgian, and he designed two Swedenborgian church buildings. The religion is based on the extensive writings of Emanuel Swedenborg (1688–1772), a Protestant theologian who devoted his studies to interpreting the Bible's Old and New Testaments. While not founding a denomination, Swedenborg hoped to inspire a "New Church." By 1787, followers in London had organized the Church of the New Jerusalem, and in the early nineteenth century, Swedenborgians established parishes in the United States. Swedenborg believed that "the church is within man, and not without him." Swedenborgians emphasize the individual's role in determining the course of his life, and they charge the individual with the task of giving his life its spiritual meaning.[5] Consistent with this religious outlook, Warren taught history with an emphasis on the role of the individual; as a leader of Arts and Crafts organizations, he promoted handicraft as a product of individual expression.

Samuel and Sarah had four children who lived into adulthood. Herbert Langford was born in Manchester in 1857. A brother, Harold Broadfield (1859–1934), was born two years later. Herbert and Harold were especially close. Harold would later teach freehand drawing under Herbert in the architecture program at Harvard and would also participate with his older brother in the Boston Society of Architects.[6]

For the most part, Herbert was reared and educated in Manchester, but he also studied in Germany. Between 1869 and 1871, he spent two years attending the gymnasia of Gotha and Dresden. During this period, wrote James Sturgis Pray, Herbert's Harvard colleague, "he received such a thorough grounding in the German language that it was ever after nearly as familiar to him as his mother tongue."[7] Warren's fluency was unusual and admired in his milieu, although a basic familiarity with German was routine. Architecture students at Harvard were expected to read texts in German by prominent historians. Years later, Warren's appreciation for German culture and German architecture in particular would lead to his involvement in Harvard's construction of the Germanic Museum.

Warren continued his studies at Owens College in Manchester, now Manchester University, between 1871 and 1875.[8] He took courses in watercolor painting and drawing with William Walker, who had in turn studied under J. D. Harding, John Ruskin's teacher.[9] Warren also attended the University of London.[10]

In 1875 Warren began working as a draftsman for William Dawes, a Manchester architect who had distinguished himself in the competition for the Manchester Town Hall.[11] The project, however, was awarded to Alfred Waterhouse and was built between 1868 and 1877.[12] Dawes was successful in competitions for school buildings and churches, building types that Warren would later pursue.[13] During this period, the enthusiasm for Venetian Gothic designs was at its height, fueled by the writings of Ruskin, including *The Stones of Venice,* published between 1851 and 1853. The so-called Ruskinian buildings, marked by polychromy in stone and brick, were loose interpretations of Venetian Gothic sources and far less academic in approach than the Gothic Revival buildings that followed at the end of the century.

A New Home in Boston

After spending a year under Dawes, Warren moved to Boston, where his parents had relocated during the 1860s.[14] While living at the family home in Roxbury, Warren began taking classes at the Massachusetts Institute of Technology, which then was located in the recently filled Back Bay. He studied at MIT for two years, from 1877 to 1879.[15] The young architect would have regularly encountered the ensemble of new buildings located nearby on Copley Square. These included the Ruskinian Gothic Museum of Fine Arts building, erected between 1870 and 1879 and designed by John Hubbard Sturgis, another Anglo-American architect who had immigrated to Boston. Sturgis impressed the American architectural community with the museum's high quality of architectural embellishment, especially its elaborate terra-cotta decoration.[16] Across the square was the New Old South Church, 1872–1874, also Ruskinian Gothic, by Cummings and Sears. And between the two buildings was H. H. Richardson's Romanesque Trinity Church, 1872–1877, whose robust forms would establish a new direction for American architecture during the next decade. The churches, like the museum, were marked by the high caliber of their ornamental detail.

During this period, Warren kept a sketchbook that he filled with pencil drawings. Produced on trips made around Boston and during a summer excursion in 1878, they reflect Warren's personal concerns rather than academic exercises. Inscribed "H. Warren—M.I.T.—Hillside—Roxbury," the sketchbook reveals several significant interests that he would pursue in later years: in colonial and federal buildings, in nature studies, and in handcrafted architectural ornament.[17]

Traveling to western Massachusetts and then to New York, Warren visited some of the region's oldest residences. One drawing, labeled "Mr. Hovey's, Greenfield [Massachusetts]," represented a federal house, monumental and noble, yet also somewhat overgrown with vegetation, picturesque in effect (fig. 2). An appreciation for American colonial and federal architecture, especially of the period's houses, was taking hold among American architects during the 1870s. In 1874 Charles McKim published one of his photographs of a colonial building, and it was soon followed by studies of similar subjects drawn by Stanford White.[18] In 1877 Boston architect Robert Swain Peabody promoted this interest in an article in the *American Architect and Building News,* and one year later Arthur Little, also from Boston, published *Early New England Interiors.*[19] American architects regarded these buildings as emblems of preindustrial times and approached them with a nostalgia that was related to that of Ruskin for the Middle Ages.

Other pages of Warren's sketchbook were devoted to botanical studies and landscape sketches in a manner that would have been considered Ruskinian. Warren rendered drawings of buds, flowers, and leaves with a precision that Ruskin promoted in his call for "truth to nature." These images probably were an outgrowth of Warren's art training in Manchester. After moving to Boston, Warren also may have come into contact with the "Ruskinians," American artists who had formed the Association for the Advancement of Truth in Art during the 1860s. One of the group's members, Charles Herbert Moore, began teaching art at Harvard in 1871.[20] Warren's landscape drawings, suggesting color tonalities and atmospheric effects through gradations of gray, were similarly consistent with Ruskin's ideas and the vistas that the Ruskinians painted in watercolor. Throughout his life, Warren painted watercolor landscapes such as these, and he exhibited at least once with his brother Harold, Moore, and Denman Ross.[21] All of them would teach architectural students at Harvard, where they encouraged close observation from nature and, through abstraction, sought to develop their students' sensitivity to design.

None of Warren's sketches represented contemporary buildings—at least, they did not capture any contemporary buildings in their entirety, as elevations or in perspective. Yet Warren did pay close attention to the new buildings in the Back Bay, focusing on their ornament. Metalwork, including iron gates, hinges, and door knockers, were drawn and

FIG. 2. Warren, pencil drawing of "Mr. Hovey's," Greenfield, Massachusetts, 1878. *Courtesy of Langford Warren.*

shown with measurements. Carved stone column capitals and bases were rendered, measured, and shown in profile. The details in the sketchbook were drawn from the New Old South Church (fig. 3) and from Richardson's Brattle Square Church, dating from 1869 to 1873. An interest in handcrafted ornament emerged in Boston during the 1870s, as exemplified by all three monuments on Copley Square, and commitment to it among both architects and artisans—including Warren—would build through the next decade and culminate in the organization of the Society of Arts and Crafts during the 1890s.

The 1878 sketchbook also provides evidence of Warren's awareness of Richardson's work. In addition to drawing details from the Brattle Square Church, in April Warren traveled to Woburn, Massachusetts, where he sketched a study of the roof tiles at Richardson's new Winn Memorial Library. The library was still under construction and would be completed that fall.[22] It seems likely that Warren also paid attention to Richardson's Trinity Church, consecrated in 1877. Years later, he would call it the architect's "masterpiece."[23] Nevertheless, the sketchbook indicates that in 1878, Warren had not focused on the robust, Richardsonian qualities of these buildings.

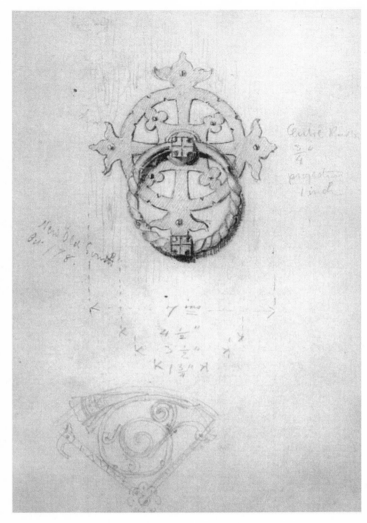

FIG. 3. Warren, pencil drawing of door pull from New Old South Church, Boston, 1878. *Courtesy of Langford Warren.*

Hired by Richardson

At the same time, Warren evidently found much to admire in Richardson's approach. He was hired by Richardson in 1879 and spent five years with him at his office in Brookline, a suburb of Boston. Warren, wrote Pray, "stood close to Richardson, and Richardson is known to have had a high opinion of his qualities."[24] The architect Charles A. Coolidge met Warren upon joining the firm. Warren, Coolidge later recalled, "had a private room at the end of the office and he took me in to work under him and with him."[25]

From a variety of sources, we can identify some of the firm's projects with which Warren was involved. Pray wrote that Warren worked on the Oakes Ames Memorial Hall at North Easton, Massachusetts, the Auburndale Station on the Boston and Albany Railroad, and Austin Hall for the Law School at Harvard University.[26] Warren also left his initials on a few of the firm's drawings, now at Harvard's Houghton Library, although most of the office drawings were not initialed, signed, or dated by anyone. Warren's initials appear on sketches for a lighthouse at Castle Hill, Newport, Rhode Island (built to a reduced design after Richardson's death); a house for Oliver Ames in Boston (unexecuted); and a working drawing for Albany City Hall.[27] In a diary, Warren referred to his involvement with the New York State Capitol, also in Albany.[28] Letters written by one of Warren's office colleagues, Alexander Wadsworth Longfellow, Jr., alluded to projects that the men worked on together. They were responsible for the drawings for the remodeled Ames Store on Washington Street, Boston, and the Ames Wholesale Store on Bedford and Kingston Streets, Boston.[29] In another letter, Longfellow observed that he and Warren were "rather riled" when Richardson gave Coolidge the honor of producing a sketch for the Malden library.[30]

What Warren had derived from his five years of work under Richardson would become apparent when he established his independent architectural practice and began designing buildings of his own. Taking the master-apprentice relationship from another perspective, one might also imagine how the men who worked for Richardson contributed to Richardson's buildings.[31] As Richardson's chief draftsman, Warren provided organizational talent in managing office projects. His familiarity with contemporary English architecture, marked by a picturesque emphasis, may have reinforced those tendencies in the firm's designs. And Warren's almost obsessive interest in architectural ornamentation, documented by the 1878 sketchbook and by his later work, clearly found expression in Richardson's buildings. The drawings for Harvard's Austin Hall, for example, show many details for decorative metalwork, including a series of renderings for andirons.[32] Whether by Warren or another architect, they reveal the extreme level of involvement that Richardson and his staff devoted to finishing and furnishing their buildings.

Warren wrote about Richardson on a number of occasions, both at the time of Richardson's death in 1886 and in later years. His admiration for Richardson's work never flagged, although his evaluation of Richardson's contribution changed. During the 1880s, what appealed to Warren was Richardson's ability to address new architectural problems. In an obituary published in the *New York Star,* signed "L.H.W." and generally recognized as Warren, he wrote, "When any new architectural problem was presented to him, he solved it for once and for all." Warren praised Richardson's solutions for libraries, as with the Winn Library in Woburn, and for office buildings, as with the Cheney building in Hartford and the Ames building on Bedford and Kingston Streets in Boston.[33] He assessed Richardson with an adulation that might be expected in an obituary, especially one written by a former employee.

At the time of Richardson's death, Warren was handling the architectural coverage for the *Sanitary Engineer,* a weekly trade journal.[34] A tribute to Richardson observed that he "succeeded in doing what others failed to accomplish thirty years ago—that is, adopting the Romanesque, and adapting it to modern uses, developing it from the point where its development was arrested in the twelfth century."[35] The idea that an earlier, unfinished architectural style could be revived and grow in modern designs was widely supported in the late nineteenth century and was reiterated by the architect Ralph Adams Cram, although at the end of the century, he and others were interested in developing Gothic.[36]

Years later, in *Picturesque and Architectural New England,* published in 1899, Warren still praised Richardson, but he now qualified his views. He described Richardson as "the most vigorous personality which American architecture has produced," and he restated his admiration for Richardson's ability to establish solutions for commercial and library buildings.[37] By this time, however, when neoclassical and Gothic Revival styles had virtually displaced the Romanesque, he observed that Richardson's influence on architecture had been transient. While expressing only admiration for his former employer's work, Warren condemned the "ignorant travesties of his manner" that were produced by so many of Richardson's contemporaries.[38] If Richardson's interpretation of Romanesque forms could not be developed successfully by others, it was Richardson's ability to mine the past for solutions to modern building problems that Warren saw as his legacy. At the turn of the century, this ambivalent view toward Richardson had become widespread. In 1901, Cram praised Richardson for his vitality and sincerity but disparaged the "shocking barbarism" that he inspired.[39]

Richardson's Library and Richardson's Men

Working in Richardson's office influenced Warren in other ways: Richardson's library and Richardson's men were both important. Warren's own writing confirms the special nature of each to him. The images that he encountered and the personal relationships that he established would stay with him throughout his life.

The library contained an extensive collection of books and photographs that the members of the staff could study.[40] When Warren left Richardson's office to travel in Europe between 1884 and 1885, he wrote letters to his brother Harold in which he repeatedly referred to images in the library. In one letter, he noted that Richardson had asked him to get a photograph of the Provençal church at Carpentras for the collection.[41] When Richardson died and Warren wrote his tribute in the *Sanitary Engineer,* he observed that Richardson's valuable library and collection of photographs were "always accessible to his draughtsmen, and he encouraged their constant reference to them."[42] Given Warren's academic inclinations, he must have relished this opportunity. Richardson's accumulation of photographs was recognized as extensive, a model collection that reflected a widespread desire by architects during the period to acquire images for study, which in turn contributed to the interest in historical revivals.

The experience in Richardson's office also connected Warren to a circle of men who would gain prominence in the late nineteenth century. The senior architect promoted a familial atmosphere, which was reinforced by the fact that his office was attached to his home.[43] In the *New York Star,* Warren explained that Richardson "was like a father to his pupils and assistants," and he described how Richardson hosted Monday night dinners with them.[44] He recalled these "evening reunions" in the *Sanitary Engineer* tribute as well.[45]

When Warren left Richardson to travel in Europe, he saw sights and stayed at inns recommended by friends from the office. In England he met Charles Coolidge, and they traveled together to Salisbury.[46] Warren later worked with several former colleagues, including Longfellow, in running the Society of Arts and Crafts, Boston.[47] And Warren would work closely with Charles McKim, another graduate of Richardson's office, when McKim designed Robinson Hall, the new home for the Harvard architecture program, in 1899.[48] The common interests of these men ranged from historicism to craftsmanship, and Warren supported their design vision through his institutional and organizational roles.

While working for Richardson, Warren enrolled as a special student at Harvard, where he attended the lectures on the fine arts given by Charles Eliot Norton.[49] Warren later wrote that he considered these lectures to have been one of the most valuable experiences in his professional training.[50] One can imagine that what stirred Warren most deeply was Norton's almost religious fervor as he preached to his students about aesthetics and the world around them.[51] In a printed syllabus distributed to students in Norton's course on Roman and medieval art, probably used during the early 1890s when Warren first taught at Harvard, Norton stated, "The true intellectual life and the moral life go hand in hand. The study of the fine arts shows us what we owe to the race. . . ."[52] Norton believed that an appreciation of aesthetics is essential to human endeavor. Warren would take a similarly moral tone when lecturing and writing on architecture.

Norton's passion for Gothic architecture and his enthusiasm for America's colonial architecture were specific interests that Warren would embrace.[53] And Norton's advocacy of Ruskin's views on the beauty of handicraft must have been appreciated by Warren, inspiring him in later years as he promoted handicraft in his architectural work, in his lectures, and in his long-term commitment to the Society of Arts and Crafts, Boston. Norton would be called upon to serve as the organization's first president.

Warren also must have found Norton's diatribes, a hallmark of his lectures, to be something of a challenge. A student's notes from one of Norton's lectures during the 1895–1896 academic year, more or less devoted to the study of ancient art, records how he attacked Richardson's buildings on the campus. "Study the system of ornamentation of Sever Hall," Norton admonished his audience. "It is more than babyish. . . . Why should Austin Hall be built as if to resist a siege? Is there any organic relation between the wings and the center? . . . As yet America has contributed very little to the arts."[54] And the swipes continued in print. The syllabus published to accompany Norton's "Fine Arts IV" reads, "The fine arts [are] the records of a race, its aims and ideals.

[Consider] what the Doric column and the Parthenon tell us of the Greek, what the Law School and Memorial Hall tell us of Americans."[55] The condemnation of the Law School building—Richardson's and Warren's Austin Hall—must have been painfully embarrassing. Norton was a brilliant curmudgeon, and Warren probably was appalled by his biting criticism while inspired by his devotion to art.

Travel in Europe

When Warren left Boston for Europe in June of 1884, he was twenty-seven years old, and he brought a trained eye to his travels. He would visit England, France, and Italy. Typical of architects of his era, he would examine the buildings that he saw by sketching them and measuring them. The trip is well documented by the letters that he wrote to his brother Harold.[56]

Warren passed the summer months in England, visiting relatives as well as various sights. Gothic cathedrals were one subject of study; he saw several, including Canterbury and Salisbury. The letters suggest that despite a childhood spent in England, he had not seen these monuments before. After visiting Chester, he praised the quality of the restoration work, a topic that was an ongoing concern to him as it was to others at this time.[57] He also revealed an interest in medieval domestic architecture. At Salisbury, he reported, "There are more fine old houses in the close . . . than I have seen together anywhere else in England."[58] The building he chose to measure most fully was Wenlock Priory, in Shropshire, the homeland of his English relatives and ancestors, and he later published his drawings and research.[59] He said nothing to Harold about the significance of the site, however, perhaps because it was familiar to them both.

Contemporary English architecture and painting were other subjects of Warren's letters. He reported to Harold that Manchester Town Hall "is certainly a very fine building," reflecting a respect for Waterhouse that he would repeat later.[60] He praised the work of Dante Rosetti, Edward Burne-Jones, and Walter Crane, revealing a bias toward those artists in the circle of William Morris.[61] At London's National Gallery, he examined the paintings of J. M. W. Turner, whose work would be shown to his students at Harvard, and Paolo Veronese. These so-called colorists, championed by Ruskin, were Warren's favorites, reflecting his acceptance of Ruskin's preferences, adopted also by Moore and Norton.[62]

Perhaps the most significant passage in Warren's letters from England was a musing to his brother in which he compared English and American cultures. "I wonder if you can appreciate at all a certain feeling of oppressiveness I experience among the lovely old things of a bygone time," he wrote. "At any rate, I prefer looking forward to looking backward and I am glad I live in a country where—in spite of ugliness and crudity—everything does in general look forward."[63] As much as Warren appreciated the beauty of the monuments of the past, he was thoroughly committed to the present. While he would always embrace historical forms for his buildings, he never glorified the past as superior to his own time. He appreciated the energy and enterprise of his age, and that of Americans in particular. Through his work, he hoped to make his contribution by promoting what he considered superior design for contemporary living.

In September Warren left England for France, and he again visited Gothic cathedrals: Notre Dame of Paris, Laon, Amiens, Noyon, and Chartres were among the monuments that he saw.[64] He praised the quality of the sculpture, and he was struck by the high caliber of the glass at Chartres. Both stone carving and glassmaking would be promoted by him later through his teaching, writing, and work with the Society of Arts and Crafts, Boston. At Laon he measured a tower, and at Chartres he painted a view of the interior.

Just as he took note of the domestic architecture of medieval England, Warren admired the domestic architecture of Renaissance France. In Lisieux, Normandy, he drew a half-timbered house from the period (fig. 4).[65] In Paris, he visited the Hotel Cluny, "a stunning old place," and he visited the châteaux in towns of the Loire Valley, including Blois and Tours.[66] Later these buildings would be discussed in his classes at Harvard.

While in France, Warren examined the restoration work of the architect Eugène-Emmanuel Viollet-le-Duc. After visiting Pierrefonds, he sent a negative report to Harold, writing, "The carving everywhere is cold and lifeless modern work."[67] Warren said nothing in his letters about new buildings by contemporary French architects, perhaps because new work was not a subject of great concern for Harold.

Warren's reports on painting, however, were frequent, no doubt due to Harold's interests as a professional artist. At the same time, they were

FIG. 4. Warren, "An Old House at Lisieux, Normandy," 1884. *From* Sanitary Engineer, *July 8, 1886.*

consistent with Herbert's own commitment to the art. He provided his impressions of the painters he saw in the Louvre, writing positively about Titian and Veronese. Titian's *Entombment,* he declared, "is perhaps the finest picture I have seen by anybody."[68] On the other hand, he told Harold that Rubens "I simply abominate." Raphael disappointed him. Warren's taste followed that of Ruskin in favoring Venetians, and he shared the commonly held distaste of the critics of his age for Baroque art and what they considered its "excess."

Warren's travels in France also reveal the influence on him of Richardson and the men whom Richardson employed. The house that Warren drew in Lisieux had been drawn by McKim in 1869, before McKim joined Richardson's office.[69] McKim may have prompted others in the office to visit it, or perhaps someone had contributed a drawing or photograph of it to Richardson's library for general use. Whatever the case, the McKim and Warren drawings are so similar that a connection through the office seems probable. Also in Normandy, Warren saw the Renaissance Manoir d'Ango, finding it "perfectly stunning." He told Harold that he must remember seeing a photo of it "at Richardson's." This manor house, with its helmet domes and large courtyard, had been visited at separate times by both Longfellow and Stanford White, graduates of Richardson's office.[70] As they walked in each other's footsteps, the architects who had been employed by Richardson came to know and admire certain buildings, not necessarily canonical today, that contributed to their designs. The images in the office photograph collection presented the men with a distinctive architectural history, one that must have been embellished by assessments of the buildings that the men shared with each other.

In the Auvergne and in Provence, Warren saw the Romanesque churches that had inspired Richardson. Warren was enthusiastic. The church at Issoire he called "the epitome of French Romanesque architecture." At Brioude, he studied the mosaic of dark brown and white sandstone, imitated in Richardson's masonry at Trinity Church in Boston. "But the color is softer and more harmonious than at Trinity," Warren wrote.[71]

When he visited the Romanesque monuments of Provence, Warren found them to be much more refined than those in the north of France. He was as enthralled by the sculpture as by the masonry. The sculpted porch of Saint Gilles especially impressed him. "It has long stood in my mind by the side of the south porch of Chartres and the porch of St. Mark's as one of the three porches of the world, and I was not disappointed," he reported.[72] The statement is revealing and defines a taste in sculpture that Warren always would favor: forms that are somewhat abstracted and marked by a classical reserve.

In February of 1885, Warren left France for Italy. Soon after he arrived, he proclaimed to Harold that medieval Italian architects were behind their French contemporaries.[73] By now Warren had rejected Ruskin's enthusiasm for Italian Gothic architecture and had embraced the outlook of Viollet-le-Duc, favoring the French. In another letter, he explained that Italian Gothic buildings imitate "forms borrowed without the least understanding of the principles that underlie them or the constructional system on which they depend."[74] Through both his teaching and his writing, Warren would later emphasize structural expression in building design. Italian Gothic sculpture also struck him as behind contemporary work in France.[75]

Nevertheless, when Warren arrived in Venice, he took pleasure in what he found. While expressing his regret over the restoration work at Saint Mark's, he was delighted with the building and its ornament; he also praised the capitals of the ducal palace.[76] Venetian painting continued to be an attraction, and he even devoted time to copying a painting by Carpaccio.[77]

Italy's architecture of the early Renaissance received Warren's greatest praise. In Brescia, he found the Piazza Vecchia especially satisfying.[78] Buildings of later periods failed to please him, however. When he visited Vicenza and saw Palladio's buildings, he admired their proportions and their dignity, but overall he found them "chilling."[79] After visiting Rome, he wrote, "The Renaissance architecture in Italy contemporary with Michael Angelo and later under Palladio and Vignola is far more disagreeable than that in England under Inigo Jones and Wren." Saint Peter's, he told Harold, was "an insignificant-looking abomination." Raphael's Stanza paintings in the Vatican also were condemned as "abominations," except for the *Disputa* and the *School of Athens*.[80] Warren's judgments of Italian architecture and painting showed a preference for balance and restraint, ideals to which he would return again and again.

When Warren wrote to Harold in June, he had left Italy, crossed the Alps, and arrived in Switzerland. "Give me a northern cathedral any day, with its great clifflike walls and its peaks rising high in air," he declared. "And for sculpture, give me those grim old prophets in the Porch of Amiens or the knights and bishops of Chartres."[81] Remembering Warren from the years when he was working at Richardson's office, Charles Coolidge observed, "I always had a feeling that Warren was a Goth at heart. . . ."[82] But Warren would not change his course abruptly. When he returned to Boston and established his own architectural practice, he would not turn his back on his five years with Richardson. Warren would take a few years to find his own direction.

~TWO~

ON HIS OWN
(1885-1893)

SOON AFTER WARREN returned to Boston, he was hired to handle the architectural coverage for the *Sanitary Engineer* while he also launched his own architectural practice. Both as an editor and as an architect, Warren demonstrated his admiration for Richardson. At the same time, he was absorbing and analyzing what he had seen in his yearlong tour of England, France, and Italy.

The young man who was setting out on his own in the fall of 1885 was unprepossessing in appearance yet animated and engaging. Winifred B. Warren remembered her father as "a small man, thin and narrow-shouldered," who gave little thought to his dress. His pants were usually baggy, and his collars were always a size too large.[1] He had a high fore-head, a light complexion, and large blue eyes. Most distinctive was his bright red beard. As for his personality, Winifred recalled, "He was im-pulsive, easily upset, alternately enthusiastic or depressed, and somewhat sentimental." One of Warren's former students and later a colleague, Henry Atherton Frost, painted a similar picture. Warren, Frost wrote, was "a little man with a tuft of hair that gave him somewhat the look of a cockatoo, a reddish round beak, and a monumental impatience, which flowed from boundless energy; and withal one of the kindliest of men."[2]

Warren probably began working for the *Sanitary Engineer* in order to supplement his income while he was starting out in his practice. There apparently was no family money to help him through this initial period. In his letters written to his brother Harold when he was in Europe, Warren commented on his tight financial situation, and daughter Winifred recalled that even in later years, her father was constantly under a strain to make ends meet.[3]

The *Sanitary Engineer* was mainly devoted to developments in building technology. Most of its articles concerned plumbing, heating, and
ventilation topics; features also described innovations relating to structural engineering. Published in New York City, the periodical addressed
a national readership. Most of its readers probably were contractors,
while some apparently were architects and tradesmen. Through this
professional affiliation, Warren was associated with the newest ideas of
his day relating to building construction.

Just when Warren began working for the *Sanitary Engineer* is not
clear; the names of the staff never appear in the periodical's masthead,
and the articles by the staff are not signed. A tribute published after
Warren's death notes that he worked for the journal in 1886 and 1887,
but he probably started in November of 1885 when the *Sanitary Engineer* began publishing a full-page drawing of a noteworthy building
on a weekly basis.[4] The line drawings were generally executed by a staff
artist and were based on photographs.[5] Because the editorial coverage
of architecture was minimal in early 1886, Warren's main responsibility
appears to have been the selection of the weekly subjects, which included the work of contemporary architects as well as historical buildings. A descriptive paragraph or two, presumably written by Warren,
usually accompanied each illustration.[6] As time went on, more articles
were published on architecture, in addition to the full-page weekly illustration, and a small line drawing, always of a contemporary building,
began appearing regularly in the text. By expanding its architectural
coverage, the *Sanitary Engineer* evidently sought to broaden its readership, catering to the architects reading the *American Architect and
Building News,* published in Boston, while still serving the readers who
shared the journal's original concerns relating to trade innovations.

During the period when Warren was working for the *Sanitary Engineer,* the architectural coverage reflected his recent association with
Richardson in a number of ways. Buildings by Richardson and by architects who worked for him appeared frequently. Illustrations were published of Richardson's gate lodge at North Easton, Massachusetts; the
Sard house, Albany; the Stoughton house, Cambridge, Massachusetts;
the Ames store on Washington Street, Boston; a number of depots in
Massachusetts; and the Gurney house in Beverly, Massachusetts. Illustrations of buildings by men who had trained under Richardson included the work of McKim, Mead, and White; T. M. Clark; and
Andrews and Jaques.[7] Two of the drawings, one of an Andrews and

Jaques building and one of work by McKim, Mead, and White, were done by Warren rather than the regular staff illustrator, as is made clear by his signature, suggesting the special relationship he maintained with these men.

In several exhibition reviews, unsigned yet presumably by Warren, he promoted Richardson's work further. An exhibition review of architectural drawings in New York City from 1886 reported, "The most interesting building by far is Mr. H. H. Richardson's splendid design for the Episcopal Cathedral in Albany, which, it is to be regretted, is not to be carried out."[8] The All Saints Episcopal Cathedral project had been developed between 1882 and 1883, when Warren was working for Richardson, and one may suspect that the young architect was especially fond of it because he had been involved with its design. When a variation of the exhibition was presented in Boston a few months later, the Richardson drawings for the Albany cathedral were not included—a disappointment that was noted in a second review.[9] In the same review, the virtues of contemporary Romanesque architecture as interpreted by Richardson and others were discussed. If, as the architect Charles Coolidge said, Warren was a Goth at heart, in 1886 he was still under Richardson's spell.

Warren published illustrations of a number of buildings that he had seen during his European travels, most of which were drawn by the staff artist from photographs. A few, though, were his own signed illustrations that he had drawn on his trip.[10] Just as Warren's European tour included visits to buildings that were particular favorites with Richardson's employees, so too did the *Sanitary Engineer* illustrations present buildings, such as the old house in Lisieux, Normandy, that reflected specific interests of the studio.[11] In addition to these, Warren selected a range of illustrations that was typical for the period. Along with Romanesque monuments from France, he published Gothic and Renaissance monuments from France, England, Italy, Germany, and Spain, as well as two buildings from Syria.

Comments in the pages of the *Sanitary Engineer* foreshadowed Warren's future preference for Gothic architecture. Influenced by the views held by the English architect Augustus Welby Pugin and the French gothicist Viollet-le-Duc, Warren advocated "straightforward honesty" in architectural construction. Recent architecture, he observed, had surpassed that of a few years earlier, when many designs were marred by the "addition of meaningless balderdash" and suffered from "constructional features having no constructional purpose."[12]

Warren also published an illustration of a Gothic Revival church, Saint James the Less, located in Falls of the Schuylkill, Pennsylvania, built in 1846 from plans furnished by the Cambridge Society, England, after measured drawings of Long Stanton church, Cambridgeshire.[13] With its simple massing, steeply pitched roof, open bellcote, and wall buttresses, it looked very much like Warren's later churches. The publication of this church may be recognized as a manifestation of a return to a more academic approach to Gothic architecture that was gathering steam during the late 1880s. At a time when mainstream American architects were embracing the Richardsonian Romanesque for church design, documented by the illustrations of the *Sanitary Engineer* and the *American Architect and Building News,* architects who had worked for Richardson, including McKim and Warren, turned their attention to the English parish church. In 1886, for example, McKim, Mead, and White designed Saint Peter's Church in Morristown, New Jersey, inspired by fifteenth-century sources.[14]

The pages of the *Sanitary Engineer* published during Warren's tenure reveal his appreciation for English colonial and federal-era American buildings, another interest that was growing among architects during the decade. In a review of an article about American architecture that had run in the *Builder,* an English publication, the English writer was criticized because he did not "seem to realize that the delicate and simple colonial work lasted as long as it did. It did not come to an end with the Declaration of Independence, but lasted even to the first years of the present century."[15] Warren would soon design colonial-inspired buildings of his own that were marked by this delicacy and simplicity. During Warren's association with the *Sanitary Engineer,* he introduced illustrations of colonial and federal architecture, including details and measured drawings, further encouraging an understanding of this work.[16]

The education of the architect was a topic that Warren promoted on several occasions. The review of the article in the *Builder* noted that while the English author had reported on the work of William Ware at MIT and Columbia, the author also "might have spoken of the schools at Cornell University under Prof. [Charles] Babcock and at Champaign, Ill., under Prof. [Nathan] Ricker. . . ."[17] In April of 1887, under the title "Regarding the Study of Architecture," Warren published the opinions of a number of leading educators and architects, who generally agreed that formal study of architecture before working in an office was the most desirable course for an aspiring professional to take.[18]

Warren's coverage of architectural exhibitions in the journal suggested his growing personal belief in the educational value of such displays. In the review of architectural drawings shown in New York in 1886, readers were told that such exhibitions "will, if properly conducted, help to educate public taste and so increase the demand for good work."[19] Later Warren would organize several major exhibitions for the Society of Arts and Crafts, Boston, and would express the same objectives.

By the beginning of 1888, Warren had resigned from his editorial position. An illustration of a house that he had designed was featured in a February issue of the journal, and it seems likely that the appearance of his own architectural work signaled his departure from the staff.[20]

Marriage and Change

The architect's personal life was changing. Just a few months earlier, in November of 1887, he had married. His bride was Catharine Clark Reed, daughter of the Reverend James Reed, minister at the Swedenborgian church on Boston's Beacon Hill.[21] James Reed was a graduate of Harvard College, where he established long-lasting friendships with Brahmin classmates Phillips Brooks, minister of Richardson's Trinity Church, and Henry Lee Higginson, a philanthropist who founded the Boston Symphony Orchestra and helped Harvard purchase Soldiers Field for an athletic complex. The Reed family lived on Beacon Hill in a house on Louisburg Square, home through the years to many of Boston's leading citizens. Reed would outlive Warren, and he seems to have been a significant figure in his new son-in-law's life.[22]

Katie, as Catharine was called, maintained the household and reared the couple's four children. Winifred, the eldest, remembers her mother as "even-tempered" and "unsentimental."[23] Like Herbert, Katie painted in watercolors, mainly before she married. Both appreciated the beauty in nature, and they enjoyed taking their children on country walks.[24]

The Warrens settled in Waban, a rural area of suburban Newton, in a colonial house that Reed bought for them as a wedding present.[25] Built as a farmhouse sometime between the mid to late eighteenth century, it is two stories high with a shallow hipped roof, a room on either side of a central entrance hall, and two chimneys at the rear.[26] By the time the Warrens moved into the house, it was already recognized for its historic interest and would soon be illustrated and discussed in *King's Handbook of Newton, Massachusetts,* published in 1889.[27]

While Warren must have recognized the simple appeal of the house, he also proceeded to alter it (fig. 5). He added an oriel window over the front entry, a columned porch to one side, and a two-story ell to the rear. The entry portico may have been added by him, too. He would rework colonial buildings with surprising freedom throughout his career, even as he rued the damage being done by restorers of historic European monuments. Perhaps he believed that such colonial architecture was incomplete, as he had regarded the Romanesque, and that the role of the modern architect was to finish it for contemporary use.

Winifred surmised that her father had more to do with selecting the furniture for the house than did her mother.[28] Secondhand shops in Salem were his source for dining room chairs and other old Windsor chairs, which he favored. "He chose them not primarily because they were old, though he was always history-minded," she wrote, "but because he considered them greatly superior artistically to anything presently being made."[29]

The house itself was painted yellow with white trim, and a wooden fence enclosed a formal garden that Warren laid out in the front yard. From the front door, straight paths radiated in five directions, defining regularly shaped flower beds, which included larkspur and—a Continental touch, unusual for New England—red and purple anemones. The path that led down the middle of the garden ended at a wooden seat that Warren had designed and hired a craftsman to make; this collaboration was of the sort that he would later encourage.[30]

Soon after Warren set up his architectural practice, he moved into office space at 9 Park Street.[31] The building had been designed as a house by Charles Bulfinch and was constructed between 1803 and 1804. The setting and the location across the street from Bulfinch's State House and the Boston Common must have pleased him. He maintained his office at this address through 1899. Later the Society of Arts and Crafts, Boston, would open a showroom here.

Yet even while savoring the refined elegance of the federal architecture around him, Warren made a comment in a letter that suggests he would have shared the chagrin expressed by Henry James a few years later over the changes taking place in Boston. Writing about his visit to the

FIG. 5. Warren, remodeled colonial house, Newton, Massachusetts, 1888. Photographed with Gertrude Warren and Catharine and Herbert Warren, holding Winifred. *Courtesy of Elizabeth Warren Stoutamire.*

United States between 1904 and 1905, after being abroad for a quarter of a century, James was dismayed to find that Boston's immigrants had taken possession of the Common. "For no sound of English, in a single instance, escaped their lips; the greater number spoke a rude form of Italian, the others some outland dialect unknown to me," he observed.

He had to look past them, as through a grating, to see " 'my' small homogeneous Boston of the more interesting time."[32]

Warren articulated a similar distaste for Boston's immigrants in one of his letters from Europe to his brother. The Germans, he said, he liked, but he wished the Irish could be kept out. The Italians weren't as bad, as "they don't much bother us and aren't likely to."[33] Although Warren did not explain his views, he probably considered Boston's teeming tenement population undesirable and even threatening. Moreover, Boston had just elected its first Irish-born mayor.[34] Society as a whole identified and judged people by their country of origin. In Boston the established community considered the American "race" fundamentally an English race. Warren's ongoing assertions about the Englishness of American culture may be better understood against this backdrop.

The buildings that Warren designed during the first years of his practice reveal that he was influenced by his five years under Richardson in many ways. Following Richardson's approach, Warren produced buildings that were defined by broad, sheltering roofs and large, full volumes. Richardson's trusswork was another feature developed further by the young architect. And Warren promoted well-crafted architectural detail, a mark of Richardson's buildings relating to his interest in the ideas of Ruskin and Morris.

During the second half of the 1880s, Warren designed several Romanesque buildings that were extensions of his years of working under Richardson. Other buildings from this period featured Richardsonian characteristics, yet they also showed original ideas. What is perhaps most significant is that even during his first years of independent practice, a time when he was producing faithful Richardsonian designs, Warren was exploring entirely new directions. By the beginning of the 1890s, he had solidified his ideas and had completely abandoned a Richardsonian Romanesque approach. When designing in the medieval tradition, he favored Gothic models—specifically English models. He also turned to American colonial and federal buildings as well as English Georgian buildings as sources of inspiration. The shift was away from a Latin-inspired architectural tradition to one that was Anglo-Saxon. Richardson's bold, massive forms, so admired by Warren during the 1880s, were rejected by him during the first years of the 1890s as he pursued thinner, finer forms and details.

This paradigm shift gradually took hold in American architecture,

with those who had worked with Richardson, such as McKim and Warren, leading the way. The reversal may be explained by the fact that
they and their clients preferred models, whether Gothic or Georgian,
that were lighter than the Romanesque. Then again, these historical
sources may have appealed to the younger architects who had worked
with Richardson in part because they were reacting against the exag-
gerated weight of his Romanesque revival.

By examining a few of the buildings that Warren designed between
1885 and 1893, from the time he established his own practice until he
began teaching at Harvard, we can see how he reconsidered Richardson's ideas and developed this new, lighter style, based mainly on English and American sources. We can also see how Warren collaborated
with artisans, affirming Richardson's approach, in following a Ruskinian
direction that prepared the way for his involvement with the Society of
Arts and Crafts. During this period, Warren settled on a personal philosophy about architectural design, producing a range of buildings that
would soon be identified as compatible with the taste of the fine-arts
faculty at Harvard.

Minneapolis Library and Museum Design

Warren's design for the Minneapolis library and museum building was
indebted to Richardson in many respects. Developed soon after Warren
had returned from his travels, it suggests a continuation of the work he
had done in his former employer's studio. In January of 1886, the Building Committee invited seven firms to submit competition proposals.[35]
Although Warren's design was not selected, a perspective illustration
and plans were published in the *American Architect and Building News*
in September (figs. 6, 7, 8).[36] Warren adopted the block-like massing
and the formal triple-arched entrance that were features of Albany City
Hall, a building on which he had worked. His towers, on the other
hand, repeat the roofline and proportions of the tower in the reentrant
angle of Richardson's Converse Memorial Library, Malden, Massachusetts, another building to which he contributed. Checkerboard patterns
of dark and light stone, a feature of Austin Hall at Harvard, appear on
the proposed library's frieze and in the gable fields. A band of frieze
sculpture over the main entrance reflects Richardson's further embellishment of his buildings.

FIG. 6. Warren, "Competition Design for Library and Museum Building," Minneapolis, Minnesota. *From* American Architect and Building News, *September 25, 1886.*

The plan features an entry hall at ground level, dominated by a grand staircase that rises before the visitor and then continues around a large light well. The library's card catalogue room and main reading room are one flight up, and the building's upper two stories accommodate galleries dedicated to the fine arts and the natural sciences. The museum floors are organized around an open court. Although the concepts of the staircase and organization around the square court are not distinctive, Richardson's Allegheny County Courthouse in Pittsburgh may have been a source in Warren's mind. One also may wonder whether Warren's proposal was noticed by McKim when he planned the Boston Public Library in 1887. The plan of McKim's building is dominated by a similar staircase and open court scheme.

Cathedral of Saint John the Divine Design

A second competition that Warren entered was for the Cathedral of Saint John the Divine, the Episcopal cathedral that would be built in New York City and was conceived as a national church.[37] The contest began in December of 1888, and Warren's entry (figs. 9, 10) was published in the *American Architect and Building News* in December of 1889.[38] In 1891, Heins and La Farge were awarded the commission.

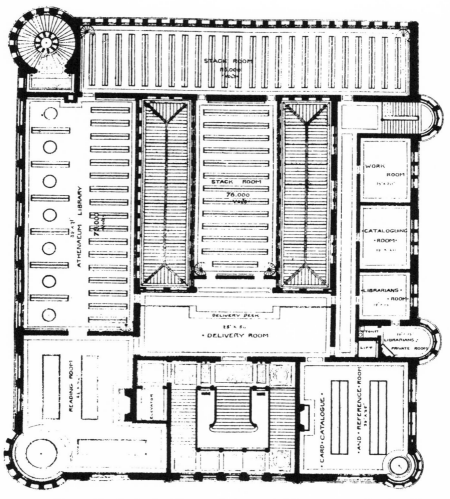

FIG. 7. "Competition Design for Library and Museum Building," Minneapolis, plan of first floor. *From* American Architect and Building News, *September 25, 1886.*

Warren's admiration for Richardson's Albany Cathedral is evident in his reworking of its design for his proposal.[39] The symmetrical main facade, featuring a rose window and a pair of towers, reflects Albany; Warren's transept facades are even more similar to those of Albany. Yet while Warren designed a Romanesque building that in massing and detail reflects Richardson, he incorporated a variety of other sources, in-

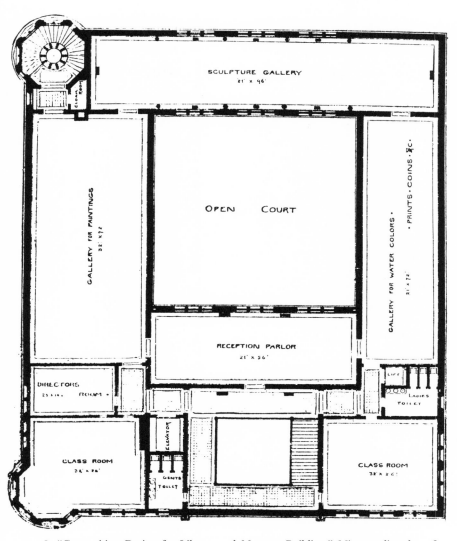

SCULPTURE GALLERY
21' x 96'

CLOAK ROOM

GALLERY FOR PAINTINGS
32' x 72'

OPEN COURT

GALLERY FOR WATER COLORS
21' x 72'

PRINTS · COINS · &c ·

RECEPTION PARLOR
21' x 56'

DIRECTORS ROOM
25' x 16'

LIFT

LADIES TOILET

CLASS ROOM
31' x 26'

ELEVATOR

GENTS TOILET

CLASS ROOM
31' x 26'

FIG. 8. "Competition Design for Library and Museum Building," Minneapolis, plan of
second floor. *From* American Architect and Building News, *September 25, 1886.*

FIG. 9. Warren, "Competitive Design for the Cathedral of St. John the Divine," New York City. *From* American Architect and Building News, *December 14, 1889.*

spired evidently by his European trip. The wide west facade, with its towers projecting beyond the building's main vessel, is English in approach. The gabled portals of Warren's design allude to those at Laon and, to a lesser extent, to those of the transepts at Chartres. And the dome and interior plan reveal a debt to Florence Cathedral. In general, Warren's proposal is less vertical than the Richardson design and more stable. Warren was also responding to other contemporary architecture. His weighty Romanesque church crowned by a dome is consistent with German designs of the period. Modern amenities are another feature of Warren's plan, reflecting an increasing desire for church buildings that would serve modern needs: lavatories and space for the storage of chairs are located and marked. Despite these modifications and enhancements, however, Warren's design reveals his continuing admiration for Richardson through the 1880s.

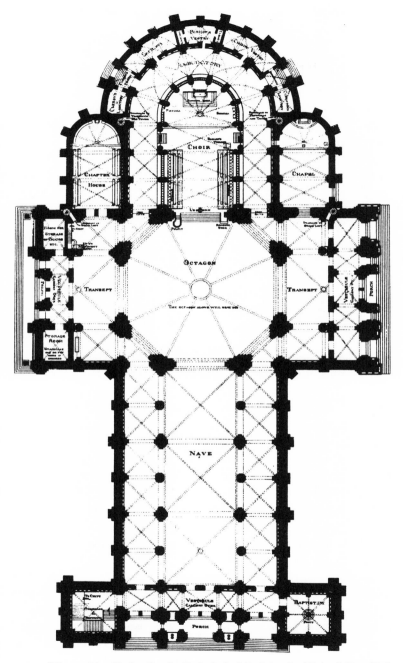

FIG. 10. "Competitive Design for the Cathedral of St. John the Divine," New York City, plan. *From* American Architect and Building News, *December 14, 1889.*

George Burdett House and Renfrew Park

One of Warren's important early suburban residential projects may be profitably compared with Richardson's country houses. The George Burdett house (fig. 11), located in Brookline, was built between 1887 and 1888.[40] While the shingled house is not indebted to any one source, it incorporates the eyelid dormers, hefty tower, and breadth of massing to be found in Richardson's country houses, such as the Ames gate lodge in North Easton, the Stoughton house in Cambridge, and the Paine house in Waltham, Massachusetts. Yet because shingled houses of this character were common in Boston during the 1880s, with other architects such as William Ralph Emerson contributing to the type, Warren's Burdett house should not be analyzed as indebted solely to Richardson.

Warren produced dozens of these shingled country houses, mainly on a smaller scale, during the late 1880s and early 1890s. In one instance, he designed an extensive complex for a resort near Newport, in Middletown, Rhode Island. Called Renfrew Park, it was conceived to include stables, a casino with tennis courts, and houses. An illustration of several of the proposed buildings was published in the catalogue of the first exhibition of the Boston Architectural Club in 1890 (fig. 12), and construction of the complex began in 1891.[41] Only the houses and the community stable were finished, however. With their broad roofs and simple, full volumes, the buildings are consistent with Richardson's houses as well as the shingled country houses of the period. More unusual is the classical shell motif that fits into the three roof dormers of the design for the casino building. The detail indicates that Warren was examining a widening range of historical sources, in this case adopting a decorative form associated with eighteenth-century Newport.

Charles J. Page House

During this period, Warren designed several distinguished residences in urban settings. The houses were brick, and all included the large round arches and taut walls that characterize Richardson's masonry work. The houses also were embellished with stone sculpture and ironwork, giving them an artistic quality, not unique to Richardson's buildings but shared by them.

FIG. 11. Warren, George Burdett house, Brookline, Massachusetts, 1887–1888. *Courtesy of the Brookline Preservation Commission.*

The house for Charles J. Page on Westland Avenue in Boston (fig. 13), dating from 1888, was most Richardsonian in feel and consistent with contemporary adaptations of the type, with its simple massing based on a rectangular plan, round turret at one corner, steeply pitched roof, a round-arched entry, and a number of arched windows. Marble colonnettes and ornamental iron balconies enriched the main facade. Prominently sited on a corner lot at the entrance to the newly developing area of the Fenway, the Page house was well publicized in architectural periodicals.[42] While Richardsonian in several respects, it also presented two new elements that were appearing in American architecture and that would become favorites with Warren: diaper patterns of dark brown-and-red brick and Flemish stepped gable ends, the gable treatment being a revival of English prototypes.

The Page house was described as "especially noteworthy for its artistic interior, a line in which Mr. Warren is very successful."[43] The main hall (fig. 14) ran through the center of the first floor, leading to the rear of the house where the staircase rose four steps, then turned and continued to rise along the rear wall. The configuration of the staircase,

FIG. 12. Warren, Renfrew Park, Newport (Middletown), Rhode Island, 1890. *From* Catalogue of the First Annual Exhibition of the Boston Architectural Club, *Boston, 1890. Reproduced courtesy of the Trustees of the Boston Public Library.*

twisted balusters, and wood paneling were all features of houses de-signed by Richardson, although again these features were not unique to him. To the right of the hall was the parlor, to the right rear was a small study, and to the left was the dining room (fig. 15). It was dominated by a large, round, brick arch that embraced built-in seats on either side of the fireplace—an inglenook arrangement Warren would have remem-bered well from Richardson's office.[44]

A few years after opening his practice in Boston, Warren established a second office in Troy, New York.[45] His father had once lived there, an uncle resided nearby, and Warren evidently believed he had enough connections in the area to justify the investment.[46] Warren's evaluation proved to be sound, and he received a number of commissions in Troy and its environs.[47]

Saratoga Racing Association Buildings

Perhaps the most interesting of Warren's designs dependent on his Rich-ardson years were his buildings for the Saratoga Racing Association at Saratoga Springs, New York, near the Troy office.[48] Commissioned in 1891 and completed the following year, the complex included a grand-stand for the observation of horse races, seating five thousand, a club-

FIG. 13. Warren, Charles J. Page house, Boston, 1888. Demolished. Photograph by Soule Art Co. *Courtesy of the Society for the Preservation of New England Antiquities.*

house, and a betting ring (fig. 16). With this project, Warren applied a Richardsonian approach to an emerging typological problem.[49]

Warren's design for the grandstand brought a new sense of style to a building type that had been more utilitarian. The first grandstand at Saratoga, built in 1864, had been long and rectangular in plan and covered with a simple pitched roof.[50] One year later, the track owners erected an uncovered public stand, and a similar pitched roof was added to it in 1876.[51] These structures were demolished for the new building designed by Warren. One source for inspiration may have been the grandstand overlooking the baseball field of Boston's South End Grounds, constructed in 1871.[52] The pyramidal and conical roofs at its two ends gave it some of the character that Warren would have sought. Yet it was busy in a way that was typical of 1870s designs, and the overall massing lacked vigor. Warren gave the Saratoga grandstand a dramatic roofline. At its center is a high dominating pavilion with four steeply sloping hips that fall from a horizontal ridge, with two subsidiary

FIG. 14. Page house, hall and staircase. Photograph by Soule Art Co. *Courtesy of the Society for the Preservation of New England Antiquities.*

peaked roofs below, all covered in slate and surmounted by gilded finials. Extending to either side of this center mass are wings covered with pitched roofs, each end terminating in a high, pyramidal roof that matches the pair at the center. The grandstand roofline recalls the steep roof of Richardson's Oakes Ames Memorial Hall, which in turn was inspired by European models from the northern Renaissance. At Saratoga, Warren preserved the picturesque effect of the Richardson design. Supporting the grandstand's vast roof is an elaborate system of wood trusses, reinforced by iron strapping and carried on simple posts. The building's spare, functional seating area, dominated by its support system, resembles any number of grandstands. At the same time, the trusswork of the Saratoga grandstand is especially complex, and Warren would have drawn on his experience with Richardson in working it out.

To one end of the grandstand was the clubhouse, which has since been engulfed by new construction. An early photograph shows that it was rectangular in massing, with a pitched roof and three hipped gables. At each end of the building was a broad, conical roof, vaguely medieval

FIG. 15. Page house, dining room. Photograph by Soule Art Co. *Courtesy of the Society for the Preservation of New England Antiquities.*

in effect. The clubhouse served association members and included a ladies' parlor and a buffet.[53] At the other end of the grandstand was the betting ring, paved inside and covered with a broadly sloping roof.[54] A monitor roof was added later. The betting ring has since been demolished. While extremely simple, this rectangular structure with its flaring, overhanging eaves recalls the Japanese architecture that influenced Richardson and others, especially in Boston, beginning in the 1880s.[55]

Scripps Mortuary Chapel

Most of the buildings designed by Warren during the first years after he left Richardson's office followed an evolutionary pattern, sharing many qualities of Richardson's designs while reflecting Warren's multiplying interests. But the Scripps mortuary chapel complicates the story (fig. 17). With it, Warren began testing new waters, revealing his indepen-

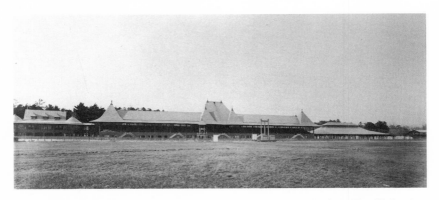

FIG. 16. Warren, Saratoga Racing Association buildings, Saratoga Springs, New York, 1891–1892. Clubhouse at left, with grandstand and betting ring. Betting ring demolished. *Photograph courtesy of the George S. Bolster Collection of the Historical Society of Saratoga Springs.*

dence from his master even as he praised him and was emulating his work in other projects. The chapel that represents Warren's first deviation from Richardson's Romanesque is a Gothic building designed for James E. Scripps, the wealthiest man in Detroit. It is located in the city's Woodmere Cemetery. Scripps wanted a Gothic design, and Warren embraced the opportunity. While on his European trip, Warren sent Scripps sketches for the chapel; the design was completed in 1886, and the chapel was built the following year.[56] It was therefore designed during the same year as McKim, Mead, and White's Saint Peter's Church in Morristown, New Jersey. Both English-derived churches represent early examples of what might be called the academic phase of the American Gothic Revival, which flourished at the turn of the twentieth century.

Scripps, a newspaper magnate, was a native of London and an advocate of Gothic architecture.[57] He built the family chapel after the death of a twelve-year-old son in 1882; he and his wife also had lost a daughter several years earlier. Not wanting to visit the graves in the harshness of winter, he conceived the idea of erecting the chapel with the tombs in its marble floor. At first Scripps considered erecting a chapel after a specific English Gothic example, but eventually he abandoned the idea, deciding instead to commission a new design. It was to be modeled after English Gothic churches of the thirteenth century, "the period of the best development of Gothic art," as he described it.[58] While the chapel was being erected in 1887, a newspaper article explained, "An

FIG. 17. Warren, Scripps mortuary chapel, Woodmere Cemetery, Detroit, 1886–1887. *Courtesy of Richard Smith Joslin, Cambridge, Massachusetts.*

important consideration with Mr. Scripps in expending so much upon this work is the desire to create in Detroit a really pure example of the Gothic architecture of which he is so enthusiastic a lover, and thereby encourage the development of this beautiful style in this city."[59] The architect had to be a scholar, and he needed to know Gothic architecture from firsthand experience. While the question of how Warren received this commission remains to be answered, Warren's English background and academic leanings were attributes that would have appealed to Scripps.

The chapel was built with a simple rectangular plan, with coursed sandstone ashlar and a steeply pitched roof. Stained glass was ordered from Bell and Sons in London, and the decorative sculpture was carved in Boston, presumably by John Evans, who had worked for Richardson and for Warren.[60] The ensemble included a tympanum featuring a Christ in Majesty flanked by kneeling angels, executed with the restraint and slightly abstracted quality of thirteenth-century examples. Most important was the chapel's construction: it was built with ribbed groin vaults of stone and brick. Outside, the thrust of the vaults was offset by wall buttresses. Warren would pursue this interest in vaulting, based on an academic study of historical models, in the years ahead, both in his teaching and in his practice.[61]

William B. Strong House

Another noteworthy building by Warren is the large house that he designed for William B. Strong, located in Brookline (fig. 18).[62] Like the mortuary chapel, it represents a departure from Richardson and the routine designs of the late 1880s and is an early example of a type that became popular during the 1890s. Begun in 1887 and finished the following year, the house demonstrates how Warren explored a new direction in design while still producing more conventional residences, such as the shingled Burdett house, which was erected next door at the same time. Strong was president of the Atchison, Topeka, and Santa Fe Railroad Company. How the design was developed is not known, but clearly Strong was supportive of it, if not the source. What makes the Strong house unusual for its date is the way it combines a breadth of massing, overhanging roof, and a classically treated entry, framed by Tuscan columns surmounted by a Doric frieze (fig. 19). The choice of stucco finish also is unusual for the 1887–1888 date. While the house presents a type that would become standard during the 1890s, the conventional country house for the late 1880s in the Boston area was shingled, more compact, and more complex in its massing.

Warren was not alone in pursuing this new direction, however. In 1888, Andrews and Jaques, based in Boston, produced the Perkins house in Beverly Farms, Massachusetts, which is related in design (fig. 20). Published in the *Engineering and Building Record,* formerly the *Sanitary Engineer,* the Perkins house is the first example in that publication of the broad, stucco-finished residences that would soon become so popular and that ultimately would be identified as an Arts and Crafts style.[63] The fact that Warren, Robert Andrews, and Herbert Jaques had all worked together under Richardson suggests some ex-

FIG. 18. Warren, William B. Strong house, Brookline, Massachusetts, 1887–1888.

planation for this precocious development at virtually the same time. The implication is not that Richardson contributed to this direction. Rather, this coincidence suggests how ideas continued to be explored among these men as they stayed in contact with each other throughout their careers.

During the late 1880s and early 1890s, architects including Warren

FIG. 19. Strong house, entrance portico.

adopted an approach to design that would continue through the 1920s. The same architect commonly produced buildings that were explicit in their imitation of historical sources—such as Warren's Scripps mortuary chapel—and also designed work that could be described as eclectic, mixing historical references or making only vague historical allusions, based on academic study—such as the Strong house. These more in-ventive designs developed from the mixed references of Queen Anne

FIG. 20. Andrews and Jaques, "Residence of Miss Perkins," Beverly Farms, Massachusetts, 1888. *From* Engineering and Building Record, *September 15, 1888.*

architecture of the 1880s. During the 1890s, American architecture—and especially Boston architecture—responded to the emergence of a more intense and systematic study of architectural history, and the results varied surprisingly. Warren was early in pursuing this direction, producing not only revival designs but also designs that were more inventive while grounded in a study of the past.

The Strong house anticipates the 1890s country house ideal in another respect: the way in which it is connected to the landscape. It is handsomely sited on a hill, overlooking a valley, and the house features a terrace defined by a balustrade. This integration of the house with the landscape would be developed by Arts and Crafts architects, including Warren, at the turn of the century, especially with their grander residential projects.

Troy Orphan Asylum

By the early 1890s, Warren's preference for Gothic over Romanesque architecture was established. When he received the commission for the Troy Orphan Asylum in 1891, now demolished, he designed a Gothic complex that evoked English architecture of the Tudor period. It was well publicized and was considered one of Warren's major projects.[64] The complex (fig. 21) featured steeply pitched slate roofs with dormers and two stair towers. Warren also incorporated the stepped gable ends and the brown-and-red patterned brickwork of his Page house, and he gave the building its Gothic cast with a sparing use of tracery in a few of the windows. The asylum was taut and its decorative elements, such as the tracery, were thin as Warren abandoned the heavier forms of the 1880s. The building was treated with a restraint that was typical of Warren's mature work.

The commission also allowed Warren to pursue his interest in landscape design.[65] This concern was one that Richardson and Warren shared, and Warren no doubt appreciated Richardson's collaborative efforts with Frederick Law Olmsted, the landscape architect. All three men worked had worked together at the Oakes Ames Memorial Hall in North Easton, and the landscaping issues at that site would have appealed to Warren, who would later require his students to learn about garden design and would hire Frederick Law Olmsted, Jr., to teach landscape architecture at Harvard. At the orphan asylum, Warren developed an integrated building and landscape plan (fig. 22) that connected the interior spaces with outdoor play spaces for the children. At the far end of the building, the night and day nurseries opened onto a large infants' playground, enclosed by a brick wall. Elsewhere, two large terraces provided play areas for boys and girls. The main building led through a cloister to a chapel, built a few years later.[66] The intermediate space of the covered passage, connecting indoors and outdoors, exposed the children to fresh air, yet it would have sheltered them on days when the weather was inhospitable. Warren would continue to design walled gardens and terraces, especially in his residential projects, including some on a relatively small scale. These features interested other architects of the era, but they appeared with special frequency in Warren's work.

Lincoln Town Hall

Living in a colonial house and working in a Bulfinch-designed federal house, Warren was an enthusiastic proponent of Colonial Revival architecture. Clients in the Boston area, many of Yankee stock, readily

FIG. 21. Warren, Troy Orphan Asylum, northwest view, Troy, New York, 1891. Demolished. *From American Architect and Building News, March 10, 1900. Reproduced courtesy of the Trustees of the Boston Public Library.*

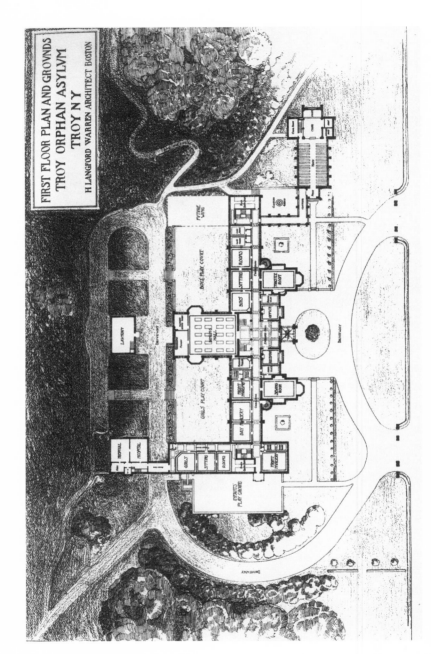

FIG. 22. Troy Orphan Asylum, plan. *From American Architect and Building News, August 11, 1900.*

embraced this new trend. His town hall for Lincoln, Massachusetts, dating from 1891 to 1892, reflects his interest (fig. 23). For a municipal building, Warren favored allusions to colonial and federal architecture, not medieval architecture, in part to convey an image of the American "race" and in part to suggest American democratic traditions. Working in the shadow of Bulfinch's State House, Warren must have admired the fine, thin beauty of its classical forms. Warren's town hall, today called Bemis Hall, has a similar attenuated elegance in its details, from the entrance, which is indebted to Palladio, to the tall thin pilasters on the facade's second story. Warren would develop similar Colonial Revival designs for all of his later municipal building projects.

The town hall was laid in Flemish bond, with bricks placed alternately lengthwise and crosswise, to enhance the strength of the walls. The use of Flemish bond for the town hall was praised in an 1891 newspaper article, which noted that while this bond was an unusual feature in the United States, it was more common in Europe.[67] In a subsequent publication and in his later buildings, Warren would promote this approach as structurally superior. The brick headers of the first story were burned black, which enhanced the basketwork pattern and emphasized the bond that was of such importance to him.

Inside the building, the light effect continues. Warren again designed thin, attenuated forms, such as the elongated Corinthian columns of the entry hall (fig. 24). The interior also was light in its palette; the newspaper article from 1891 recorded that the woodwork was painted "cream white." This lighter palette was being introduced in Boston at this time and contrasted dramatically with the dark walnut woodwork and painted olive green and terra-cotta interior finishes of the 1870s and 1880s.[68]

On the second floor, a large meeting hall presents something of a surprise, departing from classical references with a ceiling dominated by trusswork. The stained trusses suggest vaguely medieval associations. Warren would pursue this interest in trussed ceilings through his mature years. He also would continue to produce eclectic combinations of classical and medieval sources in his later work.

The Strong house, the Troy Orphan Asylum, and the Lincoln Town Hall set forth the directions that Warren would follow in the years ahead. By the early 1890s, when many American architects were still designing Richardsonian Romanesque buildings, Warren had abandoned the weighty forms for a lighter approach—an approach that would become more widespread within a few years. He also had embraced historical

FIG. 23. Warren, Lincoln Town Hall (Bemis Hall), Lincoln, Massachusetts, 1891–1892. *From An Account of the Celebration by the Town of Lincoln, Mass., of the 150th Anniversary of Its Incorporation, 1904.*

English and American architectural models, demonstrating that he could incorporate their components into his designs in a scholarly way. Yet he could work with some freedom as well, mixing his sources in a manner that would soon become commonplace among Boston and American architects.

Writing for the Architectural Press

While Warren devoted much of his attention to developing his architectural practice during the late 1880s, by the first years of the 1890s he had begun writing articles for the architectural press. Possibly solicited, they appeared in new publications. Although Warren's work at the *Sanitary Engineer* was not credited, it must have been known among the architects who submitted their projects to him for illustration.

In 1891, Warren contributed "Notes on Wenlock Priory" to the first issue of the *Architectural Review.*[69] The article was accompanied by measured drawings that Warren had made of the priory church, located

FIG. 24. Lincoln Town Hall, staircase.

in Shropshire, when he visited England in 1884. In his essay, he blocked out the history of the priory, explaining that it had been an important Cluniac foundation, and then he discussed how its ties to the French order had led to its takeover by English kings. Thus Warren associated the priory with a cultural identity, which would be a routine direction that he would take in his architectural history lectures. Warren then described the plan of the entire complex and the plan of the priory church. Its vaulting interested him, not surprisingly, in light of the vaulting he had designed for the Scripps chapel and his continued enthusiasm for structural analysis.

A year later, Warren contributed an article to the first issue of the *Brickbuilder*, titled "A Few Neglected Considerations with Regard to Brick Architecture."[70] He again raised structural considerations. He promoted the bonding of brick walls through their depth, condemning walls built with a veneer of face brick, arguing that bonded walls are not only stronger but also more beautiful. He commented on the desirability of surface patterns, such as diaper patterns resulting from the use of "hard-burned brick." Joints, he wrote, should be emphasized as an element of design, and he praised the beauty of common brick, rejecting the thin joints that accompanied the laying of pressed brick in American buildings of the late nineteenth century. For good examples of brickwork, he encouraged the study of brick buildings of the more distant past.

Just how to approach the buildings of the past was the subject that Warren contemplated in the *Architectural Review* in 1893.[71] He argued that if precedent were disregarded entirely, we would have "constructions absolutely utilitarian, devoid of ornament, devoid of style, bald, bare, and uninteresting."[72] Warren wrote that to make the best use of precedent, the architect must thoroughly understand it, through "a scholarly and thorough training in the knowledge of the great historic styles. . . ."[73] Yet Warren also warned of the dangers of simply copying sources. "Precedent should be studied with a view to gaining familiarity with the best use of architectural language," he wrote, "just as a writer studies the best examples of literature with a view to perfecting his style."[74] Once the forms of the past are understood, the architect can develop designs that are coherent and that address specific problems and modern needs. Warren wrote that merely imitative architecture "is unprogressive and abortive."[75] It is important to recognize that Warren considered himself progressive. As an authority on the architecture of the past, he was able to adapt historical forms in ways that conveyed the values that he shared with his mainly Anglo-Saxon clients while also being original.

Warren always thought of himself as an artist, and he continued to paint and to exhibit his work during the late 1880s and early 1890s. When he exhibited his watercolor paintings in 1890, a newspaper critic identified him with the artistic group that had developed around Harvard's Charles Herbert Moore, with whom Warren's brother Harold had studied. Also contributing to this exhibition was Denman Ross, who was related to the Warren brothers through marriage.[76] Ross would later gain recognition for his courses on abstract design at Harvard. In the 1892–1893 academic year, Warren lectured on the art of the Renaissance at the School of the Museum of Fine Arts, where Moore also was lecturing.[77]

Warren gravitated to organizations. He was active in the Boston Society of Architects and was secretary from 1891 until 1895.[78] He participated in the annual exhibitions of the Boston Architectural Club, and he entered competitions, achieving recognition for a design for Boston's Copley Square in early 1893.[79]

In May of that year, he wrote to his brother Harold that he had been asked to begin an architectural department at Harvard. Warren told his brother that Harvard president Charles W. Eliot had said that if the program succeeded, he would expect to build on it in subsequent years. Warren assured his brother, "I am going to make it succeed."[80]

~THREE~

AN ARCHITECTURAL
PROGRAM FOR HARVARD
(1893)

Hᴏᴡ ɪᴛ ʜᴀᴘᴘᴇɴᴇᴅ that Warren was asked to develop Harvard's architectural program is not entirely clear, but he did have supporters and qualifications for the job. Most important was the endorsement he received from several prominent men who advised Harvard's president, Charles W. Eliot. Warren mused to his brother Harold, "It is odd to be cordially supported by such opposite poles as Prof. Norton and Mr. Moore, and Professors Ware and Arthur Rotch—not to mention Mr. Cabot, Mr. Peabody and Robert Andrews."[1]

Both Charles Eliot Norton and Charles Herbert Moore were theorists and idealists, who had developed a widely respected fine-arts program at Harvard. By this time, Warren was known by Norton, with whom he had studied during the 1880s, and Warren was known by Moore, with whom he and his brother exhibited. The fact that Warren was an exhibiting watercolorist would have appealed to both professors. Warren was an artist-architect. He also was a budding historian. Even as a young man working for Richardson, Warren "displayed a surprising familiarity with general history and literature besides architectural knowledge, which in after years fitted him so peculiarly well as a scholar and teacher," observed Charles Coolidge.[2] Warren's work at the *Sanitary Engineer,* involving the selection of illustrations of buildings of historical interest, and his articles in the architectural press would have commended him further to Norton and Moore. And then his foray into teaching at the School of the Museum of Fine Arts would have been considered especially relevant.

The leaders of the architectural community, including William Ware, Rotch, Edward Clarke Cabot, Robert S. Peabody, and Andrews, would likely have endorsed Warren as a fellow professional. They evidently respected the designs that he had produced after setting up his own practice. They probably also believed that this intense, spirited man possessed the kind of personality that would succeed at building a new department for Harvard. Warren's role in Richardson's office as a chief draftsman and his participation as an officer in the Boston Society of Architects may have suggested his potential to be effective in an institutional setting.

Then, too, President Eliot must have viewed Warren favorably. Eliot must have formed some opinion about Warren when he was working for Richardson on Austin Hall at Harvard.[3] Furthermore, Warren's interest in landscape architecture would have been viewed positively by Eliot. His son Charles was a landscape architect and, as it happened, had opened an office at 9 Park Street, where Warren was working, in 1886.[4] And while far from the most important factor, Eliot is known to have held a high opinion of Warren's uncle, Cyrus Warren, who had lectured at Harvard under Eliot on organic chemistry; teaching at Harvard at this time was still in many respects a family affair.[5]

In other respects, Harvard under Eliot was changing dramatically. During the period of his presidency, from 1869 until his retirement in 1909, he transformed a less-than-rigorous, provincial educational institution into a nationally recognized university. He and his deans actively sought students from throughout the country as they strengthened the undergraduate college and the professional schools. Both in the United States and abroad, Eliot became recognized as an authority on higher education.[6] He probably identified Warren as someone who was sufficiently ambitious.

The first course that Warren taught was "The Development of Architectural Styles, with Especial Reference to the Greek and Roman Architecture."[7] Harvard's annual report for the academic year 1893–1894 shows that the course was listed under "The Fine Arts," with other courses taught by Moore, who lectured on delineation and design as well as on the history of art from the Middle Ages through the Renaissance. Norton did not teach that year. From the beginning, Warren's architecture program was closely allied with the Department of Fine Arts at Harvard.

Having been hired with the blessings of Norton and Moore, Warren not surprisingly planned a program of architectural study that was consistent with the preferences articulated by Ruskin. Years earlier, in 1865,

Ruskin had told the Royal Institute of British Architects, "My wish would be to see the profession of the architect united, not with that of the engineer, but of the sculptor."[8] In addition, Ruskin argued that the architect should be trained as a scholar, well versed in literature and philosophy. Warren would express the same view repeatedly.

Architectural Education in the Nineteenth Century

By the end of the nineteenth century, architectural education had become institutionalized in Europe and in the United States. Among the European schools, the Ecole des Beaux-Arts in Paris was generally recognized as the leader for the training of young architects.[9] Richardson had studied there, and a growing number of Americans were enrolling there by the end of the century. Students at the Ecole participated in a system of juried competitions and attended lectures taught by members of the Ecole faculty. Beginning in 1883, one of these competitions was offered to encourage the study of architectural history from an archaeological perspective. Students were required to draw a Greek or Roman monument or some portion of it. Lectures on architectural history also were offered, but attendance was not required.[10] For the most part, students received design instruction through their affiliation with an office, or atelier, of an architect. The Ecole system emphasized clear axial planning and finely rendered presentation drawings. The French school also was associated with a stylistic tradition that was classical and ornate.

German architectural education was less centralized. Leading programs were found at the Bauakademie in Berlin and in polytechnical schools in Munich, Karlsruhe, and several other cities.[11] By the late nineteenth century, German students spent two years studying technical subjects, then worked for the government, and finally finished their training by taking advanced professional courses. The dominant academic figure in Berlin was Karl Bötticher, who promoted a classical architecture based on ancient Greek sources.[12]

In England aspiring architects entered the profession through a pupilage system.[13] Students paid a fee to join an architect's office, where the training took place over a period of about five years. Students also could attend lectures at the Royal Academy of Arts in London. In 1840 King's College at the University of London began offering formal architecture classes in which engineering and construction issues were emphasized. Three decades later, in 1870, the Royal Academy opened an evening school under R. Phené Spiers, who had trained at the Ecole. Spiers directed the Academy school until 1906. The program that he developed featured visiting critics, an approach that architect William R. Lethaby remembered as "good fun, but anarchy."[14] The Architectural Association, founded by students during the 1840s, began offering courses by a paid faculty in 1891. A year later, a full-time, three-year program was introduced at King's College, University of London, directed by Banister Fletcher. In 1896 he published an architectural history textbook to assist him in his teaching and for which he would become recognized.[15]

Courses on engineering and architecture were offered in the United States through the nineteenth century. In 1865, the Massachusetts Institute of Technology appointed William R. Ware to launch the country's first fully developed architecture program; the first classes were offered in 1868.[16] A graduate of Harvard College, Ware also had worked in an atelier run by Richard Morris Hunt. Hunt had studied at the Ecole, and through him, Ware became familiar with Ecole training and practice. When he established the architecture program at MIT, he was strongly influenced by the French approach, including its method of design. Within a few years, Ware engaged Eugène Létang, a product of the Ecole, to teach the design courses. Ware left his position in 1881 and was succeeded by Theodore M. Clark, a former member of Richardson's staff. Clark's experience with Richardson evidently was valued and perhaps noted by the men who considered Warren for Harvard. Clark directed the MIT program until 1888, when he was followed by Francis Ward Chandler. As an architect who had trained at the Ecole, Chandler further strengthened MIT's French-style instruction that Létang continued to provide.[17]

Soon after the department was launched at MIT, programs were instituted at the University of Illinois and at Cornell University. The program at Illinois began in 1871 with courses taught by Harald M. Hansen, who had studied at the Bauakademie in Berlin, and was soon taken over by Nathan Ricker, who also studied in Berlin and was most inspired by the technical emphasis of the German schools.[18] The same year, Charles Babcock established the program at Cornell. Babcock had trained under Richard Upjohn, an English-born architect working in New York City, and was most influenced by the English office system.

Six other American programs followed, five of which survived, before the program at Harvard was opened.[19] Of these, the program that was begun at Columbia University in 1881 was noteworthy in that it set a precedent for Harvard.[20] The architecture program at Columbia was directed by Ware, and it differed from the MIT program in the way that it emphasized architectural history. Ware's courses were augmented by lectures in architectural history taught by Alfred Dwight Foster Hamlin, who began teaching at Columbia in 1882 and who published a textbook for the discipline in 1896.[21] As at MIT, the Columbia program was strongly influenced by the Ecole, which Hamlin had attended.

A Course of Study for Harvard

The course of study that Warren developed for Harvard shared certain characteristics in its curriculum with other American programs in architecture. Like the others, the Harvard program was conceived as self-sufficient; it trained students in design through classes taught by the faculty rather than in architects' offices or ateliers. Also like other American programs, the Harvard program assumed that the entering student was inexperienced and in need of introductory courses to the profession.

The Harvard program differentiated itself from other programs through the extent to which the students took architectural history—in three yearlong courses, all taught by Warren. Given Ware's interest in a strong architectural history curriculum in his program at Columbia University, one can understand why he expressed his support for Warren to Harvard's president Eliot. The Harvard program, in fact, would steep its architecture students in even more hours of architectural history than the program at Columbia.[22]

Warren believed that through a close examination of historical models, the student would acquire a vocabulary and an understanding of design that could then be applied to current architectural problems. Warren wrote that "if, from the constant tracing of these laws of design as exemplified in the work of Greece, of the Middle Ages and of the Renaissance in Italy, the observance of these principles has become second nature to him, [the architect] will have no difficulty in applying them to new conditions and in inventing new forms or new modifications. This is what I mean by Scholarship in Architecture."[23] A similar outlook appears to have motivated Hamlin and Fletcher, who wrote their architectural history textbooks to provide their architecture students with models that would contribute to their own designs.[24] While Warren did not publish a textbook, at his death he was praised for his brilliant teaching of the history of architecture. John Taylor Boyd, Jr., one of Warren's students who also studied at the Ecole, wrote in the *Architectural Record*, "It is not exaggerating to say that nothing surpassed [Warren's teaching of architectural history] in any school in the world."[25]

Warren admired certain aspects of Ecole training. He praised the French emphasis on monumentality, balance, and proportion in a building's plan and mass, and the insistence that a building's plan relate to its exterior expression.[26] Yet Warren also rejected much of the Ecole approach that was widely embraced by American programs. In 1897, the *American Architect and Building News* wrote that every architectural school in the country "except the one at Cambridge" had adopted the French method and the Beaux-Arts style.[27] Indeed, Warren most emphatically rejected the Beaux-Arts classicism that was so characteristic of the French school. He wrote that "in so far as it encourages a taste for extravagant and overloaded ornamentation, and tends to destroy delight in simple and quiet work—in so far as it does these things, the French influence is deeply to be deplored."[28] Boyd wrote that Warren's resistance to Beaux-Arts style required great courage at a time when the "Paris faction thought it presumptuous for any school to teach anything but the style of the Beaux-Arts."[29]

Of the various approaches to architectural education introduced in England during the nineteenth century, Spiers's visiting critics program at the Royal Academy of Arts appears to have provided the most intriguing example for Warren. Spiers had been friends with Richardson, a connection that may have caused Warren to consider Spiers's innovation more closely. By the end of his third academic year at Harvard, Warren proposed to his design instructor that they hire visiting critics. The instructor, George F. Newton, wrote to Warren: "This seems to me a serious experiment. It never has been done in any of the great architectural schools and it might be the case of too many cooks. . . ."[30] Newton was afraid that a program of visiting architects would confuse the students.

Despite Newton's reservations, Warren pressed ahead and implemented the program of engaging prominent architects as "Lecturers in Architectural Design."[31] The guest instructors were mainly from Boston and included Peabody, Coolidge, R. Clipston Sturgis, and Edmund Wheelwright, along with Frank Miles Day from Philadelphia. Warren

believed that the guest instructors offered expert instruction in special-
ized areas to advanced design students, and he proudly described this
feature of the Harvard program in the *Architectural Record*.[32]

English, French, and German theorists all contributed to Warren's
design philosophy. Warren wrote that students at Harvard were taught
"to appreciate that beautiful architectural forms are organic expressions
of structural functions."[33] His student Fiske Kimball wrote that Warren's
"criteria of admiration were the essentially mediaeval ones of Ruskin's
Seven Lamps and Viollet-le-Duc's *Discourses,* with a strong emphasis on
structural rationalism."[34] Yet Warren's outlook was not limited to that of
the medievalist; his outlook was distinguished by what Kimball called a
"broader historical catholicity," which included an appreciation for an-
tique and Renaissance architecture. Warren was well versed in the writings of his German contemporaries, including Bötticher, and adapted
their interest in Greek architecture to his design theory. Beginning students were taught to appreciate the Greek orders as beautiful expressions
of structure, Warren wrote.[35]

Kimball noted that Warren's critique of monuments adhered narrowly
to an analysis of the buildings as structural expressions and provided
"no real analysis of spatial or plastic form."[36] This approach had its
limitations, as Kimball recalled:

I was a docile youth, but I couldn't help discovering one thing about this system:
it was (and is) absolutely impossible to deduce a design by the light of reason
alone on the basis of structure and function. These factors still admitted many
alternative forms, with no criteria for choosing between them.[37]

Yet Warren's outlook, a reworking of views that a wide range of European authors promulgated during the second half of the nineteenth century, was accepted by Boyd, who wrote the tribute to Warren published
in the *Architectural Record.* Boyd did not question the limitations of this
perspective. At the time of Warren's death, in 1917, Boyd described how
Warren taught that beauty in architecture derives from its artistic expression of construction. Boyd explained that Warren presented these
ideas through the study of abstract design, as distinct from the study of
architectural history.[38]

Harvard's original architecture program enrolled undergraduates. In
1894 the program was officially announced as a department of the
Lawrence Scientific School, and a full complement of courses was of-

fered the following year. By the 1906–1907 academic year, the program was moved to the Graduate School of Applied Science, and the department began offering a master's degree in architecture. In 1912, a separate School of Architecture was established under the Faculty of Graduate Schools of Applied Science. Two years later, a Faculty of Architecture was created, with Warren appointed as its dean.[39] Thus over time, the emphasis of architectural studies at Harvard shifted to the graduate level, and the program gained greater autonomy from other departments.

Yet Warren also was a member of Harvard's Department of Fine Arts. In 1912, his courses were listed in the university register by the department, and they continued to be offered by the department until his death.[40] Warren took an active role in the department, teaching graduate students as well as undergraduates, and serving as a dissertation adviser.[41]

The curriculum that Warren developed for the architecture program reinforced his desire to train architects who would be more like artists than engineers. Early on, the program was recognized for its fine-arts emphasis. The *American Architect and Building News* reported in 1897 that the Harvard program had been "founded particularly for the cultivation of architecture as a fine art" and that "its students have generally been prepared by a much fuller artistic development than is possessed by those who matriculate at the older architectural schools."[42] Many of the men who joined or visited the department faculty also were involved with the Society of Arts and Crafts, Boston. Their taste was more English than French, and the architects among them shared Warren's interests in the Gothic Revival and Colonial Revival as opposed to Beaux-Arts classicism.

Hiring New Faculty Members

The faculty hired by Warren taught courses that advanced an aesthetic orientation. In 1894 George F. Newton joined the department to teach courses in design. Newton was hired on the recommendation of Robert S. Peabody, for whom he had worked, and he continued to teach in the department for ten years.[43] In his own practice, Newton produced many Gothic Revival churches.[44] In 1899, Denman Ross began teaching theory of design, emphasizing abstract design principles in a manner that was complementary to Warren's course on abstract theory of architecture.[45] Three years later, the painter and Arts and Crafts frame maker Hermann Dudley Murphy began teaching life drawing, and soon after, Harold Warren began teaching freehand drawing.[46] Guest architects included Ralph Adams Cram, known primarily as a medievalist, and C. R. Ashbee, a leader in the English Arts and Crafts movement, who lectured on history.[47] In 1897, the department determined that it was weakest in structural and engineering subjects—an irony, given Warren's theoretical emphasis on structure as the basis for design—and so to strengthen these areas, courses in building construction and carpentry were added.[48]

Warren's most notable achievement in rounding out his faculty came in 1911 when he brought Eugène Duquesne to Harvard to direct the teaching of architectural design.[49] Duquesne had not only attended the Ecole; he was a recipient of its highest attainment, the Prix de Rome. Duquesne was the first Prix de Rome winner to teach architecture in the United States. As Warren observed in describing this coup, Duquesne left behind a secure government position, a place on the Jury for Architecture at the Ecole, and his atelier in Paris. In lobbying Duquesne, Warren was supported by the American ambassador to France at the time, Robert Bacon (a Harvard graduate who had served as Theodore Roosevelt's secretary of state), as well as the French government.[50]

Duquesne's approach to design was compatible with Warren's and somewhat unusual for a winner of the Prix de Rome. His successful project was a church that was "frankly unsymmetrical" and was inspired by Florence Cathedral, "especially in the treatment of the great dome."[51] Warren probably viewed this project with appreciation in light of his own proposal for the Cathedral of Saint John the Divine, also inspired by Florence Cathedral. Warren wrote enthusiastically about how Duquesne was committed to the principles that were similar to those behind the Harvard program: "that structure and design in architecture are necessarily one, that the structure must be expressed in the design; consistency; restraint of design. . . ."[52] He added that Duquesne's "breadth of view" included an admiration for English medieval and early Renaissance architecture—"somewhat unusual among French architects."[53] When Duquesne wrote "The Teaching of Architecture" for Harvard's *Architectural Quarterly* a year after his appointment, he emphasized these same ideals. He also described how much time the Harvard students spent studying architectural history—Warren's domain and a Harvard specialty—and working in the drafting room—his domain and the basis of the Ecole education.[54]

Kimball, who was a student at Harvard when Duquesne arrived, explained that luring Duquesne to the architecture program was a response to the problems that had arisen from transforming the department into a graduate program.[55] For years, Harvard students had majored in architecture as undergraduates and had then gone to Paris for further study. When the department transformed itself into a graduate program, it was left with just a few students. "There was thus one moment, indeed, when I was actually the only student at Harvard in advanced design," Kimball recalled. By bringing an architect from an Ecole atelier to his program, Warren hoped to compete with the Ecole. The fact that MIT had long employed a design professor from the Ecole, if not a winner of the Prix de Rome, also motivated Warren to hire a French architect.[56]

Kimball recognized that Warren was drawn to Duquesne because the two men had sympathetic approaches to design. In other respects, however, Duquesne was not a good match for Harvard. "Simple, modest, issued no doubt from a petit-bourgeois or peasant background, Duquesne felt out of place in social Cambridge, was never happy there, and left as soon as he could," wrote Kimball. Duquesne also must have missed the opportunities to design prestigious government projects. He left Harvard in 1914, ostensibly because of the outbreak of World War I.

Duquesne's brief stay at Harvard met with mixed reviews. Kimball was less than enthusiastic. "The absence of any real transition from Warren or Cram to Duquesne left the students pretty well bewildered," he wrote. Yet other former students viewed Duquesne more positively. Boyd, who received his master's degree from Harvard's School of Architecture, had joined Duquesne's atelier in Paris before Harvard recruited him.[57] In Boyd's estimation, Warren's luring of Duquesne to his faculty was a brilliant move, and he praised the Frenchman as a theorist and as a planner.[58] George Harold Edgell, who wrote his dissertation under Warren, taught art and architectural history in the Department of Fine Arts, and became dean of the Faculty of Architecture in 1922, remembered Duquesne as an important addition to the department. Years later, Edgell would follow Warren's example by bringing another winner of the Prix de Rome to the architecture faculty.[59]

Warren was a capable recruiter, and he played a significant part in establishing Harvard's program in landscape architecture. He tried to hire Charles Eliot, the president's son, but young Eliot declined after being advised against it by his mentor, Frederick Law Olmsted.[60] President Eliot and then Warren pursued Frederick Law Olmsted, Jr., who ultimately accepted the Harvard position.[61] In a letter to Warren from Biltmore, North Carolina, where Olmsted was working at the Vanderbilt estate in 1897, Olmsted expressed his willingness to direct the course of study.[62] In 1899, Warren wrote to Eliot about how he had reviewed the proposed curriculum with Olmsted and found it acceptable.[63] The following year, Olmsted launched the program, and from that point, the School of Landscape Architecture emerged and grew alongside the School of Architecture.[64] Warren maintained an active interest in landscape architecture through the rest of his career, culminating with his role as dean of the Faculty of Architecture, which included professors teaching in the landscape school.

A Building Designed for the Study of Architecture

In the last weeks of 1901, the faculty and staff members of the university's achitecture programs completed their move into Nelson Robinson, Jr., Hall (fig. 25). The building's architect was Charles McKim, who had designed the Johnston Gate, the first component of Harvard's Memorial Fence, in 1889. Warren had hoped his own firm would be hired to build his department's new home, but members of the Harvard community opposed the idea.[65] Henry Lee Higginson, a corporation member, argued that an outside architect should be employed as a matter of propriety and that in any case Warren would be involved with the planning.[66] Higginson recommended McKim, a choice that was more than satisfactory for Warren. Warren established the types of rooms and the dimensions that he wanted, and he described where the rooms should be located. It also was his wish to use the red brick and limestone trimmings that McKim had chosen for the Johnston Gate, and these materials were adopted.[67] While not discounting McKim's contribution, one may evaluate Robinson Hall as a building that is a reflection of Warren: his taste and his vision of architectural education.

During its first years, the department established itself in a former house on Holmes Field, near the Law School. By 1897, the program

FIG. 25. Charles McKim, Nelson Robinson, Jr., Hall, Harvard University, Cambridge, Massachusetts, 1899–1901. *Courtesy of the Harvard University Archives.*

had moved into the Carey Athletic Building, which was renamed the Rotch Building, located in the same vicinity.[68] The new architecture building came about after the death of a Harvard undergraduate whose parents sought to memorialize him, and for whom the building is named. It was the first building in the United States constructed solely to serve the needs of an architectural program. Through its materials, its massing, and its siting, the structure was intended to harmonize with the other buildings of the college. Two stories in height, Robinson Hall is a simple rectangular block with a symmetrical facade, and it is classically detailed.

The plan of Robinson Hall (fig. 26) was organized around a two-story Hall of Casts, a large rectangular court that one traversed upon entering the building.[69] Casts were a standard teaching tool of architectural schools both in Europe and in America; the two-story-high court of Robinson Hall was designed to accommodate full-size casts of columns of the classical orders made from major Greek and Roman monuments. The first floor also featured a large lecture room, where Warren taught architectural history. In it were two stereopticons placed side by side for the projection of lantern slides that Warren and the students

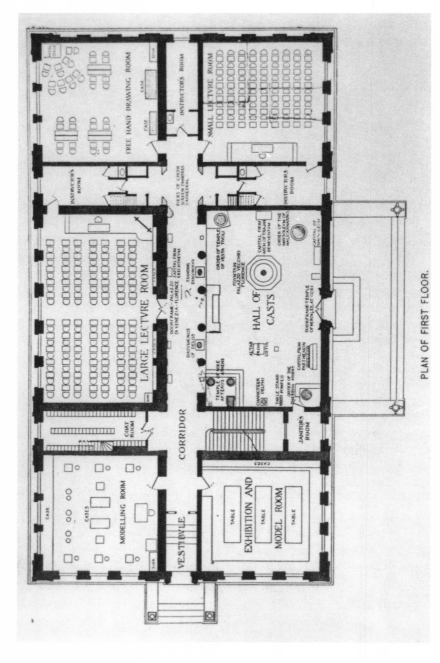

PLAN OF FIRST FLOOR.

FIG. 26. Robinson Hall, plan of first floor. *From* Harvard Engineering Journal, *June 1902.*

could compare. Norton had lectured without slides, but teaching with slides had become the norm by the turn of the century.[70] A small lecture room was located across the hall. Two additional rooms supported the department's fine-arts emphasis: one room for freehand drawing and one room for wax modeling. Yet another room was dedicated to displays of models that demonstrated construction methods and displays of samples of building stone. This room was the only space in the building dedicated to the more technical aspects of construction. The most significant space of the second floor (fig. 27) was the large drawing room, which ran the length of the building. This room was the Harvard response to the atelier, and it was staffed with a design instructor throughout the day. A small drawing room also was located on the second floor, to serve the teaching of classes and for critiques. In another corner of the second floor was the library, which connected to the large drawing room so that the students could easily consult their references.

The choice of casts, paintings, and art objects displayed in the building reflected Warren's favorite works in architectural and art history, expressed in his youth in his letters from Europe and clarified in his subsequent teaching and writing.[71] In addition to casts from standard Greek and Roman monuments, such as the Temple of Athena Nike at Athens, were casts from Laon, Chartres, and Florence Cathedral. They were installed by John Evans, the sculptor with whom Warren worked professionally and who was a colleague in the Society of Arts and Crafts.[72] In 1916 the Hall of Casts was graced with a model of the Cathedral of Saint John the Divine, a loan from Cram, who was by this time in charge of the cathedral's design and construction.[73] Original paintings and copies of paintings that were hung throughout Robinson Hall represented artists known as colorists and in the Ruskinian pantheon, including Tintoretto and Carpaccio, Turner, and Ruskin himself. A collection of textiles, embroidery, and prints owned by Denman Ross was exhibited for the study of design; this display was directly related to the involvement of Ross and many other members of the department with the Society of Arts and Crafts, Boston.

The Robinson family donation included generous funding to purchase aids for teaching. In 1907, Warren reported that the architecture program owned about 8,000 lantern slides. By contrast, the Fogg Art Museum, where art history was taught, owned 3,643 slides.[74]

In planning the new library, Warren and McKim probably discussed and analyzed their memories of Richardson's library. The architecture

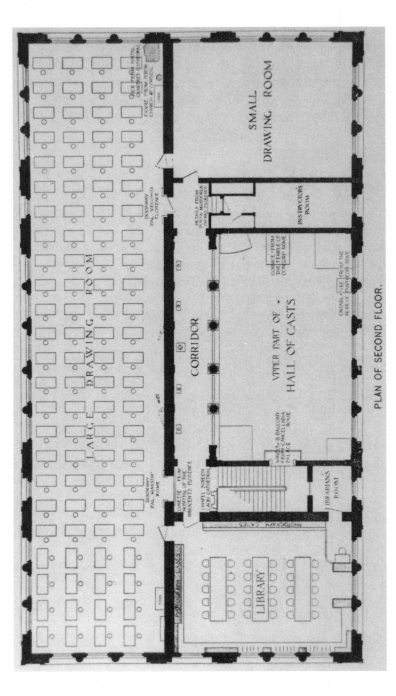

LARGE DRAWING ROOM

SMALL DRAWING ROOM

CORRIDOR

VPPER PART OF · HALL OF CASTS

LIBRARY

LIBRARIANS ROOM

INSTRUCTORS ROOM

PHOTOGRAPH CASES

PLAN OF SECOND FLOOR.

FIG. 27. Robinson Hall, plan of second floor. *From* Harvard Engineering Journal, *June 1902.*

library was conceived as an inviting place, with red walls and dark oak trim, large tables, and comfortable chairs.[75] By 1907, the library contained about 10,000 architectural photographs, all indexed and cross-referenced so that they could be studied as monuments and as sources for various architectural features.[76] The library also held nearly 1,400 volumes. This collection was complemented by more than 8,000 books on the fine arts in the university library. In 1908, Charles Coolidge donated money to the department for Warren to use for books and photographs; again one might imagine that memories of time spent in Richardson's library were shared.[77]

Despite the apparent satisfaction of the faculty with the building, Norton was displeased. In 1904, he wrote "A Criticism of Harvard Architecture Made to the Board of Overseers," published in the *Harvard Graduates Magazine*.[78] He deeply regretted that the building for an intended School of Architecture was not a model of good design, finding the building lacking in beauty and "out of harmony" with Sever Hall. He deemed Robinson Hall one of a long series of failures at the university over the past fifty years, including Richardson's Sever Hall, the Fogg Museum (the old Fogg building, by Richard Morris Hunt), and McKim's Memorial Fence. He concluded by emphasizing the need to develop a plan for future buildings and the need for a review system for new buildings when they were proposed. Although Warren must have been stung by Norton's attack on Robinson Hall, Warren also could be critical and would strive to play a role in the planning and design of Harvard's buildings.

Warren's Courses in Architectural History

Warren's courses on the history of architecture formed the foundation of the Harvard architecture program.[79] More than an examination of buildings, the lectures were colored by Warren's deeply held moral conviction that emphasized the importance of the individual in society, a perspective that was reinforced by his Swedenborgian and Anglo-American upbringing. Warren saw history in terms of the rise and fall of the individual in a political sense, and as he presented his history of architecture, he sometimes implicitly and sometimes explicitly revealed how periods marked by self-determination coincided with excellence in architecture. Norton, noted for vehement moralizing in his lectures, had made similar associations in his telling of history, identifying golden ages of Greece and the Middle Ages.[80] Warren's narrative was less strident and farther ranging. He led the student through the ancient world, culminating in classical Greece, and then through the Roman period. His narrative continued through the Middle Ages, focusing on the emergence of Gothic architecture in France, his study of the period ultimately concluding with the development of the English parish church. Warren next covered the Italian Renaissance, then passed over the Alps to examine the northern Renaissance, concluding with Georgian England. Despite his high regard for German authors, Warren devoted only a little attention to German architecture, and he focused even less on that of other countries beyond England, France, and Italy. Consistent with his Arts and Crafts orientation, Warren presented stained glass and ironwork to his students. Also reflecting his Arts and Crafts interests, he discussed residential buildings from the northern Renaissance and later, and he lectured on garden design.

In 1912, Warren wrote "The Study of Architectural History and Its Place in the Professional Curriculum."[81] In it he restated views that he had expressed years earlier in the *Sanitary Engineer* and in the *Architectural Review*. He argued that architects should not take an archaeological approach to their study of earlier buildings. Rather they should seek to penetrate the underlying meaning of architectural form.[82] Warren concluded that by studying the past, architecture students would develop their taste. He believed that contemporary architects should strive to understand the principles underlying past styles in order to build a vital artistic tradition.[83]

Throughout most of his career at Harvard, Warren's architectural history courses were presented as a three-year sequence, with the first year devoted to the study of ancient architecture, the second year devoted to the study of medieval architecture, and the third year to Renaissance and modern architecture. Although his appreciation for Gothic architecture suggested that he was a medievalist—and at his death, Cram described him as such—he was equally appreciative of the classical tradition.[84]

The purpose of Warren's ancient-history course was to teach the student to recognize the logic and beauty of the orders and classical architecture in general.[85] First, however, he discussed Egypt, Mesopotamia, and Persia, relating the geography and the culture of each civilization to its architectural traditions. After presenting this background, he introduced the Doric and Ionic orders. When Warren discussed the Athenian acropolis, he told his students that its monuments represented "the best period," that is, the fifth century B.C.[86] On the other hand, Hellenistic architecture was an "over-luxuriant Greek style."[87] Through the course of his three years of lectures, he sought to demonstrate that buildings that were spare in their ornamentation were superior to those that were more elaborately embellished. Restraint was a virtue.

Warren's lectures on Roman architecture focused on methods of vaulting, including domes, and on the use of concrete. He noted that sometimes the Romans had built vaults with flat tiles set in cement, and he related this development to modern construction, mentioning the vaulting in Guastavino tiles at the Boston Public Library, designed by McKim.[88] Roman architecture, according to Warren, was marked by lavish ornament and was a "departure from Greek simplicity and refinement."[89] He did, however, credit the Romans for their use of marble veneer. "The Romans always felt their material," he said, adding that they "didn't try to make plaster look like marble etc."[90] This focus on honesty of materials was heavily promoted by Ruskin and others during the nineteenth century and was a theme that Warren repeated in his role as a leader in the Arts and Crafts movement.

Students read the works of German and French authors, as well as works in English.[91] Some of the authors, such as Josef Durm and Auguste Choisy, emphasized construction.[92] Others, including Georges Perrot and Charles Chipiez, established geographic and cultural characteristics as a basis for their interpretation of architecture.[93] Warren synthesized these perspectives for his students, and this synthesis was the basis of a manuscript that he had nearly completed when he died, published posthumously in 1919 as *The Foundations of Classic Architecture*.[94] On his exams, Warren always included questions to determine that his students had learned the orders, while Roman vaulting was another favorite subject of inquiry.[95]

Honesty and Beauty in the Middle Ages

Just as Warren's course on ancient architecture was cast to demonstrate a progression toward the Greek architecture of the fifth century B.C., followed by a decline, so too was Warren's medieval course cast to demonstrate a progression, in this case toward the Gothic architecture of the twelfth century in France.[96] By the time students finished this course, they would have understood that peak periods in architecture were marked by a restrained approach to design and ornamentation.

Structural developments were emphasized. Warren analyzed the emergence of Byzantine domes on pendentives, Romanesque barrel and groin vaults, and Gothic ribbed groin vaults supported by buttresses.[97] Warren praised the Gothic building's structural honesty, in the vaulting system and in its subsidiary elements, while he condemned the "structural falseness" found in much late Gothic work.[98] By the thirteenth century, as Gothic builders erected walls covered "with tracery forms which have no structural significance," Warren saw decline. Equally troublesome was the use of gables over door arches and niches "without constructive meaning."[99] Again the students were taught that forms should be derived from structural need.

Warren's recounting of medieval architectural history led the student to conclude that, as was demonstrated in the study of the ancient world, good government and good architecture coincide. Following Ruskin's analysis, expressed in the *Stones of Venice*, Warren explained how the Venetians, with an elected doge, enjoyed peace and lived in an open environment, contrasting with the "grim, defended forts of the continent."[100] Students learned how Gothic architecture emerged with the growth of communes.[101] Warren explained that Noyon was one of the first French towns to receive a charter, and not coincidentally, the town built one of the first Gothic cathedrals. "The nave was the people's meeting-place, where the guilds met and where business was transacted," Warren said.[102] The rise of the craftsman accompanied the flourishing of a golden age. When discussing developments in England, Warren explained how the parish church was the people's church. He described how wardens were appointed to look after the church, and he pointed out that these meetings were the forerunner of town meetings. "The English parish church is the most beautiful building that Christianity ever produced," Warren pronounced, implying that its beauty derived in part from its institutional character.[103]

The craftsman also contributed in a material way to the beauty of the Gothic churches. In expressing his admiration for the medieval craftsman, Warren was restating the perspective of Ruskin. At the same time, Warren was articulating views that he began promoting in 1897 in his work with the Society of Arts and Crafts, Boston. Warren was especially attentive to stone carving, focusing on the sculpture of Chartres, Laon,

Reims, Amiens, and Wells.[104] Wood carving, such as the sixteenth-century work at Amiens Cathedral, also received attention and praise.[105] While pursuing his main interest in abstract design, he was not interested in issues of naturalism in figural sculpture. As one might expect, Warren considered the stained glass at Chartres to be its crowning glory. In general, he was partial to twelfth-century glass for its decorative quality, but he found merit in thirteenth-century examples as well, where the drawing was better.[106] In his discussion of glass, Warren referred his students to the window by William Morris and Edward Burne-Jones at Richardson's Trinity Church in Boston as a good example of the contemporary revival.[107] Medieval ironwork also received attention, with Warren noting that the designs always showed an intimate relation to the material and the use.[108] Referring to the ironwork, he said, "The medieval idea was to take something practical and make it beautiful"— a recurring Arts and Crafts theme.[109]

Although Warren's lectures emphasized churches, he did discuss other building types. When he showed his students examples of domestic architecture, such as the house of Jacques Coeur and the château of Josselin, he pointed out how dormers were placed where they were needed, based on interior room requirements, and without concern for regularity. By casting this observation in a positive light, he lent support to a picturesque approach to design.[110] When he presented major English Gothic monuments, he paid special attention to the Perpendicular towers and windows that were favorite models for the architects of his circle, including Newton and Cram.[111]

For the medieval course, students read works by Choisy and Viollet-le-Duc, reinforcing Warren's interest in structural development.[112] Moore's *Development and Character of Gothic Architecture*, published in 1890 and dedicated to Norton, also focused on structure.[113] William R. Lethaby's *Mediaeval Art: From the Peace of the Church to the Eve of the Renaissance*, published in 1904, acknowledged decorative as well as structural objectives of the Gothic builders, consistent with Lethaby's interests as a member of an English Arts and Crafts guild.[114] On their exams, Warren's students were asked to describe vaults and to draw them, and they were asked to compare French Gothic buildings with English Gothic buildings. On one exam, they drew a Perpendicular Gothic window, while on another, they described the relationship between the parish and the parish church in medieval England.[115]

Warren focused on medieval architecture when he wrote the entry on

Provence and Languedoc for Russell Sturgis's *Dictionary of Architecture and Building*, published in 1901 and still a recognized reference work.[116] Discussing the Romanesque monuments of Provence, Warren observed how the buildings were almost devoid of ornamentation yet were admirable in their proportions and "constructive simplicity." The abbey church of Saint Gilles, Gard, and its sculpture, which he had admired on his European trip in the 1880s, also were discussed and praised.

The Renaissance and the Modern Point of View

The third course in Warren's survey of architectural history, on the "Renaissance and Modern Styles," corresponded to the chapter Warren wrote for a survey book, *The Fine Arts: A Course of University Lessons on Sculpture, Painting, Architecture, and Decoration*, edited by Edmund Buckley, from 1900.[117] Organized as a series of lectures, Buckley's *Fine Arts* claimed to be the first comprehensive work on the fine arts published in America. Its contributors were academics and recognized authorities, such as Russell Sturgis. Warren's chapter, "Architecture: Renaissance and Modern," emphasized Renaissance Italy while also covering the architecture of other cultures and later periods.

It was Warren's belief that the Renaissance marked "the beginning of the modern point of view and of modern civilization."[118] Borrowing from Jacob Burckhardt, Warren explained that while the medieval period was characterized by little consciousness of individuality, this new, modern period was characterized by an awakening sense of individuality. He did not attempt to clarify this point with respect to the observations he had made in earlier lectures about the emergence of individual identity during the Middle Ages. Apparently Warren considered the emergence of individualism to have been a matter of degree, with a greater self-awareness marking Renaissance man.

Recognizing the new role of the architect, Warren presented this period as a history of the achievement of individuals.[119] His method followed a long-standing approach, dating to the Renaissance with Giorgio Vasari's *Lives of the Most Eminent Italian Architects, Painters, and Sculptors*, from 1550. Filippo Brunelleschi was discussed and praised for his role in the design of the dome of Florence Cathedral. Then with the career of Leon Battista Alberti, a turning point was established. Warren explained that while the architects until this time had been builder-craftsmen, Alberti was a learned scholar and the first architect in the modern sense. Alberti was a designer. Although Warren clearly admired the spontaneity and corporate relationships of earlier craftsman-builders, he did not condemn the scholar-architect; rather, Warren presented his emergence as inevitable. Warren also believed that the development of individualism during the Renaissance was inevitable and positive. Questions pertaining to the relative roles of designer and craftsman, along with individual and collective efforts, would be more fully explored by Warren in his activities with the Society of Arts and Crafts, Boston. For Warren, the finest work of the Renaissance was done by Raphael, Antonio da Sangallo, and Jacopo Sansovino.[120] Their buildings were more robust and less lavishly decorated than those of the early Renaissance, Warren wrote, implying again that restraint is a virtue. With Michelangelo, the decline began: architecture became illogical and mannered. Warren belittled the Laurentian Library in Florence, with its columns and brackets that carry nothing, serving only a decorative function.

Warren passed over the Baroque period in Italy mainly with words of scorn. "Nearly all connection between structure and design now disappeared, and theatrical splendor of effect was the ideal aimed at," he wrote. He condemned the broken pediments, curved facades, twisted shafts, and other "debased forms."[121] In turning to the architecture of the French Renaissance, Warren found charm in the way the buildings were medieval in spirit, even when classical forms were grafted onto them. The extravagance of the French Baroque period did not appeal to Warren, although he considered the gardens of Versailles to be magnificent.[122] Warren wrote more briefly about the Renaissance architecture of Germany, which he found quaint and picturesque, and of Belgium and Holland, which he related to the German.

When Warren introduced the architecture of the English Renaissance, he described it with special warmth. He said of its country house tradition, "In the expression of homely comfort and sweet domesticity no style ever equaled it."[123] He explained how a cozy effect was achieved through a smallness of scale, including small window lights and low stories. While he praised the houses that mixed Gothic with Renaissance elements, he also praised the purer classicism of Inigo Jones, who preserved the "homelike expression of earlier English work."[124] Sir Christopher Wren similarly preserved this quality, Warren wrote. He also expressed admiration for Wren's Gothic spires with classic detail and Wren's dome for Saint Paul's Cathedral in London.[125]

Although Warren's chapter covered developments in architecture through the nineteenth century and into modern times, his Harvard lectures appear to have ended with the eighteenth century. His reference books and exams suggest the limit of his "Renaissance and Modern" course. Like most of his colleagues, he didn't believe most nineteenth-century architecture had much merit. The recommended books for this course mainly addressed the Renaissance in Italy, with a few others devoted to France, Germany, and England.[126] Warren also recommended books by Reginald Blomfield, a leading English architect and academic who had participated in the Arts and Crafts Exhibition Society and the Art Workers Guild.[127] In his *History of Renaissance Architecture in England*, Blomfield praised Wren and condemned John Vanbrugh, articulating views shared by Warren. Blomfield's book *The Formal Garden in England* argued that a house and its garden should be designed together. On his exams, Warren emphasized the development of the dome, residential design, and garden design.[128] Students described the development of the English house from the time of Henry VIII to the Georgian period, and they wrote about the work of Jones and Wren.

The most noteworthy historian missing from Warren's sources was Heinrich Wölfflin. Years later, Kimball recognized this absence:

Although Wölfflin's *Renaissance und Barock* had appeared in 1888, the year I was born, and his *Klassische Kunst* in 1901 [actually 1898], Wölfflin's works and even his name were never referred to at Harvard in my day, and it was only by subsequent personal effort, with all the difficulty inherent in a total change of youthful mental habits, that I ultimately became able to see in abstract spatial and plastic terms.[129]

Wölfflin's engagement with spatial and plastic issues and his appreciation of Baroque qualities must have seemed useless to Warren, who, as Kimball noted, considered structure the driving issue in architecture and the Baroque period corrupt and debased. Kimball would ultimately publish extensively on the eighteenth century and become an authority on Rococo design.

Warren admired early American architecture, elevating formal study of it to an unusual level for the period. Boyd wrote that Warren "was chided not only for appreciating Colonial architecture, but teaching it in design problems."[130] Judging by his exams, Warren appears to have included colonial American architecture in his "Renaissance and Modern" course on an occasional basis.[131] Warren wrote about American architecture in *Picturesque and Architectural New England*, published in 1899, and in his chapter for Buckley's *Fine Arts*.[132] A register of the lantern slides acquired for the department also reflects the faculty's—including Warren's—enthusiasm for colonial and early federal buildings.[133] In his writings, Warren explained how the craftsman-builders of the seventeenth century were working in the medieval English tradition. These buildings he admired for their picturesqueness. Warren explained how the buildings of the eighteenth century, while influenced by English classicism, still were generally the work of craftsman-builders, and he praised their "sober restraint" and "modest qualities."[134] The department owned lantern slides of the Royall house in Medford, Massachusetts, the Lee mansion in Marblehead, Massachusetts, the Old State House in Boston, and many other examples of the colonial and federal periods. Slides of recent buildings were rare but predictable, including McKim's Boston Public Library and Richardson's Trinity Church.

While Warren's interpretation of history was generally typical for the turn of the twentieth century, his particular approach may be better understood through a comparison with that of his contemporaries. Henry Adams, for example, was hired by Harvard's president Eliot in the early 1870s to teach medieval history at the college. During the following decade, Adams built a house designed by Richardson when Warren was working for the firm.[135] Adams and Warren circulated in overlapping orbits. In *The Education of Henry Adams*, written in 1906, Adams described his struggle to understand the forces of history.[136] Like Warren, Adams favored the Middle Ages and America's English colonial past. Both historians also identified a unity of spirit during the Middle Ages, and both recognized the greater complexity of the modern age. But Adams was fundamentally pessimistic about his own time. He left his teaching position at Harvard after just a few years and spent the rest of his life as a writer and an observer, longing for a superior past. Warren, on the other hand, was optimistic about his world and the future. In a complex society, he was actively engaged as an architect and as an educator. Far from seeing the past as a retreat, Warren examined it for lessons to build upon.

Eliot's Harvard accommodated a range of views. While the members of this elite community shared a regard for history, the degree to which they felt this attachment varied, with Adams at one end of the spectrum and Norton close by. At the other end of the spectrum was Eliot, who, while of Brahmin stock, began his teaching career at Harvard by re-forming science education and then devoted his presidency to pedagog-ical innovation.[137] Warren's outlook toward past and present placed him in the middle of the spectrum, which no doubt was why he fit Harvard so well.

In many ways, Warren's narrative of architectural history resembled that of Hamlin and Fletcher, presented in their textbooks. As might be expected from teachers of future architects, all three historians conveyed a belief that admirable architecture had emerged repeatedly in the past. The message they conveyed was that a serious student in the modern age would be able to apply history's lessons successfully. Warren's pre-ferred periods also were favored by Hamlin and Fletcher. Yet Warren's enthusiasm for the English parish church and the English country house was distinctive. Hamlin, by contrast, expressed a reverence for the ar-chitecture of the Italian Renaissance, which was consistent with his back-ground as someone trained at the Ecole.

Student Architecture Projects and Research Papers

The Harvard students' architecture projects reflected Warren's prefer-ences in terms of their designs and their types. In the early years of the program, Warren sought to give the students practice in "picturesque planning" in addition to practice in more monumental, formal plan-ning.[138] Therefore, students during the 1896–1897 academic year were required to design a country church and a country house. Also, unlike students who were trained to design in the relatively restrictive Beaux-Arts mode, Warren's students were encouraged to use forms from the past with some freedom. On one occasion, Kimball recalled with amuse-ment, Warren proudly showed one of Kimball's drawings to McKim: Kimball had audaciously applied a Gothic dogtooth ornament to a win-dow molding of a simple classical building.[139] Warren's admiration of the northern Renaissance, in which medieval and classical forms were intermingled, evidently encouraged the inventive tendencies of his more independent students. Nevertheless, most of the student work was far from flamboyant and generally adhered to either the classical or the medieval tradition.

The nature of these student designs is indicated by examples pub-lished in the *Architectural Record* from July 1907 and in issues of the

Architectural Quarterly of Harvard University, published between 1912 and 1914. The buildings, by and large, were classically composed and detailed. The massing tended to be block-like, and the facades typically were organized with a sequence of round-arched windows. The main mass was often surmounted by a low hipped roof, sometimes crowned by a dome. A design for a municipal courthouse, illustrated in the *Architectural Record*, is representative with its blocky massing, central dome, and rhythms of arched windows.[140] Ornament was applied sparingly. Gothic sources most often were the basis for church designs, as was the case with a student's proposed college chapel (fig. 28), published in 1912 in the *Architectural Quarterly of Harvard University*.[141] The chapel reflected English Gothic models from the Early English and Perpendicular periods, combined in an original composition.

Student thesis projects, submitted for the master's degree, suggest the types of buildings that interested Warren and his department. Listed and described in the department's records of its meetings, the building types mirrored the values of an affluent, educated New England elite.[142] Projects were more likely to be for suburban or country settings than for the city. They were more likely to be for the wealthy than for the poor. They were more likely to be for institutional than for commercial clients. Student theses included an Episcopal church, a college clubhouse, a country club, a university gymnasium, a garden pavilion, and a suburban residence, complete with terraces and fountains, a swimming pool, and tennis courts. One adventurous student proposed, and presumably designed, a complex for a wealthy urban church that would "meet the social needs of the changed community which it serves."[143] The new buildings were to be Gothic, to harmonize with the existing church. They would include a social hall with a stage, a gymnasium, a swimming pool, and a library with a children's reading room, apparently for the benefit of a recently arrived immigrant population.

Student research papers followed Warren's interests as well. In the *Architectural Quarterly of Harvard University*, a periodical founded by Warren, several essays were published.[144] Howard Moise, who later taught architecture at the University of California at Berkeley, contributed an article titled "Brunelleschi and His Influence on the Development of Renaissance Architecture."[145] Other articles selected by the Harvard journal included "Raphael as Architect" by Kenneth John Conant and "Thomas Jefferson as Architect" by Kimball.[146] Warren's appreciation of colonial American architecture inspired Conant to research and

FIG. 28. Rhodes Robertson, "A College Chapel." *From* Architectural Quarterly of Harvard University, *September 1912.*

write "Three Vanished Harvard Buildings," published in the *Harvard Illustrated Magazine*.[147] In it, he documented and presented a perspective view of Harvard's first college building, Harvard Hall, from the late 1630s, known only by descriptions from the period, along with documentation and views of two later buildings, known from an engraving.

In this youthful exercise involving the reconstruction of lost buildings, Conant engaged in a line of academic study for which he would become recognized. He would devote his career to interpreting the ruins of the French Romanesque abbey of Cluny.

Warren not only directed George Edgell in his dissertation; according to Edgell, Warren suggested the subject. Edgell wrote "The Development of the Architectural Background in the Painting of the Umbrian Renaissance" for a Ph.D. that he received in 1913, the first to be granted by Harvard to a graduate student in art history.[148] Edgell explained that by studying architectural backgrounds, "we often find the highest ideals of Renaissance architecture."[149] In working on a topic that combined studies of painting and architecture, Edgell followed Warren's broad interests in the arts. Edgell, like Warren, would straddle disciplines, teaching in Harvard's Department of Fine Arts, serving as dean of the School of Architecture, and later leading Boston's Museum of Fine Arts as its director.

During the 1916–1917 academic year, Warren lectured on architectural history in two additional programs. In the fall of 1916, Henry Atherton Frost, a member of Harvard's School of Architecture faculty, organized a course of study for women who wanted to pursue careers in architecture.[150] For many years, MIT had admitted women, producing its first graduate in 1890.[151] Frost's new program, arising from requests from the Harvard community, was named the Cambridge School of Architectural and Landscape Design for Women. It lasted until 1942 and trained a number of graduates who maintained active practices. Warren and other members of the Harvard faculty lectured to the students, and Warren lent them several hundred architectural photographs. Also during the 1916–1917 academic year, Warren lectured on architectural history at MIT.[152] By the time of his death, Warren and his perspectives on architectural history were familiar to a great many architects, especially in Boston.

Warren sought to elevate the quality of American architecture, and he believed he could be most influential by educating future architects. Yet Warren also recognized that architects could produce his idea of beautiful buildings only with the help of capable craftsmen. To encourage the training of craftsmen, he played a leading role in establishing and guiding the Society of Arts and Crafts.

~FOUR~

THE SOCIETY OF
ARTS AND CRAFTS
(1897)

ALTHOUGH BY NO MEANS working independently, Warren arguably was the most significant driving force behind the Society of
Arts and Crafts, Boston, during its first two decades. He was chairman
of the organizational meetings held in 1897, he was an editor of the
Society's magazine, he organized two of its three major exhibitions, and
he served as its president from 1904 until his death in 1917. In his
professional practice, Warren collaborated with craftsmen, including
carvers, metalworkers, and glassmakers. Yet he devoted far more hours
of his busy life to the Society of Arts and Crafts in order to educate
craftsmen and the general public about the applied arts.

Under Warren the Society pursued directions that were developed in
the architecture program at Harvard. Just as the Harvard program was
characterized by an emphasis on the study of architectural history, the
Society encouraged the study of historical models. These were presented
to its members through exhibitions and publications. Society exhibitions
included loans of historic craft objects, which were a counterpart to the
casts and paintings of historic buildings and their components displayed
at Robinson Hall. The Society also sponsored lectures and maintained
a library so that the craftsman members could better learn from the past.
Yet while the Harvard students were a fairly homogeneous group that
was young, affluent, and male, the Society membership was far more
diverse, including men and women of various ages and economic backgrounds. Members were mostly of Yankee stock, but some were Italian,
Irish, German, or Jewish. Many lived in the Boston suburbs, but others
lived in Boston or in other parts of the country.

By and large, Arts and Crafts design in America has been associated with the protomodern aspects of the movement and with such figures as Gustav Stickley, Frank Lloyd Wright, and Greene and Greene, whose work shared a lack of overt historical reference. Pottery by Boston makers, most notably Grueby, which was equally inventive, has also been associated with the movement. In recent years, however, the conservative, revival designs that were more typical of Boston have become better recognized as members of this large and diverse family.[1]

The Arts and Crafts movement in general, while embracing many aesthetic and political views, may be characterized by the works of theorists, artists, and architects who were disturbed by the negative effects of industry during the nineteenth century on the built environment, on decorative and utilitarian products, and on the laboring class. Different approaches were promoted to encourage greater individual expression in the production of industrial and decorative wares, and theorists debated ideas about how government might intervene to assist a segment of the labor force that had become virtually enslaved by the machine. These concerns were formulated in England and ultimately were adopted and recast in many ways throughout Europe and the United States.

Both individuals and groups in England established platforms and organizational models that Americans imitated. An influential theorist of the early nineteenth century was the architect Augustus Welby Pugin, who considered the Middle Ages superior to his own from both aesthetic and spiritual perspectives. Inspired by English Gothic examples, he designed Gothic Revival buildings and handcrafted furnishings. Ruskin was another important theorist. An author, painter, and the first professor of art history at Oxford University, Ruskin, too, extolled the Middle Ages and railed against the dehumanizing and ugly aspects of industrial England. William Morris shared these concerns, which he expressed through his writing, lectures, and work in developing products for "artistic" interiors, including hand-printed textiles and wallpaper.

Morris established an interior design firm in 1861, reorganized as Morris and Co. in 1875. This collaborative effort inspired other groups of artisans to band together in guilds, including the Century Guild, founded in 1882, and the Art Workers' Guild, founded in 1884. The Art Workers' Guild organized the Arts and Crafts Exhibition Society, which sponsored its first exhibition in 1888 and gave the movement its name.[2] This society's exhibitions provided the impetus for the first Arts and Crafts exhibition in Boston in 1897. Also influential for Boston was the Guild of Handicraft, organized in 1888 by the architect C. R. Ashbee in London. In 1902 the Guild of Handicraft moved to Chipping Campden in the Cotswolds; although the setting was idyllic, the location was a disadvantage from a commercial perspective, and the guild folded in 1908. Despite the organization's struggles and ultimate failure, Ashbee and the Guild of Handicraft especially interested Warren and his Boston cohorts, who admired the guild's silver and were inspired by the guild's salesrooms in London.

In the United States, a number of developments created an appreciation for craftsmanship during the decades before the Society of Arts and Crafts was organized. The American Aesthetic movement of the 1870s and 1880s may be considered a starting point. During these years, at a time when machine-made products had come to dominate everyday life, a widespread enthusiasm emerged for artistic interiors enhanced by handicraft, including pottery and needlework.[3] Richardson's contact with Morris, whom Richardson visited in 1882, provided an early direct link with the English Arts and Crafts reformer.[4] Displays of decorative objects in Richardson's home and office emulated English Arts and Crafts collections and were noted by those who encountered him, including both clients and architects. Clients such as the Glessners in Chicago, for example, took their cues from Richardson in furnishing the house that he designed for them.[5] Several of the architects whom Richardson employed—including Robert Andrews, Herbert Jaques, and Longfellow, as well as Warren—became actively involved with the Society of Arts and Crafts.

Boston during the 1870s and 1880s offered an environment that encouraged artisans working in a number of fields and media. Richardson's buildings, such as Trinity Church, demonstrated the potential of close collaboration between architects, artists, and craftsmen. New standards of craftsmanship were also offered in the stone carving of John Evans and the woodwork of A. H. Davenport, both of whom were based in the Boston area.[6] The Chelsea Keramic Art Works, an early large-scale producer of art pottery, opened near Boston in 1872. Although it closed in 1889, it set the stage for the emergence of several significant art pottery firms in the region during the 1890s: the Chelsea Pottery, 1891; the Grueby Faience Company, 1895; and the Dedham Pottery, 1896.[7]

During the 1870s and 1880s, several developments occurred in the Boston-Cambridge community that related to a growing interest in art education—developments that also would contribute to the emergence of an Arts and Crafts organization. Both individuals and institutions were striving to promote a greater popular concern for aesthetics, an objective that would be a priority for the Society of Arts and Crafts. In 1873, the State Normal Art School of Massachusetts (today Massachusetts College of Art) opened in Boston for the training of art teachers who, in turn, would instruct generations of children.[8] In 1874, Charles Eliot Norton offered his first art history classes at Harvard. They were extremely successful, and Norton's influence at Harvard and in Boston was considerable.[9] A few years later, in 1877, soon after the opening of the Museum of Fine Arts, Boston, the museum school began offering art classes.[10]

Warren contributed to the interest among Boston's cultural leaders in promoting an artistic sensibility to the broader community. In the spring of 1896, Warren participated in an effort to heighten interest in aesthetics among the young. A five-person committee, including Warren, of the Art Department of the Twentieth Century Club sponsored a prize competition on urban design in Boston for people under twenty years of age.[11] The stated purpose of the competition was to "help promote a noble civic pride and a greater interest in a more beautiful city life," apparently inspired by the 1893 World's Columbian Exposition held in Chicago.[12]

One other development helped foster a culture for the establishment of an Arts and Crafts society in Boston: this was the sponsorship of exhibitions by the Boston Architectural Club, beginning in 1890.[13] These exhibitions were presented annually, sometimes in association with the Boston Society of Architects, and were accompanied by published catalogues. Many of the architects who participated in running the exhibitions would help organize the Society of Arts and Crafts.

It was in this context—peopled by English theorists and activists, architects, and craftsmen, as well as Boston-area architects, craftsmen, and educators—that the Society of Arts and Crafts emerged in 1897. During its first two decades, the organization was characterized by the involvement of men who taught at Harvard. The Society's first and third presidents, Norton and Warren, were faculty members of Harvard's fine arts and architecture departments. Others who played leadership roles in the Society were Warren's brother Harold, Ross, Cram, Longfellow, Joseph Lindon Smith, Hermann Dudley Murphy, C. Howard Walker, and Ralph Clipston Sturgis, all of whom were members of the Harvard faculty or were visiting members. The Society of Arts and Crafts played a complementary role to the architectural program at Harvard by educating craftsmen whose products would embellish the architects' buildings and would contribute to artistic interiors.

Less important, yet also worth noting, is the fact that the early leadership of the Society included two Swedenborgians. Arthur Astor Carey, the second president of the Society, who held this position immediately before Warren, was a devoted member of the Church of the New Jerusalem. In 1906, two years after serving as president of the Society of Arts and Crafts, Carey applied to the Reverend James Reed, Warren's father-in-law, asking to be ordained a Swedenborgian minister.[14] Both Carey and Warren most likely felt reinforced in their leadership of the Society of Arts and Crafts by the activist culture that characterized the nineteenth-century Swedenborgian church. Carey, however, wanted to take the Society in a socialistic direction, focusing on the conditions of labor, whereas Warren promoted aesthetic reform, which he viewed from a moral perspective.

The conflict inherent in these two allegiances was apparent to Morris, Ashbee, and other leaders in the English Arts and Crafts movement. Because the production of high-quality craft wares was labor-intensive, they were expensive; selling them at a reasonable market price while providing adequate remuneration for the craftsman proved to be problematic. At best, these reformers found that they could succeed only when a few artisans catered to a small, affluent market. Truly widespread labor reform ultimately became an independent issue. For Warren and his supporters in the Society, the socialist concerns of Arts and Crafts ideology were destabilizing and presented a challenge. The Society would ultimately assert its conservatism, accepting the conditions of the American free-market economy.

The First Major Arts and Crafts Exhibition

The organization of the Society of Arts and Crafts was the direct result of a major exhibition that was held in Boston from April 5 to 17, 1897. It was the first large-scale exhibition devoted to handicraft to be held in North America.[15] A craftsman printer, Henry Lewis Johnson, organized it, inspired by the examples of the English Arts and Crafts Exhibition Society. Thirty-seven prominent Bostonians lent their names to a prospectus for the event, including Warren.[16] Architects were involved on several levels. Of the nine advisers, four were architects.[17] The exhibits also included work by a number of noteworthy architects. Among the products displayed were an embroidered reredos by R. Clipston Sturgis, printed work by Bertram Goodhue, and ironwork by Sturgis, Longfellow, and McKim, Mead, and White.

Before the exhibition closed, a group gathered to discuss whether to hold another exhibition the following year. Warren served as chairman of the meeting.[18] Others present were George F. Newton (Warren's junior colleague who taught design at Harvard), Walker, and Cram.[19] Although Warren was pessimistic about the prospect of holding another exhibition for several years, he appointed Cram to head a committee.[20]

When the group met again, the agenda shifted to the possibility of organizing a society. Norton was present, and he spoke in favor of such a group, "if two things can be avoided—advertising and commercialism."[21] At a meeting in May, again chaired by Warren, Norton was asked to serve as president, and the name "Society of Arts and Crafts" was agreed upon.[22] Thus from the beginning, faculty members from Harvard played a central role, and they defined their mission broadly. They were not a "Boston" society but rather a group that aspired to the status of a national organization. Other Arts and Crafts organizations were, in fact, emerging: a club in Minneapolis was founded in 1895, followed by a society in Deerfield, Massachusetts, in 1896; and in the fall of 1897, the Chicago Arts and Crafts Society was launched.[23] But the people in Boston were the most ambitious in defining their reach. In June the Society of Arts and Crafts was incorporated, with twenty-four signatories, including Norton, Warren, Walker, Longfellow, Ross, and Cram.[24]

The following fall, the members of the new organization gathered, and Norton read a statement of purpose. The Society of Arts and Crafts was dedicated to "promoting all branches of handicraft." It sought to bring "designers and workmen into mutually helpful relations" and to encourage workmen to execute designs of their own. Taking aim at Beaux-Arts design, the Society sought to counteract the desire for "overornamentation," and taking aim at incipient Art Nouveau, it sought to discourage "specious originality." Instead, the Society would insist on "the necessity of sobriety and restraint."[25]

The concept of restraint was embedded in the intertwined cultures of nineteenth-century Harvard and Brahmin Boston. Recalling the Harvard of the midcentury, Henry Adams wrote that its clergy "had given to the College a character of moderation, balance, judgment, restraint. . . ."[26] This character extended to an entire way of life, harking back to a Puritan past, and it governed Boston's elite in their political activity, their architecture, and decorative arts. Much of the craft work produced and exhibited by the Society's members adhered closely to historical models, especially from the colonial era. Nevertheless, while the taste of the Boston group was conservative when compared with that of other parts of the country, the Society and its members did somewhat inconsistently produce and promote some truly original designs, especially in art pottery and silver.

From the beginning, the Society took an educational approach in its activities. It soon opened a library and offered a drawing class.[27] During the 1898–1899 season, the Society sponsored lectures by Norton, Walker, Ross, Edward S. Morse, a specialist on Japan, and Sarah Wyman Whitman, a bookbinder and stained glass designer. Warren was scheduled to give a lecture titled "The Craftsman in the Middle Ages," but due to illness, he was replaced by Robert Andrews, his architect-colleague.[28] One may imagine that Warren's lecture would have drawn upon his Harvard lectures, with an emphasis on medieval stone carving, stained glass, and ironwork.

In 1898, Warren became a vice president of the Society and a member of the Society's Council, the governing board of the organization.[29] He would serve on the Council for the rest of his life. The Council was dominated by architects who acted as spokesmen and superiors to the craftsman members.[30]

In January of 1899, a newspaper announced that a second Arts and Crafts exhibition was being planned for the spring, and Warren was chairman. In addition to a display of contemporary work, a new feature would be a loan exhibition of historic craft objects.[31] The event was well supported by Boston's Brahmins and artistic leaders. The "Loan Collection of Old Arts and Crafts" eventually included a Venetian carved chest owned by Carey and iron candlesticks from Isabella Stewart Gardner. Loans were made by Ross, Norton, and Mrs. Frederick L. Ames, among others.[32] In the interest of teaching the public about historical design, Warren and those assisting him assembled an array of decorative objects from lenders with outstanding collections, whose treasures ultimately would repose in several Boston-area museums. The following fall, Ross began teaching abstract design to the architecture students at Harvard, suggesting that the Society's springtime loan exhibition solidified Warren's commitment to offering the subject.

The exhibition opened in April and featured about three thousand exhibits, including the work of leading designers. Visitors could see ironwork by McKim, Mead, and White, glassware by Louis Tiffany, wood carving by John Kirchmayer, and stone carving by Hugh Cairns.[33] As might be expected, the exhibition's opening reception attracted established names in Boston society.[34] Yet while appealing to the more affluent Bostonians, the exhibition also was open to the public at a reduced rate on Sunday, "for the benefit of craftsmen and others who would not have the opportunity of attending weekdays."[35] The exhibition was deemed such a success that it was extended by several days.[36]

The catalogue for the event included an introductory essay, apparently written by Warren as the exhibition chairman. The essay opened with a quotation from Morris and quoted Morris a second time with his directive, "Have nothing in your houses that you do not know to be useful or believe to be beautiful," a favorite maxim repeated by Warren.[37] After condemning "lavish decoration" and observing that simplicity has its virtues, Warren turned to the craftsman. Like Morris, he was concerned about the craftsman who had become, in essence, a machine, producing uniform and unoriginal work. But without acknowledging his differences with Morris, who was more negative about machinery, Warren stated that machinery "has wonderfully facilitated production," adding that in many crafts, mechanical processes can be done better by machinery than by hand.[38] While thus repeatedly condemning machine-made art objects, Warren accepted the machine as a tool.

A month after the Society of Arts and Crafts exhibition closed, the annual architects' exhibition opened, running from May 22 to June 3, jointly sponsored by the Boston Architectural Club and the Boston Society of Architects.[39] Among the exhibits were photographs of stone sculptures for buildings that Warren had designed.[40] Significantly, the catalogue entry attributed the work to Warren, and the sculptor with whom he had collaborated was not named. Other sources, however, document that John Evans carved at least some of the sculpture.[41] The importance of identifying the individual artisan with his work was a concern that was repeated by Warren and others involved with the Society of Arts and Crafts, yet the fact that Evans was not credited with his sculpture in the architects' exhibition reveals that this concern was more readily adopted as a theory than as a practice. It took some time for the architects, including Warren, to share the credit with their collaborators. A few years later, in the 1902 architects' exhibition, the situation had changed, and recognition was given to the various designers. Modeled work by the sculptor Hugh Cairns, for example, was shown and listed in the catalogue under his name, identified with two building projects, one of which was a church that was credited to Warren's firm.[42]

A Salesroom and a Magazine

In December of 1900, the Society of Arts and Crafts opened a salesroom to display and market the products of its craftsman members. Space for the salesroom was rented on the third floor of the Twentieth Century Club Building at Somerset Street and Ashburton Place.[43] Given Warren's past involvement with the club and his future involvement with the salesroom, it seems likely that he was at least partly responsible for this development. In establishing the salesroom, the Society also appointed a jury to accept and reject work submitted by the craftsmen for display. Warren was a member of the thirteen-member panel, which came to be recognized for its selective standards. Other members included the architects Clipston Sturgis, Longfellow, and Walker, as well as Ross.[44]

Another important early effort of the Society with which Warren was involved was the publication of a monthly magazine, called *Handicraft*. It was first issued in 1902 and ran until 1904. Carey was the editor, and Norton and Warren were the associate editors. With quotations from Ruskin, Morris, and Thomas Carlyle and articles on aesthetics and ethics, type design and enameling, the magazine represented a range of Arts and Crafts interests. It appears to have been circulated mainly among the Society's members. *Handicraft* was academic in tone, with relatively long articles often rooted in history, contrasting with Stickley's *The Craftsman*, which was first issued in 1901 and appealed to a wider spectrum of readers.

Within the pages of *Handicraft*, the tensions within the Society's leadership were subtly conveyed. Carey as editor appears to have selected the quotations, sprinkled through the issues, which consistently touched on the plight of labor. For example, a quotation attributed to Morris reads: "I am not pleading for the production of a little more beauty in the world, much as I love it, and much as I would sacrifice for its sake; it is the lives of human beings that I am pleading for; or if you will, with the Roman poet, the reasons for living."[45] By contrast, Warren's article titled "The Qualities of Carving" reflected his emphasis on aesthetic reform. After describing examples of skillfully carved sculpture from ancient Greece through the Renaissance, Warren bemoaned the "almost total disappearance of the art of sculpture" in his own age.[46] He explained with dismay that while contemporary sculptors were modelers, few executed their finished work and few were trained to carve.

In "Our Work and Prospects," published in *Handicraft* in 1903, Warren distanced himself explicitly from those with socialistic goals for the Society. "The fact of William Morris' socialism and the socialism of his friends has led both the friends of the arts and crafts movement and those who are indifferent to it, to lay too much stress on socialism as connected with artistic production," he wrote.[47] He added that a strength of the Society of Arts and Crafts was its success in "keeping those questions entirely out of our midst, in disassociating ourselves from all such questions and in attending to our own proper concerns."[48] "Proper" concerns meant aesthetic concerns. Warren considered commercialism, the subdivision of labor, and the machine all positive aspects of modern life; they were negative only to the extent that they affected handicraft.[49]

While expressing no interest whatsoever in the problems of the working class as a whole, Warren continued to associate closely with artisans and to promote their efforts. In addition to collaborating with sculptors, during the early years of the decade Warren developed at least a few designs with the silversmith Arthur J. Stone. Warren helped the English immigrant set up his own workshop, which opened in Gardner, Massachusetts, in 1901 and where Stone trained a number of apprentices.[50] In the March 1904 issue of *Handicraft*, photographs appeared of a silver loving cup that, the text reported, had been made by Stone and given to Harvard's president Eliot. The design was described as having been inspired by a Greek drinking vessel in the collection of the Museum of Fine Arts in Boston.[51] When the cup was exhibited a few years later, both Stone and Warren were identified with it: Warren was named as its designer and Stone as the one who had executed it.[52] The fact that Warren did not take credit for himself in the *Handicraft* article, which he probably wrote, suggests Warren's own uncertainty about clarifying such collaborations—even as the concept of "mutually helpful relations" between designer and craftsman was being promoted by him and the Society.

In early September of 1903, Warren and his wife visited Ashbee and his Guild of Handicraft at Chipping Campden.[53] Ashbee's experimental workshop had already inspired the creation in 1901 of a workshop in Boston, called the Handicraft Shop, for metalsmiths.[54] On this trip, Warren was especially interested in seeing how the Guild retailed its products in London. Thinking of the upstairs location of the salesrooms run by the Society of Arts and Crafts in Boston, Warren wrote to the manager, Frederic Allen Whiting: "Two things I feel convinced we must do to make a financial success: 1) have a store in the street level in a good location and 2) keep it filled with a variety of material."[55] Warren's interest in making the salesroom profitable would continue in the years ahead. He felt the need to transform the store into a model of self-sufficiency, which would have been valued both by the Society's leaders as well as by its middle-class members. Yet Warren seems to have struggled with a desire to reconcile his conflicting views about commercialism. While he was leery of the effects of commercialism on artistic endeavor, he also believed that craft products could be profitably sold on terms that he and the Society members could find acceptable, presumably in the tone of their marketing and in the quality of their work.

In the same letter, Warren encouraged Whiting to try to placate Carey, who had succeeded Norton as president of the Society, until Warren's return to Boston. Carey and Mary Ware Dennett had become frustrated with Whiting, who defended the Society's role as middleman between the craftsmen and buyers. Whiting and others were convinced that the Society had to be self-supporting.[56] Warren backed Whiting, writing to Carey that he had little sympathy for Dennett and her "very positive socialistic views."[57] Warren continued, "With many of these views many of us have little sympathy, but were they right, the only logical course would be to disband the Society of Arts and Crafts and work for the total reorganization of Society. That is another question too colossal to enter upon." Warren wrote to Dennett that while recognizing the imperfections in society, this recognition "does not lead many of us to any sympathy with socialistic doctrines, the discussion of which is no concern of a Society of Arts and Crafts."[58] Warren thus redefined the Arts and Crafts movement as it had emerged in England, rejecting its socialist underpinnings.

On November 30 of 1903, Carey resigned.[59] He wrote to Warren, "My view of the whole subject of the Arts and Crafts has deepened and assumed more of a social and less of a merely aesthetic character. . . ."[60] He added that he and Dennett were more in accord with the principles of Morris than the rest of the Society's Council members. A year later,

Carey published *Nervous Prostration and Its Spiritual Cause*, and two years after that, he took steps to pursue a career as a Swedenborgian minister.[61] Dennett resigned from the Society in January of 1904.[62] Carey and Dennett were the more extreme personalities of the Society of Arts and Crafts during its formative years. Warren, a far more conservative personality, succeeded Carey as president in 1904.

Warren's values and priorities evidently reflected those of the Society's broader constituency. In his new role as president, Warren sought to make the salesroom a sound business venture. For most of the Society's members, the opportunity to distribute their work through the salesroom was highly valued. At the same time, Warren asserted his identity as an educator, repeatedly stating that the operation of the salesroom was one component of an overall program dedicated to extending the Society's influence and to educating the broader public. This view was supported by his Harvard and architect colleagues.

During the first year of his presidency, Warren oversaw the relocation of the salesroom to 9 Park Street.[63] The new shop, located at street level, opened on September 1. It was immediately successful in attracting customers and resulted in a noticeable increase in sales.[64] In the months before the move, Whiting and Ashbee corresponded about the possibility of selling Guild of Handicraft silver through the Boston store.[65] One may imagine that Warren and Whiting wanted the silver in order to expand the Boston shop's offerings. The idea collapsed, however, because of federal import taxes.

Warren and the Society at the St. Louis Fair

Also during Warren's first year as president, the Society of Arts and Crafts played a leading part at the Universal Exposition, held in St. Louis to commemorate the Louisiana Purchase. Halsey C. Ives was chief of the fair's Department of Art, having served in the same position at the World's Columbian Exposition in Chicago in 1893.[66] Ives presented the first arts exhibition to be held in the United States that was all-inclusive, featuring the applied arts as well as the fine arts.[67]

Warren assisted Ives and the Department of Art in two capacities— as an architect and as president of the Society of Arts and Crafts. Warren became involved with the exposition in early 1903 when he agreed to serve on the Boston Advisory Committee, which reviewed entries from the region for art, architecture, and the applied arts.[68] There were three other regions: New York, Philadelphia, and "Western," which was run from St. Louis. Leading architects and designers were drawn in, with McKim, White, Grosvenor Atterbury, Tiffany, and John La Farge among the advisers to the New York committee.[69] Many of the twenty-two members of the Boston committee were members of the Society of Arts and Crafts, including J. Templeman Coolidge, Hermann Dudley Murphy, Sarah C. Sears, Joseph Lindon Smith, and C. Howard Walker.[70] Six men from the Boston committee reviewed the architecture entries: Warren, Robert Andrews, Charles Coolidge, Robert Peabody, Guy Lowell, and Edmund Wheelwright.[71] Warren also served on the international Jury of Awards, determining the medal winners in architecture.[72]

As president of the Society of Arts and Crafts, Warren promoted its commitment to the exposition's Applied Arts Division. The Society sent Whiting, its administrator and salesroom manager, to St. Louis to serve as superintendent in charge of all applied arts exhibits.[73] Whiting also served on the international Jury of Awards for applied arts, which was chaired by Walker.[74]

Whiting's participation was key to fulfilling Ives's desire to expand the nature of the Department of Art's displays. In a catalogue on the exhibits, Ives wrote, "The Art Department of the Universal Exposition of 1904 has a broader classification than has prevailed at previous International Expositions. It has broken over the line which heretofore has separated 'Fine Arts,' so called from 'Industrial Arts.' "[75] In another catalogue, Ives explained that this exposition placed the applied arts on the same plane as the fine arts. An attempt to include the applied arts had been made at the Chicago fair, he added, but few craftsmen had responded with entries. He continued, "During the '90s the Arts and Crafts movement, developing strongly in England, in certain sections of the continent, and in the United States, has made for itself a distinct and permanent place in the world of art. Here, for the first time in an exposition catalogue the initials 'A. & C.'—Arts and Crafts—appear, and the work for which they stand greatly broadens and diversifies the collections."[76] Entries designated "Arts and Crafts" therefore were recognized as being artistic as well as functional creations. Publicizing the call for entries and ensuring a high standard for the exhibits was Whiting's responsibility. His success also was a success for the Boston Society.[77]

The exhibition catalogue recognized the role of the Society in a statement under the "Applied Arts" heading. The note read, "The Executive of the Department of Art desires to acknowledge the valuable services of the Society of Arts and Crafts of Boston in assisting to bring together the varied collection. . . ."[78] Warren, however, was not pleased with just a brief statement of thanks. Acting on behalf of the Society of Arts and Crafts, Warren wrote to Ives in June of 1904, protesting the minimal recognition. He asked that in new printings of the catalogue, mention be made of the exhibitors in the Applied Arts Division who were members of the Society.[79] Warren believed that the recognition would serve not only the Society as an organization but also its craftsman members as individuals. While working toward the more ambitious goal of elevating the taste of the broader population, Warren continually promoted the Society's craftsmen.

Over the course of the next year, the shop at 9 Park Street flourished, and the Society succeeded in becoming financially independent. A percentage of all sales revenues went to the organization, covering its expenses. In 1905, the sales receipts totaled $37,000; the following year, sales receipts totaled nearly $41,000. The Society also was able to take over the entire street floor of the former house, expanding the exhibit area and providing more library and meeting space. Warren's goal of a successful salesroom had become a reality.[80]

Tenth Anniversary Exhibition

In February of 1907, the Society of Arts and Crafts marked its tenth anniversary by sponsoring another large-scale exhibition, and Warren again served as its chairman. Planning for the event began a year earlier, with Warren assisted by his architect-colleagues Longfellow, Cram, and Walker, as well as his brother Harold, who continued to teach art at Harvard; J. Templeman Coolidge, a cultural leader; Edward R. Warren, a leading art collector and connoisseur; and Daniel B. Updike, a printer.[81] Once again, when it came to the management of the Society and its activities, the architects took charge, and craftsmen were in the minority.

The exhibition catalogue opened with an introduction, presumably written by Warren, in which the Society's objectives concerning design reform were explained. In the essay, the reader was told that the craftsman must understand the forms of the past in order to develop good new designs. The goal of the Society, the essay continued, was:

. . . to encourage not mistaken seeking after new and strange forms, but the sincere endeavor after personal and individual expression in the work of the hands, rather than mere copyism and mere imitation of bygone forms. It is recognized, however, that such reproduction of old forms may be of great use, especially of great educational value at the present stage of our artistic development. . . . [82]

Both history and those who interpreted history gave direction to the Society's craftsman members. Warren's own design efforts were a case in point. In the catalogue of the exhibition, Warren was credited with three silver loving cups, one that he had designed and executed in collaboration with George P. Kendrick and two others he had made in collaboration with Arthur J. Stone.[83] One of those was the cup made for Charles Eliot. Inspired by a Greek cup in the Boston museum, it was first drawn by Warren and then crafted by Stone. The historical model, the historian, and the craftsman had contributed in a hierarchical sequence to the final product.

Other exhibits included tile and pottery by Henry Chapman Mercer, William H. Grueby, H. C. Robertson, Adelaide Alsop Robineau, and Anne Gregory Van Briggle.[84] While also inspired by a range of historical sources, from medieval tiles to Oriental pottery, the results were original and distinctive. The artisans came from well beyond New England, a result of the Society's successful effort to attract members from across the country. Mercer was from Doylestown, Pennsylvania; Robineau from Syracuse, New York; and Van Briggle from Colorado. New methods and materials were explored as well. Craftsmen were experimenting with cement, a development that paralleled the investigations by architects into concrete. Elizabeth Frances Bowditch exhibited cement garden ornaments, including a flowerpot and a dolphin's head waterspout.[85]

Warren was chairman of the exhibition's Department of Wood-Working, with assistance from fellow architects Andrews and Walker, and from Nils J. Kjillstrom, a wood-carver.[86] In an essay introducing the exhibits of this department, probably written by Warren, the quality of carved woodwork in the United States was credited to "the growth and development of the profession of architecture. . . ."[87] The major problem identified by the essay was the pressure on the woodworker to reproduce the same forms in a deadening, mechanical way. To counter this situation, architects were encouraged to pay craftsmen for quality work, rather than for mere quantity—that is, to treat the woodworker as an artist, compensating him for his time and talent.

The 1907 exhibition also included works lent by leading collectors. Objects in a wide variety of media from Europe, Japan, China, Korea, and Arab countries were displayed along with exhibits identified as "American Colonial."[88] Not included were objects from South America and Africa. This omission is not insignificant, considering the importance that African art in particular held for artists such as Pablo Picasso and Henri Matisse in Paris at this time. On the other hand, the appreciation for Oriental art, evident in the Society's loan exhibition, led American artists and architects, especially those with ties to Boston, to develop in new directions. Japanese art and architecture were studied by artists such as Arthur Wesley Dow and by architects such as Cram.[89] Oriental pottery influenced many of the Society's craftsmen.[90]

The National League of Handicraft Societies

An outgrowth of the 1907 exhibition was the formation of the National League of Handicraft Societies. For two days during the exhibition, the Society sponsored a conference for delegates from craft societies from around the country. Since the founding of the Society of Arts and Crafts in Boston in 1897, Arts and Crafts groups had been proliferating. Despite the desire to serve a national membership, the organization based in Boston had not been able to satisfy the need for craftsmen in other parts of the country to meet with each other on a regular basis. Yet once the various societies had become established, a national association seemed desirable. The Society of Arts and Crafts sent invitations to forty-five societies to attend a meeting in Boston, and twenty-five sent representatives. Almost certainly Warren was the person who conceived this gathering, probably hoping to create an alliance that could further his goals. Upon forming the National League of Handicraft Societies, the delegates elected Warren as president.[91] He served in this capacity through 1911. The national league sponsored traveling exhibits, traveling libraries, and lectures. Between 1910 and 1911, the group also revived *Handicraft.*[92]

Throughout the remaining years of his life, Warren emphasized the educational objectives of the Society of Arts and Crafts. Annual reports stressed this purpose. In the annual report for 1910, members were told, "The aim of the Society is now, as it always has been, primarily educational."[93] In 1912, members were admonished that a successful salesroom was not enough. "There are underlying questions of education," the report stated.[94] And in 1916, the message was repeated:

... the American public must be educated, the American manufacturers must be educated, and American statesmen must be educated to the importance of art in industry.[95]

Warren's tone became more strident and more political in his final years, taking on the tone of his political activity relating to the First World War.

Warren and the Society considered and implemented educational efforts that addressed both the craftsman and the public. For several years, between 1909 and 1911, the Society's leaders investigated how they might launch a school of handicraft. Courses in silver work and bookbinding were already being offered at the school affiliated with Boston's Museum of Fine Arts, and a new school of handicraft probably would have developed similar offerings. Members of the Society conferred with trustees of the museum's school, but in the end, the concept faced too many hurdles.[96]A more modest effort was the Society's development of its library for the use of its members. A list of its books was published in 1918.[97] The collection was entirely different from the readings assigned to Warren's students at Harvard, with a focus on craft and its design rather than on architecture, but the aesthetic sensibility was similar. English medieval, northern Renaissance, and colonial American topics were favored. Books by English theorists and designers, including Morris and Walter Crane, and craftsmen such as C. W. Whall and George Jack were included. The collection also contained books on composition by Dow and on design by Ross.[98]

While the Society maintained its salesrooms to market and distribute the craftsmen's work, the shop also served an educational purpose by including a space for small exhibitions. The presentations heightened the Society's public visibility and extended its influence. In January of 1913, a wood relief by John Kirchmayer, carved for Cram's All Saint's Church in Ashmont, Massachusetts, was displayed in the Society's showrooms.[99] In the fall of the same year, the Danish Society for Artistic Handicraft displayed its members' work.[100] The commercial success of the shop was also an educational exercise, at least in Warren's mind. Warren hoped that in the long run, the salesroom would inspire imitators and the Society's example would no longer be needed.[101] One may imagine that he pragmatically accepted the appeal of the salesroom to the Society's members but that he found the management of it to be wearing.

In 1915 the Society extended its reach when it responded to an invitation from *House Beautiful* to publish news and features about its craftsmen. Each month the magazine devoted a page to the Society of Arts and Crafts, bringing its work to a national readership.[102] Warren would have considered this effort, too, as educational.

In light of Warren's priorities, it seems surprising that after 1907, the Society did not undertake another large-scale exhibition. Instead, the Society participated in joint exhibitions held in 1916 and in 1917 sponsored by the Boston Architectural Club, the Boston Society of Architects, and the Boston Society of Landscape Architects.[103] Warren was devoting more of his energy to global politics relating to the First World War, and apparently no one else was willing to take on the burden of organizing a large-scale Arts and Crafts exhibition. As a result, the Society's craftsmen remained in the shadow of the architects.

The 1917 exhibition opened just a few months after Warren died, and as might be expected, Warren's contribution to the Society was recognized. The exhibition included a model and renderings of his recent architectural projects.[104] Also the exhibition included Warren's last collaborative effort with a craftsman—a stained glass window for the Germanic Museum at Harvard, directed by Warren and executed by John Oster.[105]

A close interaction between architects and craftsmen came to define the Society. This interaction was recognized as unusual and was admired by others, including Ashbee. In a letter written in 1910, Ashbee asked the Society's salesroom manager to show a visiting English architect projects "in which the craftsmen actually work *for* and *with* the architects."[106] Unlike the woodworkers and metalsmiths working for Stickley or Elbert Hubbard, a significant group of craftsmen associated with the Society of Arts and Crafts made architectural products: sculpture, tile, glass, and iron. For two decades, Warren promoted the Society's commitment to "mutually helpful relations" between architect and craftsman.

~FIVE~

AN ARCHITECTURAL PRACTICE (1893–1917)

AS BUSY AS WARREN WAS with his work at Harvard and his commitment to the Society of Arts and Crafts, he continued to maintain an active architectural practice. Although his projects were generally modest in scope, they are noteworthy because of his prominence as an educator and as a leader in the Arts and Crafts movement. Working with clients who held similar values, Warren designed buildings that illustrated and clarified ideas that he promoted in a more general way in his institutional and organizational activities. These buildings help us understand Warren's contribution to the ongoing dialogue at the turn of the twentieth century about an ideal American architecture.

The character of the designs that he produced during his mature years continued to be consistent with the work of his Boston colleagues, including Henry Vaughan, Cram, and Longfellow, to name a few.[1] While American architecture of this period was marked by its wide-ranging eclecticism, the designs of these Boston architects were based upon a more selective eclecticism in their revival of English medieval and Georgian and American colonial and federal models.[2] Because many of the architects in this group were distinguished by their involvement with the Society of Arts and Crafts and their collaboration with many of the same Society of Arts and Crafts artisans, their architectural work also represents an element of the Arts and Crafts movement.[3] As with the decorative arts, American Arts and Crafts architecture has been most closely identified with protomodern designs, such as the work of Wright and the brothers Greene.[4] The academic orientation of the Boston circle, whose adherents drew their inspiration from a particular architectural history, defined the more conservative branch of the movement.

Yet even Warren and the architects with whom he was most closely associated pursued a variety of directions in their practices. Like Vaughan, Warren was an early contributor to the academic revival of English Gothic architecture that emerged in America during the 1880s and which was embraced and championed by Cram during the late nineteenth and early twentieth centuries. Like Cram and Longfellow, Warren also experimented with Japanese architectural forms. Like Longfellow, and to a greater extent than Cram or Vaughan, Warren shared an enthusiasm for the colonial and federal revivals. This interest was actively promoted by Arthur Little and other Boston architects who turned to the work of Bulfinch and his contemporaries for inspiration.

Soon after Warren began teaching at Harvard in 1893, he entered into his first business partnership. He must have quickly concluded that he could not attend to the day-to-day demands of an architectural firm while spending so much time in Cambridge. By 1894 he had teamed up with Lewis H. Bacon, a fellow resident of Waban in the Boston suburb of Newton, and they carried out their practice at 9 Park Street in Boston, where Warren was already established.[5] The firm of Warren and Bacon lasted only about a year, however, and in 1895 Warren was again on his own, assisted by junior employees (fig. 29). A year later, he hired Frank Patterson Smith, who had studied architecture at MIT.[6] While continuing to work for Warren, Smith went into partnership with Maurice B. Biscoe, who also had trained at MIT.[7] In 1900, Warren and the two younger men announced the formation of Warren, Smith, and Biscoe; at this time, they moved their office from Park Street to Boylston Street, downhill from Bulfinch's State House.[8] A few years later, in 1905, the firm relocated to the Equitable Building on Milk Street.[9] Soon after, Biscoe left for Denver, while Warren and Smith continued their practice together, an apparently satisfactory relationship for both men that lasted until Warren's death.[10]

Smith, thirteen years younger than Warren, was soft-spoken and reserved, content to stay in Warren's shadow, content to develop and build designs that represented Warren's vision.[11] Judging by the scale and number of their projects, the firm of Warren and Smith was always small. While in his younger years Warren had entered competitions for such monumental projects as the Minneapolis library and museum and the Cathedral of Saint John the Divine in New York City, once he began teaching at Harvard, he appears to have been satisfied with smaller commissions. One may surmise that Warren preferred to maintain close

FIG. 29. Warren and his staff, early 1890s. *Courtesy of Elizabeth Warren Stoutamire.*

control over the firm's work rather than to take on bigger jobs and more staff, which would have required more management. As for how many people worked in the office, few clues have survived. The firm employed a female secretary, and a photograph of Warren with fellow members of his office, apparently taken before Smith was hired, suggests that four or five architects and draftsmen routinely worked together.

Warren and his partners were engaged almost exclusively in institutional and residential commissions. He and his partners designed a number of churches, municipal buildings, suburban and rural residences, campus buildings, and a country club. Consistent with the biases of Arts and Crafts theorists, including Ruskin and Morris, they preferred to design for leafy settings, removed from urban environments. Just as the students at Harvard were not encouraged to work on commercial buildings, Warren seems to have had little interest in commercial projects in his own practice.

On the other hand, the concern for the poor that was shared by Ruskin and Morris did not interest Warren in his professional work, just as he rejected this issue in his teaching and organizational activities. Significantly, by the last decades of the nineteenth century, a number of Bostonians actively sought to address the housing problems of the needy.

Two of Warren's close colleagues, Norton and Longfellow, took leading roles in the effort to improve conditions in urban housing, Longfellow having designed a model tenement block in Boston.[12] By contrast, with the exception of his work on the large orphan asylum in Troy, New York, Warren designed buildings for the middle and upper classes. His indifference to social issues was consistent in all areas of his activity.

The churches that Warren and his firm produced were reflections of Warren's academic interpretation of Gothic architecture as well as exemplars of what would become a Boston Arts and Crafts approach. Through his family's connections to the leadership of the American Swedenborgian faith, Warren received several important commissions. He and his partners also designed churches for other Protestant sects, including Episcopalians, Methodists, and Presbyterians. With clients who were mainly of English extraction, most of the firm's church designs were English Gothic in inspiration. This choice became widespread by the 1890s and was encouraged in books written by Warren's colleagues, including Cram, who published *English Country Churches* in 1898, and Walker, who published *Parish Churches of England* in 1915.[13]

Warren's designs for the Swedenborgians share the same stylistic orientation. Between 1894 and 1896, he and his firm worked on the National Church of the Holy City in Washington, D.C. In 1901 he and his partners designed and built the New Church Theological School chapel in Cambridge, Massachusetts, and between 1911 and 1912, they were responsible for a parish house for the Washington church.[14] The Washington and Cambridge projects provide good subjects for study because of Warren's personal and ongoing connection with them.

National Church of the Holy City

Warren's Washington church (fig. 30) was an early example of a type that gained popularity during the early 1890s and that continued to be built in the United States through the 1930s. Its most common features included an austere body and tower base, inspired by Early English Gothic churches, with a transition in the tower to an ornate Perpendicular crown. An early paradigm for this revival was Vaughan's Chapel of Saint Peter and Saint Paul, built between 1886 and 1894, for Saint Paul's School in Concord, New Hampshire.[15] The tower reflected fifteenth-century English prototypes from Somerset as well as Merton College

FIG. 30. Warren, National Church of the Holy City, Washington, D.C., 1894–1896. *Courtesy of Richard Smith Joslin.*

chapel at Oxford. During this same period, Cram's office in 1890 proposed a Perpendicular tower for the Church of the Messiah, to be located in Boston's Fenway neighborhood. The design was inspired by the tower of Magdalen College at Oxford, dating from the end of the fifteenth century. It was not built, but it was published in the *American Architect and Building News* in 1891.[16] Bertram Goodhue, too, was taken with the Perpendicular tower, incorporating one in his 1890 design for Saint Matthew's Cathedral in Dallas, which also was not built.[17] When Warren's proposal for the Church of the Holy City was being developed during the early 1890s, therefore, it contributed to a new direction in American church design.

In 1889 the Swedenborgian church in Washington burned, and by the following year, the decision was made to acquire a new site and to construct a building as the denomination's national church.[18] A corner lot was bought on Sixteenth Street, a main thoroughfare lined with large residences, including Richardson's Nicholas L. Anderson house, 1881–1883, Henry Adams house, 1884–1886, and John M. Hay house, 1884–1886. Soon after the purchase of the site by the Swedenborgians, the minister, the Reverend Frank Sewall, drew exterior and interior elevations for the new building, based on Italian Romanesque churches.[19] Sewall had traveled in Europe and evidently found the churches of Italy especially appealing.[20] Once Warren was engaged, however, he introduced an English Gothic design, which the building committee accepted.[21]

Construction of the church began in December of 1894, and the building was dedicated in the spring of 1896.[22] Built of Bedford, Indiana, limestone, the body of the church and the tower were left in a quarry-faced finish, while the belfry stone is smooth. The tower is positioned to hold its place at the corner of the street, where it rises above the neighboring houses. It dominates the gable end of the building, which is massed against it. A porch centered under the gable and pulled tightly to the tower serves as the main entrance to the church.

The church tower illustrates the relationship between Warren's design interests and his architectural history lectures. In massing and in detail, the tower is an early variation of Oxford's Magdalen tower. Like the Magdalen tower, Warren's design features two lancets in each face, crenellations, and high pinnacles—a tower already presented in the designs of Cram and Goodhue, but not built. Warren told his students that the beautiful towers of the Perpendicular phase were one of its finest features, and he singled out the towers at Canterbury and at Merton and Magdalen Colleges, Oxford.[23] A surviving elevation of the Swedenborgian church reveals, however, that unlike Cram and Goodhue, Warren hoped to deviate from the Magdalen model in one respect: he proposed adding a spire to the belfry.[24] One might be tempted to view the spire as a Victorian carryover in Warren's work. But the fact that he and his firm proposed a spire for the Epiphany Church in Winchester, Massachusetts, a decade later, in 1904, indicates that Warren found the soaring spire appropriate for his time.[25]

The Church of the Holy City incorporates the forms and decorative detail of the Early English, Decorated, and Perpendicular periods, and some of the details may be attributed to specific English sources.[26] By and large, the church presents a layering of period styles, with the lower portions modeled after Early English Gothic, the west window after Decorated designs, and the tower finished in the Perpendicular manner, as if construction had proceeded over the course of several centuries. This building of history in terms of evolving style was characteristic of the historian-architect. Yet Warren was not rigid and did not strive to produce a design that was entirely logical; the cross astride the gable above the entrance portico is Norman, for example—an earlier style positioned over a style of a later period.

Visitors entering the church pass through a vestibule under a gallery and then proceed into the sanctuary through one of three doors. The nave is wide and uninterrupted by columns—essentially an auditorium. It is severe with an exposed brick dado, plastered walls, and a trussed roof supported by iron tie-rods and chain. Framing the entry to the chancel is a large Gothic arch through which the eye focuses on narrow stained-glass lancet windows in a rounded apse (fig. 31). Between the windows, colonnettes rise to form ribs of a vault, reflecting Warren's enthusiasm for true vaulting, emphasized to his students in his lectures on Gothic architecture.

A few of the design decisions were related to the Swedenborgian liturgy. The minister, Sewall, noted the importance of the Doctrines of Baptism and of the Holy Supper, and they are acknowledged by the placement of the baptismal font, located at the front of the sanctuary in what is the secular level, and the altar, located above a series of steps in the chancel, the sacred realm. At the center of the altar, the Bible is prominently displayed on a stand. This presentation is a characteristic feature of Swedenborgian churches, as the Bible is ritually opened at

FIG. 31. National Church of the Holy City, nave and chancel. *Courtesy of Richard Smith Joslin.*

the beginning of every Swedenborgian service and closed at the end. Above the arch to the chancel, an inscription was originally lettered. It has since been painted over, but it is legible in photographs that belonged to Warren's firm. It read, "He that sat upon the throne said, Behold, I make all things new," from the Revelation of Saint John the Divine, whose visions of the Second Coming and of the Holy City play a prominent role in Swedenborg's teachings.[27] In most respects, however, the church interior suggests a place steeped in English tradition more than a place of Swedenborgian worship.

Warren's Church of the Holy City brought together the artistic production of several individuals who would soon participate in the Society of Arts and Crafts, Boston. As such, the church presents an early example of the sort of collaboration that Warren would promote through the Society after it was organized in 1897. The exterior of the building is enhanced by the gargoyles and angel label stops of the sculptor John Evans.[28] Like Warren, Evans would become a charter member of the Society of Arts and Crafts.[29] The first windows to be installed, from 1895, were produced in the Boston workshops of stained glass artisans Ford and Brooks and Donald MacDonald, future craftsman members of the Society.[30] And the lettering and painted frieze decoration were the work of L. Haberstroh and Son, who would display their work in the Society's 1897 and 1899 exhibitions. In fact, between 1897 and 1899, the Haberstroh firm would run its business from 9 Park Street, where Warren was working and where the Society would open its showroom.[31] The handcrafted and historicizing qualities of these decorative elements would become standard features among better-quality architectural projects throughout the United States within just a few years, but in the mid-1890s, the Church of the Holy City illustrated new possibilities.

New Church Theological School Chapel

The Swedenborgian chapel for the New Church Theological School in Cambridge (fig. 32) represented Warren's ideas to his colleagues and students. It was prominently sited on a corner at the edge of the Harvard campus, on Quincy and Kirkland Streets, across from Ware and Van Brunt's Memorial Hall. The chapel was built to serve both a Cambridge congregation, organized in 1888, and the theological school, which was located in a house on the Quincy Street lot, purchased in 1889. Ten years later, planning of the chapel began, and it was dedicated in 1901.[32] It was widely publicized through exhibitions, including the 1904 Universal Exposition in St. Louis, and in the architectural press.[33]

The design of the chapel is consistent with Warren's deeply felt affection for the medieval English parish church, which he expressed to his students in his lectures. It also is consistent with the broader enthusiasm for the English architectural tradition that was prevalent in Boston during this period, when the Yankee population sought to affirm its Anglo-Saxon heritage. This preference for English styles, especially in church design, was one of the regional distinctions in American architecture acknowledged by Warren in an essay that he contributed to the catalogue of the 1899 Boston architectural exhibition. He wrote that "a good deal of the ecclesiastical work in and about Boston shows a loving study of the mediaeval parish churches of England and the influence of modern English church work, such as is found, perhaps, to the same extent, nowhere else in the United States."[34] This enthusiasm was shared not only by architects such as Vaughan, Cram, and Walker, but also by artists, such as Warren's brother Harold, who exhibited watercolors that featured similar subjects. Indeed, the general form of Warren's chapel is strikingly similar to Harold's watercolor of Austerfield Church, which

was shown in the 1899 Boston architectural exhibition (fig. 33).[35] Both churches are simple rectangular masses with pitched roofs surmounted by a bellcote.

The exterior of the Cambridge chapel acquires further interest through the deep gabled porch that is centered on the main facade and the rhythm of wall buttresses running along its side elevations. The walls are built of uncoursed random rubble stone and trimmed with Bedford, Indiana, limestone. The understated texture and variegated color in the masonry were important qualities of the building. In specifications for the church, Warren wrote, "It is not desired that stone walls should be even in color, but rather that there should be considerable play of color in this stone work."[36] A few years earlier, he had published a paper titled "On the Use of Color in Architectural Design" in the *American Architect and Building News*. Echoing Ruskin, Warren noted, "If there

FIG. 33. Harold Broadfield Warren, "Austerfield Church," watercolor. *From* Catalogue of the Architectural Exhibition, Boston Architectural Club and Boston Society of Architects, *Boston, 1899. Reproduced courtesy of the Trustees of the Boston Public Library.*

is to be any beauty of color there must be some variety, as in the leaves of a green tree where light and shade add to the variety of local color. . . ." Warren argued that stone in a building should be placed "as to make slight contrasts in tint between the different blocks."[37] The exterior of the chapel is enhanced by its sculpture. Carved label stops of two lancet windows represent the beasts of the four evangelists, and the entrance porch is decorated with corbels of human heads. Models for the sculpture were executed by Hugh Cairns, a founding member of the Society of Arts and Crafts, who developed his designs with Warren.[38]

Warren collaborated with a range of artisans to embellish the interior of the Swedenborgian chapel (figs. 34, 35). The oak pews and paneling were the work of Irving and Casson, a firm whose members were associated with the Society of Arts and Crafts.[39] Tiles patterned after medieval originals were supplied by Henry Chapman Mercer to decorate the chancel floor; Mercer was a member of the Society and sold his tiles through the Park Street salesroom.[40] Angels for a limestone reredos were carved by Cairns.[41] And Warren returned to Donald MacDonald, one of the glassworkers who had made windows for the Church of the Holy City, to execute the chapel windows.[42]

Especially noteworthy were the windows of the chancel. They are grisaille—clear glass painted with linear designs—closely imitating examples from early-thirteenth-century France. A newspaper article from

FIG. 34. Chapel of the New Church Theological School, nave. *Courtesy of Richard Smith Joslin.*

the period credits Warren with the design.[43] At a time when Louis Tiffany and John La Farge were creating vibrantly colored, figurative stained-glass windows, an imitation of historic examples informed by academic study, and of grisaille in particular, was unusual. Within a few years, however, American glassworkers would embrace academic imita-

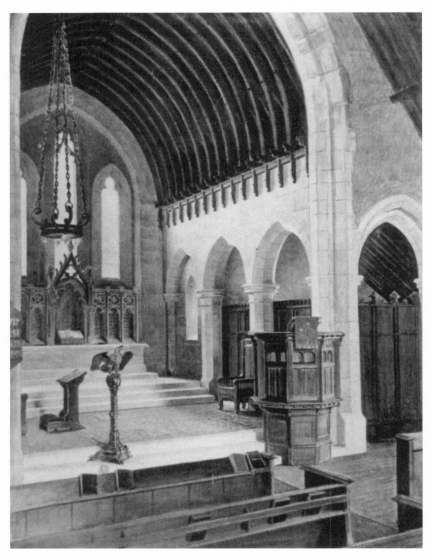

FIG. 35. Chapel of the New Church Theological School, chancel, watercolor by Warren. *Courtesy of Richard Smith Joslin.*

tion, and such designs would become more prevalent.[44] Warren's academic interests as a practicing architect again were expressed in his classroom interests. In his lectures, Warren praised the subtle beauty of French grisaille glass to his students, including that of Troyes, Soissons, and Saint Jean-au-Bois.[45]

While reviving the style of medieval sources, Warren developed designs for the glass that suited the Swedenborgian church setting. The chancel's center lancet features a dove descending to an open Bible, which reads, "In the Beginning was the Word & the Word." Congregants would have known that "the Word was with God," the quotation thus reinforcing the emphasis that Swedenborgians place on the reading of the Bible in their rituals and belief. The Bible also was given prominence in the design of the reredos, which rises around a niche where the sacred book is displayed as the focal point of the chapel.

Church of the Holy City Parish House

Warren was called to Washington again in 1911 when the Swedenborgians prepared to build a parish house for the Church of the Holy City (fig. 36). Surviving correspondence indicates that not everyone on the building committee was happy to see Warren back again. Complaints were expressed about the church's "wretched acoustic conditions" and the "extravagant chancel."[46] When Washington architect Paul J. Pelz was asked to pass judgment, however, he wrote that the church "is easily the best church in Washington," praising it for its purity of style and calling it a scholarly product worthy of its author.[47] Warren's plans for the addition were approved in the fall, and the work was begun and finished in 1912.[48]

The dominant feature of the addition is an octagonal structure that leads into a gabled rectangular block to the rear. Although the octagon has been likened to a lady chapel, it also suggests a chapter house, the seat of assembly for monks or canons governing a medieval church.[49] The structure contains a stair tower, featuring an elegantly winding staircase (fig. 37). Although not a direct imitation of the stairway to the chapter house at Wells Cathedral, Warren's design may have originated with the Wells concept. The stairs lead to a second-floor assembly hall, which also served the Sunday school. On the first-floor level, a corridor

FIG. 36. Warren and Smith, National Church of the Holy City, parish house, 1911–1912.

FIG. 37. National Church of the Holy City, parish house stairhall.

leads to a library and "ladies parlor," and the basement includes a kitchen and a dining hall.

The stairhall again illustrates Warren's interest in color in architecture, with the terra-cotta color of its brick walls enlivened by the brown of burnt headers and the blue of inset Mercer tiles. The tower design also reflects Warren's love of Gothic construction, emphasized in his teaching. An octagonal vault of brick supported by eight stone ribs crowns the hall. The most noteworthy feature of the hall, however, is the stairway itself. It was built of concrete. Cantilevered from the outer wall, it rises up and over the first-floor entry. During the 1890s, Warren and his colleagues had explored the potential of concrete in designs for the Harvard campus, and in the years that followed, Warren used it in a variety of ways.

Concord City Hall

Another building type to which Warren was drawn was the municipal building. Whether the project was a town hall or a city hall, Warren followed the stylistic approach that he settled on in his design of the town hall for Lincoln, Massachusetts, 1891–1892. Warren's municipal buildings were consistently Colonial Revival, red brick, classically detailed, and ornamented with a cupola. While most obviously derived from sources of the colonial and federal periods, the buildings also were inspired by English architecture of the eighteenth century and Italian architecture from the Renaissance, especially the fifteenth century. These periods were high points in Warren's history of secular monuments.

Of the architects in Warren's Boston circle, Longfellow was the most enthusiastic and prolific designer of Colonial Revival buildings, although during the early 1890s, his Colonial Revival projects were not institutional but residential.[50] More relevant to Warren's municipal projects were the designs of McKim. Warren admired McKim's Colonial Revival Memorial Fence for the Harvard campus, the first gate erected in 1889, designed to harmonize with the red brick colonial buildings in the Yard.[51] Warren included a photograph of the Johnston Gate in the book *Picturesque and Architectural New England*, published in 1899.[52] Warren also admired McKim's Walker Art Gallery at Bowdoin College in Brunswick, Maine, designed by McKim, Mead, and White and completed in

1894. Warren included the Walker Art Gallery along with his own Billerica, Massachusetts, Town Hall, also from 1894, as examples of good
contemporary architecture in *Picturesque and Architectural New England*.[53] In the text that accompanied the photographs of these two
buildings, Warren wrote appreciatively about the recent revival of colonial American and English Georgian buildings as well as the "direct
revival of the forms of the classical Renaissance of Italy." Warren's town
hall and McKim's art gallery share the same restrained classicism. They
are austere, with unadorned areas of brick wall, and the massing of both
buildings is horizontal and quiet.

The most prominent municipal building with which Warren was associated was the City Hall of Concord, New Hampshire, designed by
Warren, Smith, and Biscoe between 1902 and 1903.[54] It is characterized
by the same reserve that marked Warren's earlier municipal buildings
(fig. 38). The entry facade is five bays across, with the bays at each end
projecting forward slightly to create corner pavilions. A high granite
basement provides a strong horizontal effect, as do a stone stringcourse
that breaks the brick of the first and second stories and a balustrade
above the second story. Visitors to the city hall enter through a modestly
scaled classical portico, supported by unfluted granite columns. The
facade is dominated by three large arched windows on the second story,
which are emphasized by alternating brick and granite voussoirs. Coun-
tering the horizontality of the building is the Wren-like steeple that rises
above the high hip roof. Although Warren's architectural history courses
did not provide specific models for elevations such as this one, his
presentation of Italian Renaissance and English Georgian architecture,
including the work of Wren, provided the rationale for the design.

The administrative floors of the Concord City Hall have been entirely
rebuilt, but plans published at the beginning of the last century document the original disposition of the rooms (fig. 39).[55] The interior included a pronounced axial organization, a monumental staircase, and a
clear hierarchy of spaces. The visitor entered the city hall through a
vestibule and continued into a large central hall that extended through
the depth of the building and culminated with the staircase. A second
hall crossed the main hall, running laterally in either direction. At the
ends of this corridor were the tax collector's and city clerk's offices—
that is, offices most commonly frequented by city residents. This organization reflected Warren's admiration for French planning, expressed

FIG. 38. Warren, Smith, and Biscoe, Concord City Hall, Concord, New Hampshire, 1902–1903. *Courtesy of Richard Smith Joslin.*

in his teaching and in publication.[56] The fact that Warren applied French planning ideas to a civic building was not surprising, as Ecole training focused on monumental public projects. Warren's melding of French planning with other stylistic traditions was typical among his peers; Cram acknowledged this tendency.[57]

Behind the administrative block of the city hall was a community auditorium, entered from a side street. It has survived, and the interior retains some important original plasterwork. Most notable is the ornamental plaster surrounding the proscenium arch. Its acanthus leaf design was the work of Sleep, Elliott, and King of Boston and was supervised by Mortenson and Holdenson, leading decorators in Boston with whom Warren collaborated on many of his projects.[58] As with decorative elements that Warren and his craftsmen associates designed in the Gothic tradition, historical sources were a point of departure for new and original embellishment in the classical tradition.

FIRST FLOOR PLAN.

FIG. 39. Concord City Hall, plan of first floor. *From* Brickbuilder, *November 1904.*

H. Langford Warren House

Warren and his firm designed several dozen houses, mainly for suburban and country settings. A few of the projects were extremely large, but most were residences for the upper middle class. By the 1890s, Warren had abandoned the round towers, conical roofs, and other elements of the Queen Anne revival, although these forms were still widespread in American domestic architecture. Warren's houses were marked by a breadth of massing and an overall balance. Stylistically, they were eclectic in their historical references; what unified them was their basis in English and American architectural traditions.

Warren wholeheartedly embraced the English enthusiasm for the country house, which he emphasized in his architectural history lectures and which he and members of his department presented to the students at Harvard as a basis for design problems. He extolled the virtues of the English country house in print as well. In a review of recent English residential projects, published in a 1904 issue of *Architectural Review*, Warren declared, "It is not too much to say that no other nation has succeeded in developing a domestic architecture having the subtle and intimate charm which in the English country house makes so strong an appeal to the love of home as well as to the love of beauty."[59] He praised these houses for their "quiet and restrained beauty" and for their "sympathy with the surrounding landscape." The English architects whose residential designs were most admired by Warren included Ernest George and Peto, John Belcher, and Mervyn Macartney.[60]

Warren's perspective was well girded by a broadly based interest in the country house held by American architects at the turn of the twentieth century. Writing in the *American Architect and Building News* in 1899, Warren commented on the success of American country-house design, contrasting it with the inadequacy of French work in this area.[61] By this time, many American architects took their inspiration from colonial- and federal-era sources. In *American Renaissance*, published in 1904, Joy Wheeler Dow described the appealing qualities of American colonial and federal houses, attributing their character to English tradition.[62] Boston architects, including Warren, were especially attracted to these models, most commonly producing frame houses sheathed in clapboard or shingles. They also referred to English models in designs of brick, half-timber, and stucco.

Yet regional variations in American residential design were becoming apparent, and Warren recognized the regional distinctions that were taking hold. As he noted in an exhibition catalogue essay from 1899, New York architects were more likely to emulate French styles.[63] Large houses in the Beaux-Arts tradition were more commonly designed for New York clients, such as those who built the outstanding examples in Newport, Rhode Island. At the same time, East Coast designs, generally inspired by historical sources, contrasted with the more abstract designs, stripped of historical references, that were being developed in the Midwest and on the West Coast. Nevertheless, despite regional preferences, all of these strains intermingled to some extent; Warren's work was a high-style version of an eclectic approach that could be found in residential design throughout the United States during this period.

What Warren's residential designs shared with the houses of more protomodern architects was an integration of spaces, especially on the main living level. Rooms connected with other rooms through wide pocket doors, and they opened to the outside through glazed doors. Mediating between the indoors and outdoors were porches, which in turn led into walled gardens that often connected with more natural landscape settings. The desire of American architects to integrate spaces, within a house and between its interior and exterior, was widespread and included the architects of the Midwest and the West Coast. Warren encouraged this sort of unity in residential planning, and he believed American domestic architecture surpassed that of the English in this respect.[64] Although Warren viewed this approach to planning in terms of its unity, it also was characterized by a transparency of spaces—a planning concept that architects would develop in the succeeding decades of the century.

Warren's ideas about residential design take form in the house that he designed and built for his family in 1904. It is located in Cambridge on Garden Terrace, a short walk from the Harvard campus. The site that he chose backed on the grounds of the Harvard observatory. Many of Warren's clients also purchased sites that would benefit from protected views, and even today, the Warren house and its grounds remain buffered from nearby traffic and campus activity.

Like the much larger English country houses, the Warren house features an entrance facade and a garden facade (figs., 40, 41, 42). It has a brick foundation and a stucco cladding. The dominant mass of the house is a rectangular block, sheltered under a steeply pitched roof, reminiscent of seventeenth-century designs. The entrance facade challenges conven-

FIG. 40. Warren, Herbert Langford and Catharine Warren house, Cambridge, Massachusetts, 1904. *Courtesy of Elizabeth Warren Stoutamire.*

tion and symmetry with the door, triple-casement window, and gable all aligned to the left of center, while two windows are dropped to illuminate interior stairs. The garden facade, by contrast, recalls the eighteenth century, with symmetrically banked windows flanking a pedimented door in a classical composition.

The main floor of the house is planned in the unified way that Warren valued and that was typical of early-twentieth-century American residential interiors, with public rooms connected to each other by wide doorways. Because the house is built into a hill, one enters a story below the main level. Inside, the visitor passes through a vestibule, enhanced by classical pilasters, built-in seats, and leaded glass sidelights, and arrives at a reception hall. A winding staircase, reminiscent of the winding staircases of colonial houses, leads to the main floor. There a spacious hall leads through double doors to the living and dining rooms (figs. 43, 44), which connect through a pair of pocket doors. The living room, in turn, leads through a door to the garden, which is at grade level on this side of the house, and the dining room opens through doors to a porch that also connects to the garden.

The house has a number of handcrafted elements that reflect Warren's

FIG. 41. Herbert Langford and Catharine Warren house, entrance. *Courtesy of Elizabeth Warren Stoutamire.*

involvement in the Society of Arts and Crafts. The entry door includes two handblown bull's-eye windows, and the house includes a number of casement windows of leaded glass. The floor of the entry-level reception hall is decorated with Mercer tiles, medieval in inspiration, featuring birds, dragons, and a fleur-de-lis motif. The tiles are embedded in polished concrete—a modern choice, although its finish required handwork and skill, so that the selection was consistent with the concepts of craftsmanship and quality that Warren and the Society promoted. The wood fireplace mantel in the living room is decorated with carved potted palms, while the mantel shelf in the dining room is sup-

FIG. 42. Herbert Langford and Catharine Warren house, garden facade with Catharine and children. *Courtesy of Elizabeth Warren Stoutamire.*

ported by corbels carved with an acanthus leaf pattern. Also in the dining room are door casings decorated with corner blocks carved with floral and foliate motifs, each pair in a different design.

The garden, while not large, is terraced with brick and stone retaining walls. The main wall, surmounted by a brick balustrade, was built at a right angle from one side of the house. Stone stairs, running through the main wall, connect one level of lawn to another and establish the garden's dominant axis. This formality reflects Warren's interest in contemporary English garden design and, more specifically, the writings of Reginald Blomfield, whose works were assigned to the Harvard students.

Everett D. Chadwick House

The house designed and built by Warren and Smith for Everett D. Chadwick in 1909 (fig. 45) is similar to the Warren house in many respects. Located in Winchester, Massachusetts, the Chadwick house also includes a street facade and a garden facade, its garden elevation overlooking a small lake. The street elevation is classically organized

FIG. 43. Herbert Langford and Catharine Warren house, living room with Arthur and James Warren. *Courtesy of Elizabeth Warren Stoutamire.*

around a central entrance, and the classicism is emphasized through vaguely Georgian detailing, including the pediment over the center bay and the fanlight over the front door.

The plan of the house (fig. 46), published with photographs of the exterior in the *American Architect*, reveals the same concern for a coherent relationship among public areas as was taken with Warren's house.[65] The living room and dining room, both offering views of the lake, connect to each other across a central hall. Both rooms have double

FIG. 44. Herbert Langford and Catharine Warren house, dining room with James Warren. *Courtesy of Elizabeth Warren Stoutamire.*

pocket doors, which, when opened, allow for an integration of the spaces. As in the Warren house, the dining room of the Chadwick house connects through a door to a covered porch, which in turn leads to a terraced garden. Yet while the Warren house was designed for a sloping site, the Chadwick house was built on a level site. The front door is axially aligned to lead the visitor through a central hallway to glazed

FIG. 45. Warren and Smith, Everett D. Chadwick house, Winchester, Massachusetts, 1909. *From* American Architect, *January 7, 1914.*

double doors that open to the garden beyond—a plan that was a favorite with Warren and Smith in their residential work.

What distinguishes the Chadwick house from other houses by Warren and Smith is the fact that it was constructed of reinforced concrete.[66] Brick quoins and window surrounds soften the effect, as do brick belt courses. The concrete surface is pebbly, with a pleasing texture that derives from the use of a coarse aggregate that was cleaned after the poured mixture had set and the wood forms were removed. The idea of building houses in concrete was being pursued across the country during this period, but because of the expense involved, the material was never widely adopted. When it was chosen, it was valued as a durable, high-quality product, consistent with the fine materials promoted by Arts and Crafts theorists and designers.

Another person who was constructing a house in concrete at this time was Mercer, Warren's cohort who sold his tiles through the Society of Arts and Crafts. Mercer built his house, Fonthill, between 1908 and 1910 in Doylestown, Pennsylvania.[67] Yet while the Chadwick and Mercer houses date from the same years, the Chadwick house is refined in

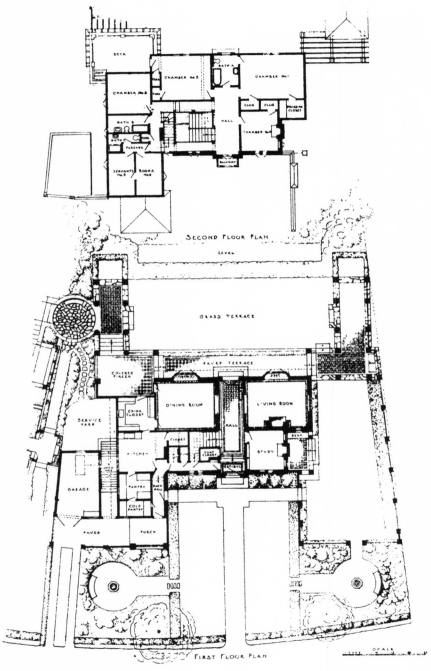

FIG. 46. Chadwick house, plan of first floor. *From* American Architect, *January 7, 1914.*

appearance while the Mercer house is characterized by a certain rawness. The walls of the Mercer house are marked by the impressions left by the wood forms, the result of a higher proportion of cement to aggregate and the choice of a finer aggregate than was used for the Chadwick house. Mercer's house, like Mercer's tiles, has an uneven appearance, an appearance that is appealing because of its irregularity and imperfection. Paradoxically, while Warren liked this quality—championed by Ruskin—to a certain extent, he did not favor it for work in concrete.

George B. Upham House

One of the grander houses designed by Warren and Smith was the country estate of George B. Upham in Claremont, New Hampshire, dating from 1912. The firm had designed a town house for Upham, an attorney and businessman, in Boston ten years earlier.[68] The house in New Hampshire is spectacularly sited on the brow of a hill overlooking the Connecticut River. Built of brick, shingles, and stucco, the house again was conceived with two facades (figs. 47, 48). It consists of a main rectangular mass that is classically organized and detailed on both elevations, with large pavilions flanking both sides. Porches defined as discrete spaces are located around the building's perimeter. One porch, on the facade overlooking the river, features a long row of two-story square columns, reminiscent of the colonnade at George Washington's home at Mount Vernon, Virginia. Warren had written about the dignity of such Virginia mansions and illustrated Mount Vernon in the chapter on Renaissance and modern architecture that he contributed to *The Fine Arts: A Course of University Lessons,* published in 1900.[69]

A private road originally brought the visitor to the entrance on the side of the house that overlooks a terraced formal garden. One enters a hall defined by Tuscan columns and a curved Doric entablature. A flying staircase circles up to the second floor, in a manner reminiscent of the cantilevered staircase of the parish house of the Swedenborgian church in Washington, D.C. Crowning the space above the stairway is a domed ceiling. On the main level, the entry hall continues through the depth of the house to a wide glazed door and sidelights, through which one sees a panoramic view of the river valley. Living room and dining room flank either side of the hall in a continuously flowing space. Both rooms include sash windows that extend to the floor and that can be raised to

FIG. 47. Warren and Smith, George Upham house, "Upland Court," river facade, Claremont, New Hampshire, 1912. *Courtesy of Richard Smith Joslin.*

the ceiling, opening the house completely to its porches and the out-of-
doors.

In addition to the customary Arts and Crafts materials favored by
Warren and Smith, including hand-carved woodwork, ironwork, and
Mercer tiles, the exterior of the house is enhanced by a collection of
historic tiles embedded in its walls. The tiles come from variety of
cultures, including Chinese, Turkish, Italian, and Spanish, representing
bits of architectural history. Whether assembling the collection was
Upham's idea or that of his architects is not known, but it clearly was
in keeping with Warren's inclinations. Mercer, too, shared this interest
in tile and embedded an outstanding and diverse collection in the walls
of Fonthill. Another influential example of this concept of incorporating
architectural artifacts of museum quality into the fabric of one's house
was Fenway Court, Isabella Stewart Gardner's house in Boston, built in
1902, which Warren knew well.[70]

Campus design also engaged Warren and his firm, and their campus
projects relate to their work for a country club. These projects involved
the challenge of associating buildings with each other through their materials and their style, through their siting, and, in some cases, through
their relationship with the natural landscape. Warren's interest was consistent with his championship of landscape architecture and, more specifically, the establishment of the School of Landscape Architecture at
Harvard under Frederick Law Olmsted, Jr. Both the campus and the
country club presented idealized settings, places of respite from com-

FIG. 48. "Upland Court," garden facade. *Courtesy of Richard Smith Joslin.*

mercialism and the congestion of urban life. They also were private and exclusive, bastions of Anglo-Saxon culture. As with much work of this period, the designs that Warren and his firm produced were alternately regressive and progressive, historical and protomodern.

Carey Cage and Soldiers Field Gates, Harvard University

Warren was involved with a number of projects on the Harvard campus. Two of them called on Warren to address inadequacies with existing facilities, the library and the first fine-arts building, both of which have since been demolished.[71] Warren's most important work for Harvard was for Soldiers Field, the new athletic grounds acquired by Harvard in 1890, located across the Charles River from the Cambridge campus.

In 1897 Warren designed the Carey Cage in association with Lewis J. Johnson, professor of civil engineering (fig. 49). Demolished in November of 1995, the building was one of Warren's more inventive efforts. In form, its broad, tiered, pagoda-like roof with flaring corners reflected the interest in Japanese architecture that was explored by Boston archi-

FIG. 49. Warren in consultation with Lewis J. Johnson, Carey Cage, Soldiers Field, Harvard University, Allston, Massachusetts, 1897. Demolished. *Courtesy of the Harvard University Archives.*

tects in Warren's circle during the 1890s. Even before Cram and Longfellow, Warren had adopted a broad, flaring roof in his design for the betting pavilion at Saratoga Springs, dating from 1891 to 1892. In 1894, Cram and Goodhue designed the Arthur Knapp house in Fall River, Massachusetts, as a Japanese residence, and they added an accompanying teahouse between 1895 and 1898, which was similar to Carey Cage with its low massing and monitor roof.[72] Longfellow designed several buildings that reflected an interest in Japanese architecture, including a barn for William Weld in Brookline, dating from 1893, and his island station proposal for the Boston Elevated Rail Road, from 1898.[73] Yet in Warren's teaching and his writing, he expressed not a word about Japanese architecture. His development of this roofline seems to have derived from a purely formal interest, which was reinforced by the academic interest of his peers. Even more important to Warren, however, were Richardson's train stations—direct sources for Warren in further developing the idea of the broad, flaring roofline. Having contributed to the design of at least one of the stations, Warren returned to them for inspiration. In this respect, Richardson's work had entered into Warren's narrative of architectural history, providing additional concepts for his design development.

Carey Cage was one of Warren's more eclectic projects, with its walls built of brick, half-timbering, and stucco, in a loosely Elizabethan manner. This rustic combination may have seemed appropriate for a structure that was situated at the edge of an open athletic field. Longfellow took a similar approach with the Weld barn, combining half-timbering with a broad, Japanese-inspired roofline.[74] Complementing the half-timbering and brick of Carey Cage were handwrought decorative iron details, evocative of an earlier, if undetermined, age. These included large iron hinges on the doors and iron brackets with spiraling ends under the eaves (fig. 50).

At the same time, the building was experimental and forward-looking. Its walls were built in modular panels, which became apparent when the building was demolished.[75] The interior of the building revealed its structural elements (fig. 51). It was framed in steel, making Carey Cage the first steel-framed building on the Harvard campus. The roof was supported by an elaborate steel-trussed system, a further development of Warren's interest in wood trusswork.

Warren also was involved with the design of the Soldiers Field fence, made of reinforced concrete (fig. 52). It was with this project, dating from 1897 to 1900, that the use of concrete was tested for subsequent construction at the field. The gates, with finials on their piers and elaborate ironwork incorporating the Harvard crest, alluded to the gates designed by McKim for Harvard Yard. Brick trim further connected the new gate with the main campus buildings. The question of how to finish the concrete was an issue. With this fence, a heavy aggregate, picked clean after the forms were removed, was first used at Harvard and by Warren. He also designed a concrete superintendent's lodge, which was demolished in the 1960s.[76] The construction of the gates and piers represented a collaborative effort between Warren, Johnson, and Ira Hollis, professor of mechanical engineering.[77] The success led to the ambitious construction in concrete of the Harvard stadium, which included steel framing and precast concrete seating. The stadium was the largest ferroconcrete structure in the world when it was finished in 1903. While McKim was hired to develop its classical design, Warren supported the effort by placing it in a historical context, writing an article about ancient stadia and circuses.[78]

FIG. 50. Carey Cage, brackets.

Slocomb Hall, Proctor Academy

In 1909, Warren and Smith designed several buildings for the campus of Proctor Academy, located in Andover, New Hampshire, northwest of Concord. The work probably came to the firm through Smith's family connections, although Warren could have been recommended through Harvard's president Eliot, who was involved with Proctor Academy because of its Unitarian affiliation.[79] After a boys' dormitory burned, Warren and Smith were retained to design and build a new brick boys' dormitory, later named Gannett House. Along with this commission, the firm designed a girls' dormitory, Cary House, of frame construction.[80] They also rebuilt a stable to serve as a gymnasium, called Slocomb Hall.[81] Prior to this campaign, the academy had been a modest enterprise, organized around a single classroom building, in a tiny New England village. The new dormitories were picturesquely sited to overlook a newly planned, irregularly shaped green.[82] They were loosely

FIG. 51. Carey Cage, interior trusswork.

colonial in effect, conceived to enhance the aura of the simple eighteenth- and early-nineteenth-century buildings nearby.

The transformation of a onetime stable into Slocomb Hall (fig. 53) was one of several reconstruction projects that Warren and Smith oversaw in their practice through the years and was typical of a broader interest in reworking eighteenth- and early-nineteenth-century buildings.[83] The original stable was substantially rebuilt, with enormous rectangular windows inserted into each of its gable ends. The scale of these openings was totally modern, yet the windows were designed with small panes, reminiscent of colonial windows. The interior of the new gymnasium (fig. 54) revealed the architects' same enthusiasm for trusswork that was evident with Carey Cage, although the Proctor project was not as technically advanced as the design for Harvard. Slocomb Hall was rebuilt with an extensive new system of wood beams and trusses under its pitched roof, resulting in an effect that was more medieval than colonial. With the stable left largely intact, the installation of the large windows with the small panes, and the addition of the trusswork inside, the end product was paradoxically both historical in its origins and in

FIG. 52. Warren in consultation with Ira N. Hollis, Soldiers Field gates, Harvard University, Allston, Massachusetts, 1897. *Courtesy of the Harvard University Archives.*

the design of its new components and thoroughly modern in its eclecticism.

Flowers Memorial Hall, Huntingdon College

Warren and Smith's work for Proctor Academy in 1909 was followed immediately by a commission to design the main building along with a campus plan for the Woman's College of Alabama, located in Montgomery. Today a coeducational institution, renamed Huntingdon College, it was established by the Methodist Church. The campus was planned around a natural amphitheater, with the John Jefferson Flowers Memorial Hall serving as the central building. It was designed to include the college's administrative offices and a chapel without fixed seats, allowing it to double as an assembly hall—in essence, a multipurpose room.[84]

While Warren and Smith seemed partial to colonial designs for New England campuses, especially when early buildings survived, for the Woman's College of Alabama they designed a Gothic Revival building that was similar to the firm's work for the Troy Orphan Asylum. On one facade, the massing of the chapel projects at right angles from the administrative part of the building (fig. 55). Its high, sheer brick walls are buttressed by brick piers that alternate with large lancet windows.

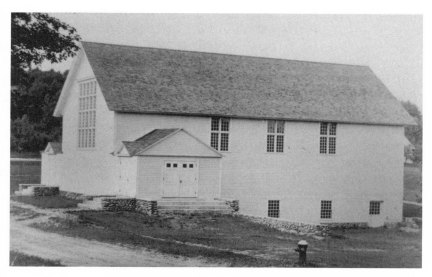

FIG. 53. Warren and Smith, Slocomb Hall, a stable reconstructed as a gymnasium, Proctor Academy, Andover, New Hampshire, 1909. *Courtesy of Richard Smith Joslin.*

The building's opposite facade is long and low, with little embellishment except at the entry, which is emphasized by an oriel window and sculpture. Inside the entrance hall, stone ribs support a true vault of brick, again a reflection of Warren's devotion to Gothic construction. The chapel roof is trussed, in a manner reminiscent of the trusswork of Slocomb Hall at Proctor Academy (fig. 56). Indeed, the chapel and the academy gymnasium have much in common, with their high walls and large windows under trussed, gabled roofs. While Slocomb Hall was an inexpensive project and the Flowers Hall chapel far more ambitious, the two represent the essence of Warren's ideal architecture. They are restrained, they emphasize structure, and they suggest associations with English and American architectural traditions. While serving the modern needs of their clients, they incorporate historical references that clearly convey their cultural assertions.

Winchester Country Club

Yankee traditions were affirmed when Warren and Smith remodeled an early-nineteenth-century farmhouse and barn for the Winchester Coun-

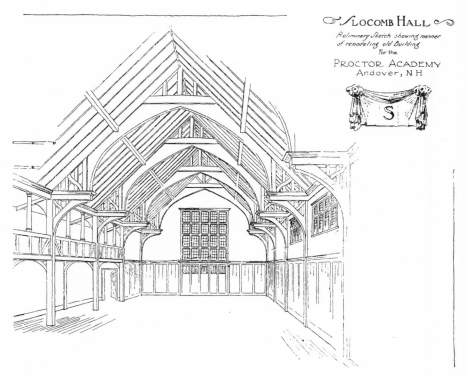

FIG. 54. Slocomb Hall, interior. From *Proctor Academy Catalogue*, 1909–1910. *Courtesy of Proctor Academy.*

try Club in 1916.[85] Its original members had organized a golf club in 1897, and in 1902 they purchased a house and land on the Arlington-Winchester border (fig. 57). The club's first president, John Suter, was rector of the Winchester Episcopal church and also a client of Warren and Smith.[86] By the very nature of those involved, the club was an extension of its members' Yankee and English identities.

In what was to be the first of several projects at the country club, the later phases directed by Smith after Warren's death, the firm of Warren and Smith rebuilt the barn to accommodate a social hall and locker rooms (figs. 58, 59). A large fireplace was constructed at one end of the former barn, and a large bank of windows with small colonial-style panes was inserted into one of the gable elevations. Inside, wood posts support a second floor that was built around the perimeter of the

FIG. 55. Warren and Smith, Flowers Memorial Hall, Woman's College of Alabama (today Huntingdon College), Montgomery, Alabama, 1909–1911. *Courtesy of Richard Smith Joslin.*

structure, while a large area in the center of the room rises two stories, creating a kind of great hall for country club parties. The walls were plastered so as to expose the wood framing, adding to the rustic and vaguely English effect. The preservation of the old homestead and barn was a testimony to the continuity of the Yankee society that had invested in it, and the new elements reinforced the message in a readily comprehended visual language.

Three additional projects warrant consideration to further clarify Warren's views about architecture. All three are buildings on the Harvard campus. Two of the projects were designed by other architects and were constructed under the direction of Warren and Smith. They are the Cruft Laboratory, dating from 1913 to 1915, designed by Eugène Duquesne, and the Germanic Museum, designed by German Bestelmeyer in 1911 and built between 1914 and 1917. In both cases, Warren was motivated to support the work of these architects, forgoing the opportunity to work on projects designed in his own office, in order to promote his other interests. The third building was neither constructed nor

FIG. 56. Flowers Memorial Hall, interior of chapel. *Courtesy of Richard Smith Joslin.*

supported by Warren. It is Widener Library, designed by Horace Trumbauer and built between 1913 and 1915. This building represents an approach to architecture that Warren found objectionable.

Cruft Laboratory, Harvard University

The Cruft Laboratory (fig. 60) is a building that is so unassuming that it has been all but ignored in modern study of the Harvard campus.[87]

FIG. 57. Winchester Country Club, Winchester and Arlington, Massachusetts, facade of early-nineteenth-century farmhouse. *Courtesy of Richard Smith Joslin.*

One may deduce that once Warren had lured Duquesne to Cambridge, Warren realized that Duquesne needed to reestablish his architectural practice. In France, the winner of the Prix de Rome had received government commissions, whereas no such work would be forthcoming in the United States. Warren probably appealed to the administration at Harvard for help. In 1913, Duquesne developed a master plan for the campus and neighboring commercial property, and he designed the Cruft Laboratory.[88] The master plan calls for the adoption of Georgian-inspired designs to develop a more coherent campus, while the Cruft Laboratory serves as an example of what he had in mind. It is a red brick building, sparingly detailed with a pediment over its centrally positioned door and dentil molding under its eaves. Warren must have discussed the design with Duquesne, and the result is consistent with Warren's own work.

In addition to lacking commissions, Duquesne had no atelier, the student-staff office that was a part of the French system. Surviving records show that the Cruft building was constructed entirely under Smith's supervision, while Duquesne was consulted for just a few design decisions after work had begun.[89] Structurally the building presented some

FIG. 58. Warren and Smith, Winchester Country Club, reconstruction of barn for social hall and locker rooms, 1916. *Courtesy of Richard Smith Joslin.*

problems, as it was to be a high-tension laboratory for the study of electrical engineering. The foundation is concrete, the floors are rein-forced concrete, and the exterior and interior of the building include concrete "cast stone" and concrete block. The oversight of this work fell to Smith and the consulting engineers.

Germanic Museum, Harvard University

Just as the construction of the Cruft building was nearing completion, in 1914, Warren and Smith committed themselves to the construction of the Germanic Museum (fig. 61), designed by German Bestelmeyer, a Dresden professor, in 1911. The building, located on Kirkland Street, was soon named Adolphus Busch Hall and housed the Busch-Reisinger Museum until 1987, when the museum relocated; two years later, the building was reopened as the Minda de Gunzburg Center for European Studies.[90]

Establishing the Germanic Museum at Harvard stemmed from a broader interest in museum building at the university at the turn of the

FIG. 59. Winchester Country Club, social hall, 1916. *Courtesy of Richard Smith Joslin.*

twentieth century. More narrowly, the idea fit into a desire to create museums dedicated to various world cultures.[91] The Germanic Museum was conceived to house plaster casts of great artworks from German-speaking nations, and its spaces were planned to accommodate Romanesque, Gothic, and Renaissance halls, auxiliary rooms, and a walled garden. Kuno Francke, a member of the Harvard German department, promoted the cause of the museum, and toward this end he enlisted Warren to prepare an early design.[92] Warren might well have been given the commission had donors not requested a design from a German architect. When Bestelmeyer was chosen, Warren's commitment was essential, as his firm would take responsibility for overseeing the construction.[93] Warren and Francke met Bestelmeyer in the summer of 1910 in Weimar, and after the meeting, Warren accepted the subordinate role in the project. His deep affection for German culture, established in his youth when he studied in Gotha and Dresden, explains his willingness to assist Francke and his cause.

Bestelmeyer's plans for the building were prepared in 1911, but con-

FIG. 60. Eugène Duquesne in association with Warren and Smith, Cruft Laboratory, Harvard University, Cambridge, Massachusetts, 1913–1915. *Courtesy of the Harvard University Archives.*

struction could not be undertaken at the site until the summer of 1914.[94] The timing could not have been worse. With the outbreak of the First World War that August, Bestelmeyer lost his staff and could not submit finished drawings. It fell to Warren and Smith to develop the designs as well as to oversee the construction.[95] Smith supervised the project, which involved major engineering challenges, including the fabrication of two precast concrete domes. Warren took charge of the many design details and chose the various artisans for the project. Tiles by Mercer, ironwork by Frank Koralewsky, and stone sculpture by John Kirchmayer and Roger Noble Burnham gave the building the richness that Bestelmeyer envisioned.[96] Even in 1916, as the building was nearing completion, the *Boston Sunday Herald* identified it as being both "thoroughly German" and a product of the Boston Arts and Crafts movement.[97]

Warren continued to take an interest in the building, designing stained glass windows for its Gothic chapel-like hall in collaboration with John Oster of Boston. Like the casts, the windows were developed as faithful copies and intended for study. One, a reproduction of a window from the church of Maria am Wasen in Vienna, was exhibited in the salesroom of the Society of Arts and Crafts when Warren died in 1917.[98] Because

FIG. 61. German Bestelmeyer in association with Warren and Smith, Germanic Museum (Busch-Reisinger Museum, renamed the Minda de Gunzburg Center for European Studies in 1989), Harvard University, Cambridge, Massachusetts, designed 1911, constructed 1914–1917. *Courtesy of Richard Smith Joslin.*

of strong anti-German sentiment during the war, the museum did not open to the public until 1921.

Warren would not have worked on this building had he not believed in its design. He dedicated himself to it because it was compatible with his ideals. It represented a scholarly understanding of earlier architectural models; it respected and embraced its own cultural tradition; and it was designed to showcase the work of skilled artisans, whose tile, iron, sculpture, and glass also were informed by a knowledge of historical precedent.

By contrast, Warren was far from supportive of Harvard's Widener Memorial Library (fig. 62), designed by Horace Trumbauer of Philadelphia in 1913. With its imperial staircase and colonnade overlooking Harvard Yard, the proposed library design disturbed several of Warren's colleagues, who circulated letters to each other and to Warren to see whether they could alter the decision.[99] Failing in that effort, these men were frustrated again in 1915 when Trumbauer received an honorary degree for his work. In one letter, Warren told Clipston Sturgis that he had not been consulted in this decision and that he regretted it.[100]

FIG. 62. Horace Trumbauer, Widener Memorial Library, Harvard University, Cambridge, Massachusetts, 1913–1915. *Courtesy of the Harvard University Archives.*

Ironically, a few months later the Harvard architecture faculty was castigated in a critique of the library design that appeared in the *Architectural Review*. The lead editorial, presumably written by the editor, Boston architect Frank Chouteau Brown, observed that the library "suggests the parvenu in striving to attract attention by forcing itself, in its gross physical guise, among its far better 'born and bred' associates, whose manners it might with better grace have striven to assume."[101] The author then questioned the ability of Harvard's architecture department to train the younger generation in view of the "impropriety" that had been permitted.

Yet Warren did not believe he could publicly criticize the new library to any advantage. He remained loyal to Harvard and its leadership, steadfastly silent, even while sharing the views expressed in the editorial. Widener Library was historically informed, and it had been constructed with fine materials and commendable craftsmanship. But it lacked restraint, a quality that was highly cherished by Warren and the architects with whom he was most closely associated.

~ SIX ~

FINAL YEARS

W ARREN WAS A consummate team player, a man who was an active member of a number of organizations, willing to serve on committees as well as to hold executive positions. The American Institute of Architects and the Boston Society of Architects were just two of the groups with which Warren was involved.[1] In his final years, from 1914 when the First World War began until his death in 1917, Warren also devoted a great deal of time and effort to political affairs. He met regularly with men in Boston and New York City—academics, professionals, and business leaders—who sought to influence American policy relating to the war by holding rallies and by publishing their positions. The views that Warren expressed, in calling for American support of England and France, reflected the same attachments that shaped his ideas about architectural history, architecture, and craftsmanship.

During the first weeks of August of 1914, when Germany invaded Belgium, marking the beginning of the First World War, Warren wrote to his brother Harold about his concerns for his son Arthur, who was studying in Marburg. He also reported with satisfaction that a contract had been signed and construction had begun on the Germanic Museum.[2] Yet the strong affection that Warren harbored for many aspects of German culture and that he conveyed to his children did not carry over to his feelings toward the governments of Germany and Austria, which he viewed with antipathy.[3]

By early 1915, a time when the American government was maintaining a neutral position, Warren and a group of men had begun meeting in Boston to encourage public support for the Allies. In an effort to reach a national audience, they began distributing pamphlets and submitting letters to various publications.[4] Among them was Warren's letter to the *Nation*, which appeared on April 29 under the heading "The English Tradition."[5]

In his letter, Warren identified two opposing social ideals that he believed distinguished German from English traditions. Expressing views that were typical for Anglo-Saxon Boston, he contrasted the German ideal "of the individual subordinated to the state, which is made an end in itself" with the English ideal in which the state exists "for the sake of the individual and as the servant, not the master, of the collected individuals." Warren argued that American political and social thought is fundamentally English. He wrote, "The history of the origin and development of the American nation is one chapter in the history of the development of English freedom." In emphasizing the importance of the individual, in associating this idea with English history, and in linking that history with American history, Warren restated ideas that formed the basis for his views about architecture and the Society of Arts and Crafts. His political analysis reflected not a detached judgment of whose cause was right in the war, nor a concern for its French and Belgian victims, but rather a sense of America's shared cultural values with those of England.

Warren's sympathy with England was felt by others in Boston and especially in the Harvard community. A critic of the era, Randolph S. Bourne, commented on "those foolish Anglophiles of Boston and New York and Philadelphia" who saw "uncritically in England's cause the cause of Civilization."[6] Bourne did not exaggerate. This sweeping perspective, that England's battle represented a battle for civilization, was expressed at length in several letters written to the *New York Times* by Charles W. Eliot, Harvard's president emeritus.[7]

In early 1916, between 2,500 and 3,000 men and women gathered in Boston's Tremont Temple, where they passed resolutions urging American support of the Allies—a meeting later identified as the first of its kind in the United States.[8] The speakers all had some connection to Harvard. Warren was actively involved with the Boston group, called the Citizens' League, and he helped found the New York–based American Rights League, which ultimately absorbed the Boston group.

Warren's most ambitious effort on behalf of the Allies involved writing a letter that was called "An Address to the People of the Allied Nations," for which he obtained the signatures of five hundred leading American citizens. Later referred to as the "Address of the Five Hundred," it was

published in April of 1916 throughout the United States and simulta-
neously in England and France, followed by publication in Russia, Italy,
and Japan.[9] The letter opened with a clear statement of support for the
Triple Entente and added that the signers believed they were presenting
the views of the overwhelming majority of Americans. The address expressed the signers' solidarity "with those who are struggling to preserve
the liberties of the world and the highest ideals of civilization." While
praising the great cultural contributions of Germany, the letter condemned the German invasion of Belgium and German methods of war-
fare. The address concluded by expressing the signers' desire for the
success of the Allies, the restoration of Belgium and of Serbia, and the
suppression of militarism, all seen as the hope for the "future of civilization."

The signers of the letter, from forty-two states of the Union, represented leaders in education, including more than twenty presidents of
American colleges and universities and 147 professors, as well as prominent businessmen, doctors, lawyers, clergymen, and statesmen. Among
the architects who endorsed the letter were Cram, Sturgis, Coolidge,
and Lowell. Frederick Law Olmsted, Jr., the landscape architect, provided his name. Artists included Edmund C. Tarbell, Childe Hassam,
Bela Pratt, and Daniel C. French. In the range of their backgrounds,
the signers presented a challenge to various regional and ideological
views, including East Coast pacificism and midwestern isolationism. In
August, the French issued a reply of appreciation, signed by five hundred leading statesmen, religious leaders, and artistic figures including
Auguste Rodin and the composers Camille Saint-Saëns and Claude De-
bussy.[10]

Warren's activity was one of many efforts made by members of the
Harvard community to support the Allies. Richard Norton, the son of
Charles Eliot Norton, organized and led the American Volunteer Motor
Ambulance Corps, assisting at the battlefronts.[11] Eliot, as president
emeritus, continued to lecture and write on behalf of the Allied cause,
eventually calling for American intervention. In June of 1916, he spoke
at Harvard, and the *New York Times* reported in a headline, "Eliot Says
We Must Help Allies Win War."[12] A month later, he published a long
letter in the *Times* about the ideals of the American people.[13] Religious
toleration, government resting on the consent of the governed, and freedom of speech were among the principles that he considered, observing
that they were shared by England, France, and Belgium. The historical

differences between the Allied nations were not mentioned, as he selectively emphasized a common heritage. Eliot concluded his letter by calling for active support of these nations in the war. In September, Warren wrote to his brother Harold, asking him whether he had seen Eliot's "excellent letter" in the *New York Times*.[14] Warren continued to attend meetings of the Boston group, now a chapter of the American Rights League, and he also attended meetings in New York.

In February of 1917, the American Rights League published a large advertisement in the *Times*, advocating American entry into the war. Featured in the ad were quotations from Eliot and Nicholas Murray Butler, president of Columbia University.[15] Underneath their statements, the advertisement proclaimed in boldface: "These are not the words of jingoes. They are the words of clear-headed, far-sighted, patriotic Americans." By showcasing the positions of academic leaders who were pro-intervention, the League sought to counter the outspoken intellectuals on the left who opposed American military involvement.[16] The advertisement's most important target was President Woodrow Wilson, who, as a former president of Princeton University, would have been especially sensitive to the views expressed by Eliot and Butler. With many developments converging, including the sinking of three American ships and the growing desperation of the Allies, Wilson led the nation into war during the first week of April.

While Warren's political activities were motivated by his conviction that the war was about the future of democracy in the face of autocratic governments, and even the future of civilization, he was also distressed by the damage to so many important monuments in the region between Belgium and eastern France. History, for Warren, was being destroyed. Having walked through this region on his European trip during the mid-1880s, sketching and measuring its medieval churches, he was deeply stirred by the destruction.[17] Anticipating the war's end, Warren helped lead an effort to raise money from American architects to rebuild one of the churches as a memorial to France's contribution to architecture.[18]

Warren's commitment to the construction of the Germanic Museum required even more devotion at a time when passions ran high. Strong anti-German sentiments were expressed during the period, and the Germanic Museum became the focus of protests in the Harvard community. A cast of the Braunschweig Lion, displayed outside the museum, was routinely "decorated" during the night.[19] That Warren could invest so much energy toward persuading Americans to side with the Allies against Germany even as he stood by the Germanic Museum was due to his unwavering sense of what he conceived as moral—a morality derived from his perspective on history.

Understanding Warren's idiosyncratic moral vision helps us understand the choices he made at Harvard and with the Society of Arts and Crafts. Morality to Warren did not mean addressing the housing problems of the poor, as it did to some of his colleagues, nor caring for the immigrant, as it did to his sister-in-law Elsie Reed, who worked among Boston's Jewish families.[20] Morality to Warren was a somewhat abstract commitment to the concepts of individualism, self-determination, and aesthetic expression, seen from the vantage point of political and ethnic traditions.

Warren died suddenly, succumbing to a heart ailment, on June 27, 1917, at sixty years of age.[21] His colleagues believed he died of exhaustion, his energy sapped by the added burden of his war effort.[22] Morton Prince, president emeritus of Tufts Medical School and a leader in the Boston effort to support the Allies, wrote about Warren's self-sacrifice.[23] In addition to suggesting that Warren's efforts had compromised his health, Warren's colleagues recognized that his teaching and organizational service had limited his architectural practice and prevented him from completing his books on the history of architecture, the first of which he had begun.[24]

Had he lived through the war, Warren would have been deeply saddened by events that would have touched him most intimately. The stained glass windows that he had designed with John Oster for the Germanic Museum, once installed, were smashed and destroyed by anti-German protesters.[25] Even more tragic was the death of his son Arthur, who in 1918 became a war casualty.[26]

After Warren's death, his major areas of activity were taken over by colleagues and former students who continued the general direction of his work. At Harvard, he was succeeded as dean by his former Ph.D. student George Edgell, with courses taught by Warren's longtime faculty colleague C. Howard Walker and former student Kenneth Conant, among others.[27] Sturgis succeeded Warren as president of the Society of Arts and Crafts. And Smith carried on the firm's architectural practice, adding to many of the firm's earlier projects, including the Germanic Museum.

By way of honoring his former professor, Fiske Kimball undertook the task of publishing Warren's manuscript for the first volume of a multivolume architectural history. Kimball added notes, illustrations, and a concluding chapter, as well as an introduction dedicated to Warren, and *Foundations of Classic Architecture* was published in 1919.[28] Yet another tribute to Warren was the donation of a bronze bell to the French cathedral of Noyon by a group of American architects. Dedicated in October of 1923, it replaced a bell melted down by the Germans during the war. Cram was chairman of the committee that arranged for the gift, and he almost certainly wrote the bell's inscription, honoring Warren's efforts "to bring America into the war, side by side with the Allies, to defend against the Germans the cause of justice and liberty."[29] The money that paid for the bell was the fund collected by Warren before his death, when he had hoped to lead an effort to rebuild a French church.

In his professional work, as an architect and as an architectural historian, Warren trained a wide range of men, and although it would be impossible to assess the extent of his influence, a few of the names of those who came into contact with him may be noted. In 1891, he employed Charles Greene, who later contributed significantly to the development of Arts and Crafts architecture in California.[30] While less well known, Maurice Biscoe, who worked as a junior partner with Warren, designed a number of important buildings in Colorado, including Denver, where he based his practice.[31] Another onetime partner, Lewis Bacon, later a partner with Bacon and Hill, continued to work in Boston.[32] Warren also was closely connected to George F. Newton, who taught design at Harvard and who went on to develop a significant Boston practice. Architectural students trained in Warren's program include George Washington Smith, who worked in California; Harry Little, who worked in Concord, Massachusetts; and Thomas Mott Shaw, whose Boston firm restored colonial Williamsburg and designed many campus buildings.[33]

Warren's enthusiasm for architectural history influenced a number of students, including architecture students, to pursue careers as historians. When writing about Warren for the *Dictionary of American Biography*, Conant noted, "His influence was widespread, for many teachers of the fine arts were trained at Harvard during the twenty-five years of his service."[34] Warren's students saw him in different ways. Conant appreciated Warren as a medievalist. In introducing *Carolingian and Romanesque Architecture, 800–1200*, first published in 1959, Conant wrote, "The theme of the book is carried by church architecture, but that is natural in the work of an author who is academically the heir of Herbert Langford Warren and his teachers Henry Hobson Richardson and Charles Eliot Norton, the latter an intimate friend of John Ruskin."[35] Yet other students followed different paths. While studying under Warren, Kimball had pursued studies of American architecture, and Edgell had focused on the Italian Renaissance. In 1918, Kimball and Edgell published *A History of Architecture*, which reflected features of Warren's history even as the younger men showed their independence of their former professor, writing, for example, about "functionalism" in contemporary buildings.[36]

Warren's broad knowledge of architectural history extended to his three major areas of activity: the architectural program at Harvard, the Society of Arts and Crafts, and his architectural practice. In presenting his architectural history, he emphasized the English tradition, both as an aesthetic heritage and as a political ideal. His attachment to the past resonated in the worlds of Harvard and Yankee Boston, the communities that embraced him. These people identified themselves with American and English history, which they accepted as the foundation of the American "race." They looked to the past to varying degrees, however. Henry Adams, for example, clung to it more completely, recoiling from the dynamo, his symbol of the modern age. Others, including Warren, sought to bring the past into the present. This group pragmatically accepted the benefits of industry and new technologies while erecting English Gothic and Colonial Revival buildings, tastefully embellished with handcrafted tile and iron.

At Harvard, Warren's sense of the past suited the Brahmin culture that shaped and supported the institution during the nineteenth century. More specifically, his respect for history made him successful as a colleague alongside the dominating personalities of Norton and Moore. In his commitment to teaching architecture as a fine art, he also was a good match for a social culture that regarded itself as aesthetically oriented.

In his work with the Society of Arts and Crafts, Warren represented the conservative view. When conflict arose, Warren articulated the organization's interest in design reform and its rejection of socialist concerns. After the departure of Carey and Dennett, the Society's members supported Warren's leadership, including his goal of a profitable showroom. Warren's emphasis on handiwork inspired by historical models satisfied the organization's architect-leaders, its craftsmen, and its consumers.

In his architectural practice, Warren produced designs that were consistent with those of a successful circle of men who found clients not only in New England but also throughout the United States. These designs appealed to a sector of American society, generally of Anglo-Saxon descent, that embraced a history and an image that affirmed their cultural dominance.

Warren was a link in a chain of figures who contributed to the development of architecture, design, and architectural history in America at the turn of the twentieth century. He reworked ideas from Ruskin to Norton and Morris to Richardson and conveyed his own to another generation of historians, architects, and designers, who went in new directions. Cram described Warren as "intensely human, active, enthusiastic, a crusader for all he believed worth fighting for; a propagandist, if you like; fearless and outspoken, a prophet and a teacher by nature, finding his greatest joy in working with men, or fighting with them if occasion demanded."[37] Warren was most influential through his social endeavors—through his teaching and through the organizations that he directed. In shaping the architecture program at Harvard and in leading the activities of Arts and Crafts organizations both in Boston and nationally, Warren articulated and promoted an aesthetic and a philosophical vision that confirmed the values of those who supported him. His architecture of an idealized England and a venerated New England presented a past that was attractive to many, especially in the Boston area, but also to a significant group of Americans across the country in the years surrounding the turn of the twentieth century.

APPENDIX

List of Buildings and Projects

The list below identifies buildings and projects with which Herbert Langford Warren was involved from the time when he established his own architectural practice, in descending order by date. If the work was designed under a firm name, the firm is noted. The most important sources for the list include records that belonged to the firm of Warren and Smith, now owned by Richard Smith Joslin of Cambridge, Massachusetts, and American architectural periodicals, most notably *American Architect and Building News*. I also have benefited from a preliminary list prepared by Joslin with assistance from me in 1993.

1. Scripps mortuary chapel, Woodmere Cemetery, Detroit, 1886–1887, Warren.
2. Residence for William C. Strong, Newton, Massachusetts, 1886–1887, Warren.
3. Residence for George C. Hammill, Saratoga Springs, New York, 1886, Warren.
4. Competition design for Minneapolis library and museum building, 1886, Warren.
5. Residence for George Burdett, Brookline, Massachusetts, 1887–1888, Warren.
6. Residence for William B. Strong, Brookline, Massachusetts, 1887–1888, Warren.
7. Study for residence for Charles R. Cross, Brookline, Massachusetts, 1887, Warren.
8. Apartments for Alexander Davidson, Newton, Massachusetts, 1888, Warren.
9. Boathouse, cottage, windmill, stable for E. Burgess Warren, Bolton Landing, New York, 1888, Warren.
10. Residence for Charles J. Page, Boston, 1888, Warren. Demolished.
11. Residence for Alexander Davidson, Newton, Massachusetts, 1888, Warren.
12. Residence for William R. Dresser, Newton, Massachusetts, 1888, Warren.
13. Residence for Frederick H. Henshaw, Newton, Massachusetts, 1888, Warren.

14. Residence for Chauncey B. Magee, Newton, Massachusetts, 1888, Warren.

15. Residence for Charles J. Page, Newton, Massachusetts, 1888, Warren.

16. Residence for Herbert Langford and Catharine Warren, reconstruction of a colonial house, Newton, Massachusetts, 1888, Warren.

17. Residence for S. Alexander Orr, extensive reconstruction of an existing building, Troy, New York, 1889. Demolished.

18. Competition design for Cathedral of Saint John the Divine, New York City, 1889, Warren.

19. Renfrew Park, a residential compound for J. B. Kendall, Newport (Middletown), Rhode Island, 1890, Warren.

20. Residence for C. E. Patterson, extensive reconstruction of existing buildings, Troy, New York, 1890, Warren.

21. Study for Huntingdon Park, a residential development, Boston, 1890, Warren.

22. Study for residences and apartment house for W. H. Doughty, Troy, New York, 1890, Warren.

23. Lincoln, Massachusetts, Town Hall (today Bemis Hall), 1891–1892, Warren.

24. Saratoga Racing Association grandstand, clubhouse, and betting ring, Saratoga Springs, New York, 1891–1892, Warren. Betting ring demolished.

25. Troy, New York, Orphan Asylum, 1891, Warren. Demolished.

26. Residence for Samuel Barton, Lake Worth, Florida, 1891, Warren.

27. Cliftondale, Massachusetts, Congregational Church, 1892–1893, Warren.

28. Competition design for Arlington, Massachusetts, High School, 1892, Warren.

29. Competition design for Copley Square, Boston, 1893, Warren.

30. Billerica, Massachusetts, Town Hall, 1894–1895, Warren and Bacon.

31. National Church of the Holy City, Washington, D.C., 1894–1896, Warren.

32. Residence for G. Alice Watson, Brookline, Massachusetts, 1894, Warren and Bacon.

33. Residence for Warren A. Locke, Cambridge, Massachusetts, 1894, Warren and Bacon.

34. Residence for William G. Snow, Watertown, Massachusetts, 1894, Warren and Bacon.

35. Competition design for Claremont, New Hampshire, Town Hall, 1895, Warren.

36. Residence for George P. Baker, Cambridge, Massachusetts, 1896, Warren.

37. Competition design for a New York City municipal building, 1896, Warren in collaboration with Alexander S. Jenney.

38. Carey Cage, Harvard College, Allston, Massachusetts, 1897, Warren in consultation with Lewis J. Johnson. Demolished.

39. Fence and gates enclosing Soldiers Field, gatehouse, Harvard College, All-

ston, Massachusetts, 1897–1900, Warren in consultation with Ira N. Hollis. Gatehouse demolished.

40. Residence for Mrs. A. Vogel, Cambridge, Massachusetts, 1897, Warren.

41. Chapel of the New Church Theological School, Cambridge, Massachusetts, 1899–1901, Warren, Smith, and Biscoe.

42. Chapel for Troy, New York, Orphan Asylum, 1900–1902, Warren, Smith, and Biscoe. Demolished.

43. Residence for Theodore W. Richards, Cambridge, Massachusetts, 1900, Warren, Smith, and Biscoe.

44. Residence for Robert DeCourcy Ward, Cambridge, Massachusetts, 1901, Warren, Smith, and Biscoe.

45. Development plan for road and house sites, for George A. Fernald and Samuel McCall, Myopia Hill Road, Winchester, Massachusetts, 1902–1903, Warren, Smith, and Biscoe in consultation with Olmsted Brothers.

46. Concord, New Hampshire, City Hall and Civic Auditorium, 1902–1903, Warren, Smith, and Biscoe.

47. Craigsville, Virginia, Presbyterian Church, 1902, Warren, Smith, and Biscoe.

48. Residence for George Upham, Boston, 1902, Warren, Smith, and Biscoe. Demolished.

49. Residence for M. B. L. Bradford, reconstruction of colonial house, Concord, Massachusetts, 1902, Warren, Smith, and Biscoe.

50. Study for campus plan, Wellesley College, Wellesley, Massachusetts, 1902, Warren, Smith, and Biscoe in consultation with Frederick Law Olmsted, Jr.

51. Competition design for Foundry Methodist Church, Washington, D.C., 1902, Warren, Smith, and Biscoe.

52. Residence for F. B. Cutler, Osterville, Massachusetts, 1903, Warren, Smith, and Biscoe.

53. Residence for Edward J. Johnson, "Dun-Cairn," Winchester, Massachusetts, 1903, Warren, Smith, and Biscoe.

54. Church of the Epiphany, Winchester, Massachusetts, 1904, Warren, Smith, and Biscoe.

55. Residence for Herbert Langford and Catharine Warren, Cambridge, Massachusetts, 1904, Warren, Smith, and Biscoe.

56. Study for Marlboro, Massachusetts, municipal building, 1904, Warren, Smith, and Biscoe.

57. Residence for Charles Hovey Pepper, Concord, Massachusetts, 1905, Warren, Smith, and Biscoe.

58. Major addition to Gore Hall Library, Harvard University, Cambridge, Massachusetts, 1906, Warren and Smith. Demolished.

59. Study for University Press, Cambridge, Massachusetts, 1906, Warren and Smith.

60. Elizabethan Hall, Shakespeare Society House, Wellesley College, Wellesley, Massachusetts, 1907, Warren and Smith.
61. Glens Falls, New York, Methodist Church, 1907–1908, Warren and Smith.
62. Residence for Walter S. Burke, Cambridge, Massachusetts, 1907, Warren and Smith.
63. Church of the Advent, chancel, Cincinnati, Ohio, 1908, Warren and Smith.
64. Study for Germanic Museum, Harvard University, Cambridge, Massachusetts, 1908, Warren and Smith.
65. Master plan and Flowers Memorial Hall, Woman's Methodist College (today Huntingdon College), Montgomery, Alabama, 1909–1911, Warren and Smith.
66. Gannett House and Cary House, both dormitories, and Slocomb Hall, a stable reconstructed as a gymnasium, Proctor Academy, Andover, New Hampshire, 1909, Warren and Smith. Cary House demolished.
67. Residence for J. B. Williams, Gloucester, Massachusetts, 1909, Warren and Smith.
68. Residence for Everett D. Chadwick, Winchester, Massachusetts, 1909, Warren and Smith.
69. Residence for Iver Johnson, "Flofields" (today the Dr. Franklin Perkins School), Lancaster, Massachusetts, 1910–1913, Warren and Smith.
70. Residence for Clarence E. Carr, reconstruction of federal house, Andover, New Hampshire, c. 1910, Warren and Smith.
71. Church of the Epiphany, parish hall and cloister, Winchester, Massachusetts, 1911, Warren and Smith.
72. National Church of the Holy City, parish house, Washington, D.C., 1911–1912, Warren and Smith.
73. Proctor Block, reconstruction of federal house into town office building, Andover, New Hampshire, 1912, Warren and Smith.
74. Interior alterations to Fogg Museum, Harvard University, Cambridge, Massachusetts, 1912, Warren and Smith. Demolished.
75. Garden and garage for Eben B. Page, Winchester, Massachusetts, 1912, Warren and Smith.
76. Residence for George Upham, "Upland Court," Claremont, New Hampshire, 1912, Warren and Smith.
77. Cruft Laboratory, Harvard University, Cambridge, Massachusetts, 1913–1915, Eugène Duquesne in association with Warren and Smith.
78. Study for Alumnae Building, Wellesley College, Wellesley, Massachusetts, 1913, Warren and Smith.
79. Germanic Museum (Busch-Reisinger Museum, renamed the Minda de Gunzburg Center for European Studies in 1989), Harvard University, Cambridge, Massachusetts, designed by German Bestelmeyer 1911, constructed 1914–1917, Bestelmeyer in association with Warren and Smith.
80. Jordan Hospital, Plymouth, Massachusetts, 1915, Warren and Smith.

81. Residence for the Reverend Carlton Putnam Mills, Winchester, Massachusetts, 1915, Warren and Smith.
82. Winchester and Arlington, Massachusetts, Country Club, reconstruction of an early-nineteenth-century barn, 1916, Warren and Smith.
83. Residence for George and Margaret Dobyne, "Inglelow," Beverly, Massachusetts, 1916–1919, Warren and Smith.
84. Norfolk County Tuberculosis Hospital (Olympus Specialty Hospital), Braintree, Massachusetts, 1917, Warren and Smith.

Notes

Introduction (pp. 1–6)

1. Ralph Adams Cram, "Letters to the Editor. Masters in Architecture—Langford Warren, Henry Vaughan," *Boston Transcript*, July 2, 1917.

2. Carroll L. V. Meeks, "Creative Eclecticism," *Journal of the Society of Architectural Historians*, vol. 11 (Dec. 1953), pp. 15–18; Walter Kidney, *The Architecture of Choice: Eclecticism in America, 1880–1930*, New York: Braziller, 1974; Richard W. Longstreth, "Academic Eclecticism in American Architecture," *Winterthur Portfolio*, vol. 17 (spring 1982), pp. 55–82.

Chapter 1. Early Years (pp. 7–21)

1. Richard Herndon, *Boston of Today*, Boston: Post, 1892, s.v. "Warren, H. Langford."

2. George Copp Warren, *The Part of the Warrens in the Development of Coal Tar, Petroleum Oil and Asphalt*, pamphlet dated 1928, Swedenborgian School of Religion Archives, Newton, Mass., box 72.9, W257, Warren, S. M., p. 3. See also Betsey Warren Davis, "The Warren Family," in *The Warren, Jackson, and Allied Families, Being the Ancestry of Jesse Warren and Betsey Jackson*, Philadelphia: J. B. Lippincott, 1903.

3. Davis, "The Warren Family," p. 29.

4. This information comes from a telephone conversation in April of 1999 with Elizabeth Warren Stoutamire of Tallahassee, Fla., a granddaughter of Herbert Langford Warren.

5. James Lawrence, ed., *The Story of Swedenborg and the Swedenborgian Church*, booklet published by the Communications Support Unit of the Sweden-

borgian Church, Newton, Mass.: Swedenborgian Church of North America, 4th ed., 1992.

6. Davis, "The Warren Family," pp. 30–31. Also "Harold B. Warren, Artist, Dies at 75," *Boston Herald*, Nov. 24, 1934.

7. [James Sturgis Pray], "Faculty of Architecture. Minute on the Life and Services of Dean Herbert Langford Warren," *Harvard University Gazette*, Dec. 1, 1917, p. 45. Copy on file at Harvard University Archives, HUG 1875.80. Pray, chairman of the Council of the School of Landscape Architecture, is named as author of the tribute in a handwritten note on the clipping.

8. Ibid.

9. Anthony Alofsin, "Toward a History of Teaching Architectural History: An Introduction to Herbert Langford Warren," *Journal of Architectural Education*, vol. 37, no. 1 (fall 1983), pp. 2–7. Alofsin does not provide a source for this information. Herbert's brother Harold also studied with Walker, according to a typed page, "Harold Broadfield Warren," owned by one of Harold's grandchildren, Langford Warren of Kittery Point, Maine.

10. Davis, "The Warren Family," p. 30.

11. [Pray], "Minute on the Life."

12. "Obituary. Mr. William Dawes," *The Builder*, vol. 72, no. 2821 (Feb. 27, 1897), pp. 206.

13. Warren assisted Dawes on the Victoria Hotel in Manchester. See Warren's letter to his brother, Harold Broadfield Warren, June 11, 1909, owned by Elizabeth Warren Stoutamire of Tallahassee, Fla.

14. Davis, "The Warren Family," p. 30. Samuel Mills Warren became minister of the Brookline Swedenborgian Society in 1864 and rented a house, "Hillside," in Roxbury, which he bought the following year.

15. Alofsin writes that Warren "did not take courses in the architecture curriculum; he enrolled in supplementary courses such as stereotomy, French, and German," p. 7, n. 4.

16. Margaret Henderson Floyd, "A Terra-Cotta Cornerstone for Copley Square: Museum of Fine Arts, Boston, by Sturgis and Brigham (1870–1876)," *Journal of the Society of Architectural Historians*, vol. 32, no. 2 (May 1973), pp. 83–103.

17. The sketchbook is owned by Langford Warren of Kittery Point, Maine. See Maureen Meister, "Observations of an Architect: Herbert Langford Warren's 1878 Sketchbook," *Nineteenth Century*, vol. 21 (spring 2001), pp. 3–9.

18. Leland Roth, *McKim, Mead and White, Architects*, New York: Harper and Row, 1983, pp. 29–30.

19. Ibid., p. 44. Arthur Little, *Early New England Interiors*, Boston: A. Williams and Co., 1878.

20. Linda S. Ferber and William H. Gerdts, eds., *The New Path: Ruskin and*

the American Pre-Raphaelites, exhibition catalogue, Brooklyn, N.Y.: Brooklyn Museum, 1985, pp. 193–203, 284–287.

21. "At the St. Botolph," *Boston Advertiser*, Mar. 21, 1890.

22. Jeffrey Karl Ochsner, *H. H. Richardson: Complete Architectural Works*, Cambridge, Mass., and London: MIT Press, paperback edition, 1984, pp. 174–179. The library was designed in 1876 and opened in May of 1879.

23. H. Langford Warren, "Architecture in New England," *Picturesque and Architectural New England*, vol. 1, Boston: D. H. Hurd, 1899, p. 40.

24. [Pray], "Minute on the Life."

25. Charles A. Coolidge, "Herbert Langford Warren (1857–1917)," *Proceedings of the American Academy of Arts and Sciences*, vol. 68 (Dec. 1933), pp. 689–691. Copy at Loeb Library, Harvard University.

26. [Pray], "Minute on the Life."

27. The drawings of the H. H. Richardson Architectural Archive are at the Houghton Library and are most easily examined on microfilm. The Castle Hill lighthouse is on reel 1, project 21; the house for Oliver Ames is on reel 2, project 6; and Albany City Hall is on reel 8, project 3.

28. H. Langford Warren Diary, 1884, entry recorded from Ely, Sept. 7. Property of Elizabeth Warren Stoutamire of Tallahassee, Fla.

29. Margaret Henderson Floyd, *Architecture after Richardson: Regionalism before Modernism—Longfellow, Alden, and Harlow in Boston and Pittsburgh*, Chicago and London: University of Chicago Press in association with the Pittsburgh History and Landmarks Foundation, 1994, p. 50.

30. Ibid., p. 57.

31. Floyd makes this point, ibid.

32. H. H. Richardson Architectural Archive, Houghton Library, Harvard University, microfilm reel 11, project 1.

33. L. H. W., "Mourned by Lovers of Art," *New York Star*, May 2, 1886; typescript at Loeb Library, Harvard University, p. 6.

34. Warren's name never appears in the editorial columns, although signed illustrations by him were published from time to time. His role at the journal is known from Herndon and from Pray. Both sources state that Warren handled the architectural coverage from 1886 through 1887.

35. "H. H. Richardson," *Sanitary Engineer*, vol. 13, no. 23 (May 6, 1886), p. 537.

36. Ralph Adams Cram, *Church Building: A Study of the Principles of Architecture in Their Relation to the Church*, Boston: Small, Maynard, 1901, pp. 226–227.

37. Warren, "Architecture in New England," p. 40.

38. Ibid., pp. 40–41.

39. Cram, *Church Building*, pp. 219–220.

40. See James F. O'Gorman, *H. H. Richardson and His Office—Selected Drawings*, Boston: David R. Godine, 1974; and O'Gorman, "Documentation: An 1886 Inventory of H. H. Richardson's Library, and Other Gleanings from Probate," *Journal of the Society of Architectural Historians*, vol. 41, no. 2 (May 1982), pp. 150–155.

41. "Letters from Europe Written by H. Langford Warren," bound volume of photocopies, Loeb Library, Special Collections, Harvard University, Feb. 9, 1885. Also see letters from Sept. 21, 1884, and Nov. 27, 1884. The original letters are owned by Elizabeth Warren Stoutamire of Tallahassee, Fla.

42. "H. H. Richardson," *Sanitary Engineer*.

43. O'Gorman, *Richardson and His Office*, p. 10.

44. L. H. W., "Mourned by Lovers of Art," p. 7.

45. "H. H. Richardson," *Sanitary Engineer*.

46. "Letters from Europe," Sept. 21, 1884.

47. Floyd, *Architecture after Richardson*, pp. 63–64, 371–374.

48. Herbert Langford Warren, "Architectural Education at Harvard University," and Walter Dana Swan, "Nelson Robinson Jr. Hall," both in *Harvard Engineering Journal*, vol. 1, no. 2 (June 1902), pp. 76–103.

49. [Pray], "Minute on the Life." He writes that Warren attended the Harvard classes during his last year of working for Richardson.

50. Letter from Herbert Langford Warren to Charles W. Eliot, Jan. 24, 1894, Harvard University Archives, UAI.5.150, box 110.

51. See Agnes Mongan, "Harvard and the Fogg," in *The Early Years of Art History in the United States: Notes and Essays on Departments, Teaching, and Scholars*, ed. Craig Hugh Smyth and Peter M. Lukehart, Princeton, N.J.: Princeton University, Department of Art and Archaeology, 1993, pp. 47–50.

52. "Fine Arts IV—Syllabus No. 1. Roman and Mediaeval Art," Harvard University Archives, HUC 8893.128.4, box 618.

53. Charles Eliot Norton, *Historical Studies of Church Building in the Middle Ages. Venice, Siena, Florence*, New York: Harper, 1880. Norton, "The Lack of Old Homes in America," *Scribner's Magazine*, vol. 5 (May 1889), pp. 636–640.

54. "Fine Arts III, 1895–1896," notes taken by Arthur Rindge Wendell, p. 11, Harvard University Archives, HUC 8895.328A, box 648.

55. "Fine Arts IV—Syllabus No. 1. Roman and Mediaeval Art."

56. "Letters from Europe."

57. Ibid., June 29, 1884.

58. Ibid., Sept. 21, 1884.

59. Ibid., Aug. 30, 1884. He published "Notes on Wenlock Priory," *Architectural Review*, vol. 1, no. 1 (Nov. 2, 1891), pp. 1–4.

60. "Letters from Europe," June 29, 1884.

61. Ibid., June 29, 1884; Sept. 20, 1884.

62. Ibid., Sept. 21, 1884.

63. Ibid., Aug. 26, 1884. By identifying Warren with an "antimodern" outlook, T. J. Jackson Lears failed to capture the complexity of a man whom Lears listed among his "dramatis personae." See Lears, *No Place of Grace: Antimodernism and the Transformation of American Culture, 1880-1920,* New York: Pantheon, 1981, pp. 322-323.

64. "Letters from Europe," Oct. 5, 1884; Oct. 18, 1884, and Nov. 17, 1884.

65. The drawing of the Lisieux house was published in the *Sanitary Engineer,* vol. 14, no. 6 (July 8, 1886).

66. "Letters from Europe," Oct. 5, 1884; Nov. 27, 1884.

67. Ibid., Nov. 5, 1884.

68. Ibid., Oct. 5, 1884.

69. The drawing is illustrated and discussed in Roth, *McKim, Mead, and White, Architects,* pp. 22-23. Unfortunately the drawing appears to have been lost.

70. Floyd, *Architecture after Richardson,* p. 344; Richard Longstreth, "Academic Eclecticism in American Architecture," *Winterthur Portfolio,* vol. 17 (spring 1982), pp. 63-65.

71. "Letters from Europe," Feb. 9, 1885.

72. Ibid., Feb. 13, 1885; Feb. 22, 1885.

73. Ibid., Feb. 20, 1885.

74. Ibid., follows Feb. 25, 1885 [date unclear].

75. Ibid., Feb. 20, 1885.

76. Ibid., Feb. 25, 1885.

77. Ibid., Apr. 18, 1885.

78. Ibid., Feb. 20, 1885.

79. Ibid., Feb. 23, 1885.

80. Ibid., May 27, 1885.

81. Ibid., June 30, 1885.

82. Coolidge, "Herbert Langford Warren."

Chapter 2. On His Own (pp. 22-55)

1. Winifred B. Warren (1888-1986), "My Father and My Mother," written after 1969, unpublished manuscript, original copy owned by her niece, Elizabeth Warren Stoutamire of Tallahassee, Fla.

2. Quoted in Dorothy May Anderson, *Women, Design, and the Cambridge School,* West Lafayette, Ind.: PDA Publishers, 1980, p. 11, n. 6. Henry Atherton Frost (1883-1952) was director of The Cambridge School, a school established in 1916 to teach architecture and landscape architecture to women, who were not allowed to study in the Harvard programs.

3. "Letters from Europe Written by H. Langford Warren," bound volume of photocopies, Loeb Library, Special Collections, Harvard University, Sept. 21, 1884, and Feb. 23, 1885. The original letters are owned by Elizabeth Warren

Stoutamire of Tallahassee, Fla. Also Winifred Warren, "My Father and My Mother."

4. [James Sturgis Pray], "Faculty of Architecture. Minute on the Life and Services of Dean Herbert Langford Warren," *Harvard University Gazette*, Dec. 1, 1917, p. 45. Copy on file at Harvard University Archives, HUG 1875.80. The *Sanitary Engineer* began carrying architectural illustrations on a weekly basis beginning with the Nov. 5, 1885, issue.

5. Warren may have submitted photographs for the *Sanitary Engineer* to illustrate before he joined the staff. In at least two issues from 1885, churches that Warren visited while traveling in France are published: "Church in the Village of Dorat, France," July 2, 1885 (vol. 12, no. 5), and "Church of St. Julien, at Brioude, Haute-Loire (Auvergne)," Dec. 31, 1885 (vol. 13, no. 5). Warren mentioned visiting Dorat in "Letters from Europe," Feb. 9, 1885, and visiting Brioude when writing on Feb. 13, 1885.

6. As someone who had benefited from the resources of Richardson's photograph collection, Warren sought not only to publish these images but also to assist other architects in collecting them. Late in 1885, he wrote a letter that was read at the annual meeting of the American Institute of Architects in which he protested the duty charges on photographs brought into the country by architects. Coverage of the meeting, including Warren's letter, appeared in the *Sanitary Engineer* on Oct. 29, 1885 (vol. 12, no. 22), pp. 441–445.

7. The *Sanitary Engineer* illustrated the Ames gate lodge on Nov. 5, 1885 (vol. 12, no. 23) and the Sard house on Nov. 19, 1885 (vol. 12, no. 25), when Warren may have begun his employment. In 1886 and 1887, when Warren was known to have been working for the *Sanitary Engineer*, illustrations appeared of the Stoughton house on Feb. 18, 1886 (vol. 13, no. 12); the Ames store on Apr. 15, 1886 (vol. 13, no. 20); the Auburndale, Chestnut Hill, and Holyoke stations on Oct. 14, 1886 (vol. 14, no. 20); the Waban and Woodland stations on Feb. 12, 1887 (vol. 15, no. 11); the Gurney house on Apr. 30, 1887 (vol. 15, no. 22). A "Country house near Boston" by T. M. Clark was illustrated on Nov. 19, 1885 (vol. 12, no. 25). McKim, Mead, and White's Osborn house, Mamaroneck, N.Y., was illustrated on Dec. 3, 1885 (vol. 13, no. 1); Villard house, dining room fireplace (drawn by Warren), New York, on Jan. 29, 1887 (vol. 15, no. 9); and Taylor house, Newport, on May 14, 1887 (vol. 15, no. 24). Andrews and Jaques's "Moderate Cost House," Manchester-by-the-Sea, Massachusetts, appeared in the text on Dec. 31, 1885 (vol. 13, no. 5); and "A Farmer's Cottage" (drawn by Warren), Beverly Farms, Mass., appeared in the text on Apr. 2, 1887 (vol. 15, no. 18).

8. "Exhibition of Architectural Drawings at the Rooms of the American Art Association. Second Notice," *Sanitary Engineer*, vol. 13, no. 8 (Jan. 21, 1886), p. 177.

9. "First Architectural Exhibition Under the Auspices of the Boston Society of Architects," *Sanitary Engineer*, vol. 13, no. 14 (Mar. 4, 1886), p. 320.

10. Illustrations in the *Sanitary Engineer* that reflect Warren's European travels include the house of Jacques Coeur at Bourges, France, published on Feb. 25, 1886 (vol. 13, no. 13); Romanesque and early Gothic capitals from Laon, Arles, and LePuy, France, Wenlock, England, and Siena, Italy (drawn by Warren), published on Mar. 18, 1886 (vol. 13, no. 16); stables at Marple Hall, Cheshire, England, published on Apr. 1, 1886 (vol. 13, no. 18); and house at Lisieux, Normandy (drawn by Warren), published on July 8, 1886 (vol. 14, no. 6).

11. *Sanitary Engineer*, vol. 13, no. 14 (July 8, 1886).

12. "The Exhibition of Architectural Drawings at the Rooms of the American Art Association," *Sanitary Engineer*, vol. 13, no. 7 (Jan. 14, 1886), p. 152.

13. *Sanitary Engineer and Construction Record*, vol. 15, no. 26 (May 28, 1887).

14. Leland Roth, *McKim, Mead, and White, Architects*, New York: Harper and Row, 1983, pp. 103–104. The church was built in phases, dating from 1886 to 1890, 1890 to 1892, and 1905 to 1908.

15. "English Impressions of American Architecture," *Sanitary Engineer*, vol. 13, no. 6 (Jan. 7, 1886), p. 127.

16. *Sanitary Engineer*, vol. 16, no. 10 (Aug. 6, 1887); vol. 16, no. 19 (Oct. 8, 1887).

17. "English Impressions."

18. "Regarding the Study of Architecture," *Sanitary Engineer*, vol. 15, no. 18 (Apr. 2, 1887), p. 463, and vol. 15, no. 19 (Apr. 9, 1887), p. 483. Contributors included Prof. William R. Ware, E. M. Wheelwright, C. H. Blackall, Prof. N. Clifford Ricker, Prof. Charles Babcock, Prof. T. M. Clark, Leopold Eidlitz, and Edward H. Kendall.

19. "The Exhibition of Architectural Drawings" (Jan. 14, 1886), p. 152.

20. "Interior, Residence of Geo. C. Hammill, Esq., Saratoga Springs, N.Y. H. Langford Warren, Architect," *Engineering and Building Record and the Sanitary Engineer*, vol. 17, no. 12 (Feb. 18, 1888).

21. Warren married Catharine Clark Reed on Nov. 8, 1887. See "Recent Deaths. Professor H. Langford Warren," *Boston Transcript*, June 27, 1917.

22. "Had Pastorate for 60 Years. Rev. James Reed of Church of the New Jerusalem Dies at Age of 87," newspaper clipping at the Swedenborgian School of Religion Archives, Newton, Mass., box 72.9, "Ragatz-Reed," folder "Reed, James," R 254. Reed, who lived from 1834 to 1921, served for many years as president of the New Church Theological School and between 1900 and 1919 was general pastor of the Massachusetts Association of New Jerusalem churches. He was the son of Sampson Reed, also a graduate of Harvard College, a resident of Beacon Hill, and an author on the Swedenborgian faith. His treatise, "Observations on the Growth of the Mind," 1826, was sent by Ralph Waldo Emerson to Thomas Carlyle. A copy, reissued with an introduction by James Reed in 1910, is at the Swedenborgian School of Religion Archives, box 72.9, "Ragatz-Reed," folder "Reed, Sampson," R 257.

23. Winifred Warren, "My Father and My Mother."

24. Ibid.

25. Winifred B. Warren, "Recollections of my early childhood. Our Home in Waban," written after 1969, unpublished manuscript, original copy owned by her niece, Elizabeth Warren Stoutamire of Tallahassee, Fla.

26. Located at 401 Woodward St., the house has been designated a Newton Local Landmark. See Aleca Sullivan, "Landmark Report," Apr. 30, 1997, at the Jackson Homestead, Newton Historical Society Archives.

27. M. F. Sweetser, *King's Handbook of Newton, Massachusetts*, Boston: Moses King Corp., 1889, pp. 232, 242. The house also was featured in *House Beautiful*, Dec. 1919. A copy of the article is at the Jackson Homestead in the file on 401 Woodward St. Two decades later, the house was published in *Waban: Early Days, 1681–1918*, ed. Jane Bacon MacIntire, Newton, Mass.: Modern Press, 1944, pp. 84–87.

28. Winifred Warren, "Recollections of my early childhood."

29. Ibid.

30. Ibid.

31. Warren's presence at 9 Park Street is first noted in the Boston directory of 1887.

32. Henry James, *The American Scene*, intro. by Leon Edel, Bloomington and London: Indiana University Press, 1968 (originally published 1907), p. 231.

33. "Letters from Europe," June 30, 1885.

34. Hugh O'Brien was elected mayor of Boston in 1884, intensifying the conflict between the immigrant population and the Yankees. See Lawrence W. Kennedy, *Planning the City upon a Hill: Boston Since 1630*, Amherst, Mass.: University of Massachusetts Press, 1992, p. 97.

35. The competition was announced in "Building Intelligence," in *American Architect and Building News*, vol. 19, no. 524 (Jan. 9, 1886), p. xvi.

36. *American Architect and Building News*, vol. 19, no. 561 (Sept. 25, 1886).

37. See Janet Adams Strong, "The Cathedral of Saint John the Divine in New York: Design Competitions in the Shadow of H. H. Richardson, 1889–1891," Ph.D. dissertation, Brown University, 1990.

38. *American Architect and Building News*, vol. 26, no. 729 (Dec. 14, 1889).

39. See Strong, "The Cathedral of Saint John the Divine," vol. 3, pp. 319–322.

40. The house is identified as one of Warren's more important projects in Richard Herndon, *Boston of Today*, Boston: Post, 1892, s.v. "Warren, H. Langford." See also Massachusetts Historical Commission Survey Form, no. 45/222-19, for 213 Gardner Road, Brookline.

41. *Catalogue of the First Annual Exhibition of the Boston Architectural Club*, Boston, 1890, nos. 716 and 764. The project was announced in "Building Intelligence," in *American Architect and Building News*, vol. 31, no. 788 (Jan. 31,

1891), p. xxii, as follows: "Renfrew Park, a number of frame stables, including a club stable, in one group; to be used by the occupants of the cottages on the Park." The owner was J. B. Kendall. Renfrew Park was described by Herndon in the entry on Warren, *Boston of Today*, as "nineteen elegant dwellings, a Casino, with tennis courts, etc., and large club stables."

42. *American Architect and Building News*, vol. 28, no. 696 (Apr. 27, 1889); *Brickbuilder*, vol. 14, no. 3 (Mar. 1905), illustration no. 35, p. 56.

43. Herndon, *Boston of Today*.

44. The Page house survived at 90 Westland Ave., Boston, until the summer of 2002, when it was demolished. The plan of the first floor is documented by the Building Inspection Report for 1888, vol. 26, p. 46, at the Boston Public Library. Photographs of the interior are at the Society for the Preservation of New England Antiquities, Boston, archives. For a representation of the inglenook in Richardson's study, see James F. O'Gorman, *Living Architecture: A Biography of H. H. Richardson*, New York: Simon and Schuster, 1997, p. 118.

45. Warren is listed in the Troy city directories for three years, from 1890 through 1892.

46. Betsey Warren Davis, "The Warren Family," in *The Warren, Jackson, and Allied Families, Being the Ancestry of Jesse Warren and Betsey Jackson*, Philadelphia: J. B. Lippincott, 1903, pp. 22-30. An uncle, E. Burgess Warren, lived in Lake George, N.Y.

47. Two houses in Troy received extensive recognition through exhibition and publication. One of them, the S. Alexander Orr house, was noted in the "Building Intelligence" of the *American Architect and Building News*, vol. 25, no. 699 (May 18, 1889), p. xiv. It was located at Second and Congress Streets. Its entrance was published in the *American Architect*, International and Imperial editions only, vol. 29, no. 761 (July 26, 1890). A second house, for Judge C. E. Patterson, was noted in the "Building Intelligence" of the *American Architect and Building News*, vol. 27, no. 733 (Jan. 11, 1890), p. xv. The house is located at Second and Washington Streets. Watercolor paintings of the entrances to the Orr and Patterson houses were exhibited in the *Catalogue of the First Annual Exhibition of the Boston Architectural Club*, 1890, and are listed in the catalogue, nos. 682 and 683. Photographs of the Orr and Patterson houses were exhibited in the architectural exhibition of 1891. See *Catalogue of the Architectural Exhibition Held in the New Public Library Building*, Boston, 1891, nos. 423-426. Photographs of stone carvings were recorded in *Catalogue of the Architectural Exhibition, Boston Architectural Club and Boston Society of Architects*, Boston, 1899, nos. 301 and 302.

48. The project was announced in "Building Intelligence" in the *American Architect and Building News*, vol. 31, no. 785 (Jan. 31, 1891), p. xxiii.

49. The Saratoga racetrack has been the subject of two books by contemporary historians, but the identity of Warren as its architect has not been noted. See Nancy Stout, *Great American Thoroughbred Racetracks*, New York: Rizzoli,

1991; Edward Hotaling, *They're Off: Horse Racing at Saratoga*, Syracuse, N.Y.: Syracuse University Press, 1995.

50. Hotaling, *They're Off*, p. 53.

51. Ibid., p. 66.

52. The grandstand of the South End Grounds, which stood on Walpole Street, is illustrated in Philip Bergen, *Old Boston in Early Photographs*, New York: Dover, 1990, p. 88.

53. Hotaling, *They're Off*, p. 172.

54. Ibid., p. 147. After 1902, the grandstand was moved and its wings were extended, although its roofline was maintained. At the same time, a monitor roof was added to the betting pavilion. See Stout, *Great American Thoroughbred Racetracks*, p. 228, and Hotaling, *They're Off*, p. 170.

55. The interest in Japanese architecture originated in Boston with the lectures of Edward S. Morse. See Margaret Henderson Floyd, *Henry Hobson Richardson: A Genius for Architecture*, New York: Monacelli Press, 1997, pp. 192–200.

56. "Letters from Europe," Sept. 21, 1884, and Oct. 23, 1884. Information on the chapel appeared in an unattributed newspaper article titled "A Mortuary Chapel" and dated Mar. 13, 1887. It is included in a scrapbook owned by a descendant of James Scripps, Warren Scripps Wilkinson of Grosse Pointe, Mich.

57. Warren Scripps Wilkinson informed me in June, 1999, that the wife of James Scripps had been a Warren, suggesting that there may have been a relationship between her and the young architect.

58. "A Mortuary Chapel." The sculpture from the Scripps chapel was exhibited in the Boston architectural exhibition of 1899, *Catalogue of the Architectural Exhibition, Boston Architectural Club and Boston Society of Architects*, nos. 301 and 302.

59. "A Mortuary Chapel."

60. Ibid.

61. Warren's project in Detroit had ramifications over the next few decades. The chapel project brought Warren into contact with George Gough Booth, Scripps's son-in-law, who owned an ornamental ironworks business. Booth later became a member of the Society of Arts and Crafts, Boston, and ultimately established the Cranbrook Academy of Art, in Bloomfield Hills, where an Arts and Crafts ideology was promoted. I discussed George Booth with Mark Coir of the Cranbrook Academy, Bloomfield Hills, Mich., in June of 1999.

62. Herndon, in *Boston of Today*, identified the Strong house as one of Warren's major residential projects. See also Massachusetts Historical Commission Form 45/222-20, for 219 Gardner Road, Brookline, Mass., 1980.

63. See "Residence of Miss Perkins, Beverly Farms, Mass.," by Andrews and Jaques, Boston, in the *Engineering and Building Record*, vol. 18, no. 16 (Sept. 15, 1888).

64. Warren's work on the Troy Orphan Asylum was announced in the "Building Intelligence" of the *American Architect and Building News*, vol. 31, no. 796 (Mar. 28, 1891), p. xxiii. It was illustrated along with plans in the *American Architect*, vol. 32, no. 798 (Apr. 11, 1891). Photographs were published in the *American Architect*, vol. 67, no. 1263 (Mar. 10, 1900). A plan and photographs were published in the *American Architect*, vol. 69, no. 1285 (Aug. 11, 1900). The complex was listed in the *Catalogue of the Architectural Exhibition Held in the New Public Library Building*, 1891, nos. 120, 259, 261, 309, and 310.

65. The entry on Warren in Herndon's *Boston of Today* states, "Mr. Warren has given considerable attention to landscape gardening." The arrangements of Renfrew Park and the Troy Orphan Asylum are given as examples.

66. Plans, elevations, and details for the chapel were published in the *American Architect and Building News*, vol. 69, no. 1285 (Aug. 11, 1900).

67. "Lincoln's New Town Hall," *Boston Herald*, Nov. 6, 1891. The Lincoln Town Hall was listed in the *Catalogue of the Architectural Exhibition Held in the New Public Library Building*, 1891, no. 331.

68. Appropriately and perhaps not coincidentally, the speaker at the town hall's dedication was Ogden Codman, whose family homestead in Lincoln became a showplace for Codman's promotion of the colonial style in residential decoration. For more on the town hall, see Eva Siu and Parker Croft, "Lincoln Town Hall: Lincoln, Massachusetts," paper filed at the Loeb Library, Special Collections, Harvard University, Cambridge, Mass. [1976]. See also Margaret Mutchler Martin, *Inheritance: Lincoln's Public Buildings in the Historic District*, Lincoln, Mass.: Lincoln Historical Society, 1987, pp. 52–58, and *An Account of the Celebration by the Town of Lincoln, Mass. of the 150th Anniversary of Its Incorporation*, Lincoln, Mass.: Town of Lincoln, 1904, frontispiece.

69. H. Langford Warren, "Notes on Wenlock Priory," *Architectural Review*, vol. 1, no. 1 (Nov. 2, 1891), pp. 1–4.

70. H. Langford Warren, "A Few Neglected Considerations with Regard to Brick Architecture," *Brickbuilder*, vol. 1, no. 1 (Jan. 1892), pp. 3–5.

71. H. Langford Warren, "The Use and Abuse of Precedent," *Architectural Review*, vol. 2, no. 2 (Feb. 13, 1893), pp. 11–15, and vol. 2, no. 3 (Apr. 3, 1893), 21–25.

72. Ibid., Feb. 13, 1893, p. 11.

73. Ibid., p. 13.

74. Ibid., p. 15.

75. Ibid., Apr. 3, 1893, p. 25.

76. "At the St. Botolph. Regular Exhibition of Watercolors—Some of the Most Notable Works Shown," *Boston Advertiser*, Mar. 21, 1890, newspaper clipping owned by Langford Warren of Kittery Point, Maine. "Harold B. Warren, Artist, Dies at 75," *Boston Herald*, Nov. 24, 1934, newspaper clipping at Harvard Uni-

versity Archives, HUG 300. Herbert and Harold Warren's uncle, Cyrus Warren, was married to the sister of Denman Ross. See Davis, "The Warren Family," p. 30.

77. Cynthia D. Fleming, "Instructors and Courses in the Museum School," in Trevor J. Fairbrother, *The Bostonians: Painters of an Elegant Age, 1870–1930*, exhibition catalogue, Boston: Museum of Fine Arts, 1986, p. 233. Moore taught Gothic architecture. During the 1894–1895 year, Warren taught Renaissance architecture, p. 234.

78. "Recent Deaths. Professor H. Langford Warren."

79. Warren exhibited his entry for the American Fine Arts Society in New York City in the Boston architectural exhibition of 1891, *Catalogue of the Architectural Exhibition Held in the New Public Library Building*, no. 307. His design for Arlington, Mass., High School was illustrated in the *American Architect and Building News*, vol. 38, no. 888 (Dec. 31, 1892). His design for Copley Square was among the four of twenty-two designs submitted to receive commendation in 1893. It was published in the *American Architect*, vol. 40, no. 906 (Mar. 4, 1893).

80. "Letters from Europe," May 1, 1893.

Chapter 3. An Architectural Program for Harvard (pp. 56–83)

1. "Letters from Europe Written by H. Langford Warren," bound volume of photocopies, Loeb Library, Special Collections, Harvard University, May 1, 1893. The original set is owned by Elizabeth Warren Stoutamire of Tallahassee, Fla.

2. Charles A. Coolidge, "Herbert Langford Warren (1857–1917)," *Proceedings of the American Academy of Arts and Sciences*, vol. 68 (Dec. 1933), pp. 690–691. Copy at Loeb Library, Harvard University.

3. As Richardson was traveling in Europe during the summer of 1882 while construction on Austin Hall was proceeding, Warren presumably was the architect from the office who reported to the Harvard president.

4. Keith N. Morgan, *Held in Trust: Charles Eliot's Vision for the New England Landscape*, vol. 1, National Association for Olmsted Parks Workbook Series, ed. Darlene McCloud, Bethesda, Md.: National Association for Olmsted Parks, 1991, p. 3.

5. George Copp Warren, *The Part of the Warrens in the Development of Coal Tar, Petroleum Oil, and Asphalt*, pamphlet dated 1928, Swedenborgian School of Religion Archives, Newton, Mass., box 72.9, W257, "Warren, S. M.," pp. 6–7.

6. Edward Howe Cotton, *The Life of Charles W. Eliot*, Boston: Small, Maynard, 1926; Ronald Story, *The Forging of an Aristocracy: Harvard and the Boston Upper Class, 1800–1870*, Middletown, Conn.: Wesleyan University Press, 1980, p. 179.

7. *Annual Reports of the President and Treasurer of Harvard College, 1893–94*, Cambridge, Mass.: Harvard University, 1895.

8. John Ruskin, *The Study of Architecture*, New York: John B. Alden, 1885, p. 147.

9. Richard Chafee, "The Teaching of Architecture at the Ecole des Beaux-Arts," in *The Architecture of the Ecole des Beaux-Arts*, ed. Arthur Drexler, New York: Museum of Modern Art, 1977, pp. 61–109.

10. Ibid.

11. Turpin C. Bannister, ed., *The Architect at Mid-Century: Evolution and Achievement*, New York: Reinhold, 1954, vol. 1, pp. 86–87.

12. Roula Geraniotis, "The University of Illinois and German Architectural Education," *Journal of Architectural Education*, vol. 38 (summer 1984), pp. 15–21.

13. John Wilton-Ely, "The Rise of the Professional Architect in England," in *The Architect: Chapters in the History of the Profession*, ed. Spiro Kostof, New York: Oxford, 1977, pp. 180–208. See also Bannister, *The Architect at Mid-Century*, pp. 91–93; and Frank Jenkins, "The Victorian Architectural Profession," in *Victorian Architecture*, ed. Peter Ferriday, London: Jonathan Cape, 1963, pp. 37–49. On professional practice in nineteenth-century England, see Andrew Saint, *The Image of the Architect*, New Haven, Conn.: Yale University Press, 1983, pp. 51–71.

14. Quoted in Bannister, *The Architect at Mid-Century*, p. 92.

15. Banister Fletcher and Banister F. Fletcher published *A History of Architecture for the Student, Craftsman, and Amateur*, London: B. T. Batsford, 1896. The copy that I consulted was a revised third edition from 1897.

16. Bannister, *The Architect at Mid-Century*, pp. 93–100. See also Arthur Clason Weatherhead, *The History of Collegiate Education in Architecture in the United States*, Los Angeles: n.p., 1941, submitted as a Ph.D. dissertation to Columbia University.

17. Caroline Shillaber, *Massachusetts Institute of Technology, School of Architecture and Planning, 1861–1961: A Hundred Year Chronicle*, Cambridge, Mass.: Massachusetts Institute of Technology, 1963, pp. 4–28.

18. In addition to Bannister, *The Architect at Mid-Century*, see Geraniotis, "The University of Illinois and German Architectural Education." Also see Alan K. Laing, *Nathan Clifford Ricker, 1843–1924. Pioneer in American Architectural Education*, a booklet published by the University of Illinois at Urbana-Champaign, 1973.

19. The programs were at Syracuse University, University of Pennsylvania, Columbia University, Columbian University (later George Washington), and Armour Institute of Technology (later Illinois Institute). The University of Michigan also began a program, but it closed after two years. See Bannister, *The Architect at Mid-Century*, p. 98.

20. Richard Plunz, "Reflections on Ware, Hamlin, McKim, and the Politics of History on the Cusp of Historicism," in *The History of History in American Schools of Architecture, 1865-1975*, ed. Gwendolyn Wright and Janet Parks, New York and Princeton, N.J.: Temple Hoyne Buell Center for the Study of American Architecture, Columbia University, and Princeton Architectural Press, 1990, p. 56.

21. A. D. F. Hamlin, *A Text-book of the History of Architecture*, New York: Longmans, Green, 1896.

22. Weatherhead, *History of Collegiate Education in Architecture*, pp. 68–69, has a table that provides the number of hours students spent studying architectural history, among other subjects, in America's nine architecture programs in 1898. On Columbia's program, see Theodor K. Rohdenburg, *A History of the School of Architecture, Columbia University*, New York: Columbia University Press, 1954.

23. Herbert Langford Warren, "Architectural Education at Harvard University," *Harvard Engineering Journal*, vol. 1, no. 2 (June 1902), p. 79.

24. In his introduction to *A Text-book of the History of Architecture*, Hamlin emphasized the idea that a study of architectural history is a study of "man's ability to build beautifully," p. xxi.

25. John Taylor Boyd, "Notes and Comments: Professor H. Langford Warren," *The Architectural Record*, vol. 42, no. 6 (Dec. 1917), p. 588–591.

26. Warren, "Architectural Education," pp. 84–85. See also H. Langford Warren, "The Influence of France Upon American Architecture," *American Architect and Building News*, vol. 66, no. 1248 (Nov. 25, 1899), pp. 67–68, reprint of a paper read at the thirty-third annual convention, American Institute of Architects, Pittsburgh, Nov. 14, 1899.

27. Untitled, unsigned lead editorial, *American Architect and Building News*, vol. 55, no. 1101 (Jan. 30, 1897), p. 49.

28. Warren, "Influence of France," p. 68.

29. Boyd, "Notes and Comments," p. 589.

30. Letter from George F. Newton to H. Langford Warren, Mar. 25, 1896. Harvard University Archives, UAV 322.7, series III, box 2.

31. H. Langford Warren, "The Department of Architecture of Harvard University," *Architectural Record*, vol. 22, no. 1 (July 1907), p. 140.

32. Ibid.

33. Ibid., p. 138.

34. Fiske Kimball, "Architecture at the Turn of the Century," unpublished manuscript, n.d., Fiske Kimball Papers, Philadelphia Museum of Art, archives, series 17, ssa, folder 34, p. 2.

35. Warren, "The Department of Architecture," p. 138.

36. Kimball, "Architecture at the Turn of the Century," p. 2.

37. Ibid., p. 4.

38. Boyd, "Notes and Comments," p. 589.

39. George H. Edgell, "The Schools of Architecture and Landscape Architecture," in *The Development of Harvard University Since the Inauguration of President Eliot, 1869–1929*, ed. Samuel Eliot Morison, Cambridge, Mass.: Harvard University Press, 1930, pp. 443–450. See also official registers for Harvard University, 1893–1917, Harvard University Archives.

40. *Official Register of Harvard University, 1912–1913*, Cambridge, Mass.: Harvard University, 1914.

41. Warren's ongoing role as a member of the fine-arts division of the Faculty of Arts and Sciences is noted in [James Sturgis Pray], "Faculty of Architecture. Minute on the Life and Services of Dean Herbert Langford Warren," *Harvard University Gazette*, Dec. 1, 1917, p. 45. Copy on file at Harvard University Archives, HUG 1875.80.

42. Untitled, unsigned editorial, *American Architect and Building News*, Jan. 30, 1897, p. 49.

43. Peabody's letter to Warren concerning Newton is at the Harvard University Archives, UAV 322.7, series III, box 2. Peabody described Newton as "the best man I could think of."

44. Newton designed the Unitarian Church in Winchester, Mass. (1898), the First Congregational Church of Wellesley Hills in Wellesley, Mass. (1901), and the First Baptist Church in Melrose, Mass. (1907), among many. See Douglass Shand-Tucci, *Built in Boston: City and Suburb, 1800–1950*, Amherst, Mass.: University of Massachusetts Press, 1978 (reprint 1988), pp. 177–180.

45. *Annual Reports of the President and Treasurer of Harvard College, 1899–1900*, Cambridge, Mass.: Harvard University, 1901, Harvard University Archives. The course taught by Ross was listed under "Architecture 7, Theory of Design." See also Boyd, "Notes and Comments," p. 589.

46. Murphy's course was first listed in *Annual Reports of the President and Treasurer of Harvard College, 1902–1903*, Cambridge, Mass.: Harvard University, 1904. Harold Warren's course appeared in the *Annual Reports* for 1904–1905.

47. Cram was listed in the *Official Register of Harvard University, 1908–1909*, Cambridge, Mass.: Harvard University, 1910. The *Official Register* for 1914–1915 listed Ashbee.

48. This evaluation of the department's weakness was noted in the *First Report of the Alumni in Architecture of Harvard University*, Cambridge, Mass.: Harvard University, 1932, p. 3, in Special Collections, Loeb Library, Harvard University.

49. H. L. Warren, "The Appointment of Eugene Duquesne as Professor of Architectural Design," *Harvard Engineering Journal*, vol. 9, no. 4 (Jan. 1911), pp. 243–246.

50. Ibid., p. 244. Robert Bacon, an 1880 graduate of Harvard College, served as Theodore Roosevelt's secretary of state in 1909.

51. Ibid., p. 245.

52. Ibid.

53. Ibid., p. 246.

54. E. J. A. Duquesne, "The Teaching of Architecture," *The Architectural Quarterly of Harvard University*, vol. 1, no. 3 (Sept. 1912), pp. 73–83.

55. Kimball, "Architecture at the Turn of the Century," pp. 5–6.

56. MIT's first Ecole-trained instructor, Eugène Létang, taught at MIT under Ware, Clark, and Chandler. He died in 1892 and was succeeded by Désiré Despradelle in 1893. See Shillaber, *Massachusetts Institute of Technology, School of Architecture and Planning*, p. 28. Warren pointed out that there were "Frenchmen" teaching design at MIT, the University of Pennsylvania, and Cornell in a letter to Charles W. Eliot, Feb. 12, 1909, Harvard University Archives, UAI.5.150, box 255.

57. On Boyd's career, see *First Report of the Alumni in Architecture*, pp. 41–42.

58. Boyd, "Notes and Comments," p. 589.

59. See Edgell, "The Schools of Architecture and Landscape Architecture," pp. 445–446. In 1922, Harvard hired Jean-Jacques Haffner, winner of the Prix de Rome in 1919. For more on the effort by Warren to find an Ecole-trained design professor, see Anthony Alofsin, *The Struggle for Modernism: Architecture, Landscape Architecture, and City Planning at Harvard*, New York and London: W. W. Norton, 2002, pp. 46–49.

60. See "Department of Architecture. Records of Meetings, 1902–1917," bound volume, Harvard University Archives, UAV 322.5. The entry for Nov. 27, 1908, reads: "Charles Eliot was asked by Prof. Warren to give such courses. Dissuaded by the senior Olmsted on the ground of the newness of the profession and the limitations of the field for practice."

61. Letter from Frederick Law Olmsted, Jr., to Charles W. Eliot, June 1, 1893, Harvard University Archives, UAI.5.150, box 109, folder 129.

62. Letter from Frederick Law Olmsted, Jr., to H. Langford Warren, Cambridge, Mass., Mar. 25, 1897, Special Collections, Loeb Library, Harvard University.

63. Letter from H. Langford Warren to Charles W. Eliot, Dec. 19, 1899, Harvard University Archives, UAI.5.150, box 110, folder 142.

64. Edgell, "The Schools of Architecture and Landscape Architecture," p. 444. See also Melanie L. Simo, *The Coalescing of Different Forces and Ideas: A History of Landscape Architecture at Harvard, 1900–1999*, Cambridge, Mass.: Harvard Graduate School of Design, 2000.

65. Letter from H. Langford Warren to Charles W. Eliot, July 5, 1899, Harvard University Archives, UAI.5.150, box 110, folder 142. Letter from Charles Francis Adams II to Charles W. Eliot, July 14, 1899, Harvard University Archives, UAI.5.150, box 100, folder 1.

66. Leland Roth, *McKim, Mead, and White, Architects*, New York: Harper and Row, 1983, pp. 230–231.

67. Letter from H. Langford Warren to Charles W. Eliot, Aug. 4, 1899, Harvard University Archives, UAI.5.150, box 110, folder 142. See also letter from Warren to Eliot, Oct. 21, 1899, same folder.

68. Walter Dana Swan, "Nelson Robinson, Jr., Hall," *Harvard Engineering Journal*, vol. 1, no. 2 (June 1902), p. 88. A line drawing of the house appears on p. 93. The Carey Athletic Building, 1889, was designed by Alexander W. Longfellow, Jr. See Bainbridge Bunting, *Harvard: An Architectural History*, completed and edited by Margaret Henderson Floyd, Cambridge, Mass.: Belknap Press of Harvard University Press, 1985, pp. 98–101.

69. Robinson Hall survives but was rebuilt substantially inside after the Graduate School of Design moved to Gund Hall, which was completed in 1969. Plans and descriptions of Robinson Hall as it originally was built may be found in *Harvard University, Lawrence Scientific School: Announcement of the Department of Architecture, 1901–02*, Cambridge, Mass.: Harvard University, 1901, pp. 7–9, Special Collections, Loeb Library, Harvard University; and Swan, "Nelson Robinson, Jr., Hall." Additional information may be found in H. Langford Warren, "Departments, Schools, Museums. Architecture," *The Harvard Graduates Magazine*, vol. 12, no. 47 (Mar. 1904), pp. 428–429, Harvard University Archives, HUK 435A; and Warren, "The Department of Architecture," pp. 144–150. The building is discussed and illustrated in Alofsin, *The Struggle for Modernism*, pp. 29–32.

70. Agnes Mongan, "Harvard and the Fogg," in *The Early Years of Art History in the United States: Notes and Essays on Departments, Teaching, and Scholars*, ed. Craig Hugh Smyth and Peter M. Lukehart, Princeton, N.J.: Princeton University, Department of Art and Archaeology, 1993, p. 47. The original Fogg Museum building was designed in 1893 by Richard Morris Hunt with a lecture hall ostensibly for Norton. Despite the fact that he did not project slides, those who followed him did. The hall was considered an acoustical failure, and Norton continued to lecture in Sanders Theater. See *Boston Daily Advertiser*, Sept. 25, 1894; *Boston Daily Advertiser*, Mar. 18, 1896.

71. On the casts and other exhibits, see Swan, "Nelson Robinson, Jr., Hall."

72. Letter from H. Langford Warren to Charles W. Eliot, Sept. 5, 1901, Harvard University Archives, UAI.5.150, box 110, folder 142.

73. "Department of Architecture. Records of Meetings, 1902–1917," Dec. 31, 1915.

74. Warren, "The Department of Architecture," p. 150.

75. Swan, "Nelson Robinson, Jr., Hall," p. 102.

76. Warren, "The Department of Architecture," p. 150; and Warren, "Departments, Schools, Museums," p. 429.

77. Letter from H. Langford Warren to Charles W. Eliot, Mar. 4, 1908, Harvard University Archives, UAI.5.150, box 255.

78. Charles Eliot Norton, "A Criticism of Harvard Architecture Made to the Board of Overseers," *The Harvard Graduates Magazine*, vol. 12, no. 47 (Mar. 1904), pp. 359–362.

79. Anthony Alofsin has written about Warren as a leading, if not the leading, teacher of architectural history in the United States during his lifetime. See Anthony Alofsin, "Toward a History of Teaching Architectural History: An Introduction to Herbert Langford Warren," *Journal of Architectural Education*, vol. 37, no. 1 (fall 1983), pp. 2–7; and Alofsin, "Tempering the Ecole: Nathan Ricker at the University of Illinois, Langford Warren at Harvard, and Their Followers," in *The History of History in American Schools of Architecture*, ed. Wright and Parks, pp. 73–88. Alofsin's analysis was based on Warren's *Foundations of Classic Architecture* (published posthumously by Kimball), lecture notes on Warren's medieval course taken by Kenneth John Conant, and Warren's reading lists. Other students' lecture notes, printed syllabi, printed exams, and other articles by Warren contribute to my analysis.

80. Norton's outlook is discussed in Frederic Cople Jaher, *The Urban Establishment: Upper Strata in Boston, New York, Charleston, Chicago, and Los Angeles*, Urbana: University of Illinois Press, 1982, p. 85.

81. H. Langford Warren, "The Study of Architectural History and Its Place in the Professional Curriculum," *The Architectural Quarterly of Harvard University*, vol. 1, no. 2 (June 1912), pp. 37–44.

82. Ibid., p. 37.

83. Ibid., p. 44.

84. Ralph Adams Cram, "Letters to the Editor. Masters in Architecture—Langford Warren, Henry Vaughan," *Boston Transcript*, July 2, 1917.

85. Roger Bigelow Merriman, "Notes in Architecture 1a, 1896–97," Harvard University Archives, HUC 8896.305.1a, box 654. C. Howard Walker, "History of Architecture," Special Collections, Loeb Library, Harvard University, Rare NA200.W252, 2 vols. These volumes of typed notes were owned by Walker and contain his bookplate; in 1938 they were given to the architecture library by Joseph Hudnut, a former Warren student who became dean of the School of Architecture in 1936. Although Walker's notes are not dated, a reference to the devastation in Reims, France, suggests that the lectures were given after the outbreak of World War I in 1914.

86. Merriman, "Notes in Architecture," Apr. 7, 1897.

87. Ibid., Apr. 26, 1897.

88. Ibid., May 14, 1897. Also Walker, "History of Architecture," vol. 1, p. 133.

89. Merriman, "Notes in Architecture," June 2, 1897.

90. Walker, "History of Architecture," vol. 1, pp. 138–139.

91. Reference books are listed in published announcements for Warren's

courses. See *Harvard University. Lawrence Scientific School. Announcement of the Department of Architecture,* Cambridge, Mass.: Harvard University, 1900–1901, in Special Collections, Loeb Library, Harvard University. See also succeeding years.

92. Josef Durm's *Die Baukunst der Griechen* (1892) and *Die Baukunst der Etrusker und Römer* (1885) were recommended as was Auguste Choisy's *L'art de bâtir chez les Romains* (1873).

93. Georges Perrot and Charles Chipiez, *A History of Art in Ancient Egypt* (1883), *A History of Art in Chaldaea and Assyria* (1884), and *A History of Art in Persia* (1892).

94. Herbert Langford Warren, *The Foundations of Classic Architecture,* introduction by Fiske Kimball, New York: Macmillan, 1919. It was reviewed by William H. Goodyear, "The Foundations of Classic Architecture," *The American Architect,* vol. 117, no. 2306 (Mar. 3, 1920), pp. 269–274. Warren also prepared the art for *Vitruvius: The Ten Books on Architecture,* trans. Morris Hicky Morgan, Cambridge, Mass.: Harvard University Press, 1914.

95. I consulted the following printed exams in the Harvard University Archives: "Harvard University Examinations, 1911–1912, June 1912," "Architecture 1a," HUC 7911, box 278; "Examination Papers. Mid-Years 1912–13," "Fine Arts 3a (Architecture 1a)," HUC 7912, box 278; "Harvard University Examinations, 1912–1913," "Fine Arts 3a (Architecture 1a)," HUC 7912, box 278; "Harvard University Examinations, 1913–1914," "Fine Arts 3a (Architecture 1a)," HUC 7913, box 278.

96. Kenneth John Conant, "Notes Taken in Fine Arts 4a," 1914–1915, Harvard University Archives, HUC 8914.328.4, box 846. See also Walker, "History of Architecture," vols. 1 and 2.

97. To reinforce his students' understanding, Warren required them to build large-scale models of Byzantine and Gothic vaults. See Warren, "The Department of Architecture," p. 136. An example of a student model is illustrated in Alofsin, "Tempering the Ecole," p. 80.

98. Walker, "History of Architecture," vol. 2, p. 70.

99. Ibid., pp. 111–112.

100. Ibid., vol. 1, p. 203.

101. Ibid., vol. 2, p. 39; Conant, "Notes Taken," p. 33.

102. Walker, "History of Architecture," vol. 2, p. 53.

103. Ibid., p. 180. Walker typed this last statement in quotation marks, as if to underscore Warren's emphasis.

104. Ibid., pp. 80, 95, 187.

105. Ibid., p. 136.

106. Ibid., pp. 81–84.

107. Ibid., pp. 86–87.

108. Ibid., p. 88.

109. Conant, "Notes Taken," p. 54.

110. Walker, "History of Architecture," vol. 2, pp. 130–131.

111. Ibid., 173–178.

112. See *Harvard University. Lawrence Scientific School. Announcement of the Department of Architecture,* 1900–1901, for the reference books listed by Warren. See also succeeding years. He recommended *L'Art de bâtir chez les Byzantins* by Auguste Choisy (1883) and the *Dictionnaire raisonné de l'Architecture française* by Eugène-Emmanuel Viollet-le-Duc (1854–1868).

113. Charles Herbert Moore, *Development and Character of Gothic Architecture* (1890).

114. William R. Lethaby, *Mediaeval Art: From the Peace of the Church to the Eve of the Renaissance* (1904).

115. I consulted the following printed exams in the Harvard University Archives: "Examination Papers. Mid-Years 1912–13," "Fine Arts 4a (Architecture 1b)," HUC 7912, box 278; and "Harvard University Examinations, 1912–13," "Fine Arts 4a," HUC 7912, box 278. I also consulted two printed syllabi: "Fine Arts 4. Gothic Art. Artists of the Renaissance," undated but apparently used during the 1914–1915 academic year, HUC 8914.128, box 844, pp. 2–26 and 34–35; "Fine Arts 3. The History of Art. Roman, Byzantine, Romanesque, Gothic," undated but apparently for Fine Arts 3a, which ran from 1913–1916, HUC 8914.128, box 844, pp. 2–33.

116. H. Langford Warren, s.v. "France, Architecture of: Part X; Provence and Languedoc," in *A Dictionary of Architecture and Building,* ed. Russell Sturgis, New York: Macmillan, 1901.

117. Edmund Buckley, ed., *The Fine Arts: A Course of University Lessons on Sculpture, Painting, Architecture, and Decoration, in Both Their Principles and History,* Chicago: International Art Association, 1900. See the chapter by H. Langford Warren, "Architecture: Renaissance and Modern," pp. 190–234. Study brochures were issued a few years later, with Warren named as a contributor. See *The Fine Arts: Study Brochures,* ed. Edmund Buckley, Chicago: National Art Society, 1907, "Study Brochure No. 3," "Questions upon Architecture," pp. 16–20; "Study Brochure No. 4," "Answers to the Questions upon Architecture," pp. 9–17. No student notes from Warren's "Renaissance and Modern" course seem to have been preserved, so the chapter that he wrote for Buckley's book is especially important. Some notes that Warren made for this course, however, have been filed at the Harvard Archives. They are dated 1895. See Harvard University Archives, HUG 1875.105.

118. Warren, "Architecture: Renaissance and Modern," in Buckley, *The Fine Arts,* p. 191.

119. Ibid., p. 194.

120. Ibid., p. 205.

121. Ibid., p. 209.

122. Ibid., p. 213.

123. Ibid., p. 218.

124. Ibid., p. 219.

125. Ibid., pp. 219–220.

126. See *Harvard University. Lawrence Scientific School. Announcement of the Department of Architecture,* 1900–1901 and succeeding years, for the reference books listed by Warren. Some of the authors whose works they read included Jacob Burckhardt, John Addington Symonds, Eugène Müntz, and Wilhelm Lübke.

127. Reginald Blomfield, *The History of Renaissance Architecture in England, 1500–1800* (1897), *The Formal Garden in England* (1892), and *A History of French Architecture from 1494 to 1661* (1911). The *History of French Architecture* was used only briefly and was replaced by William H. Ward, *The Architecture of the Renaissance in France* (1911). Blomfield promoted French classicism, seeing the French Renaissance as a period in which classical design ultimately triumphed over the medieval, whereas Ward considered the French Renaissance a period of interchange between medieval and classic approaches, a view that was closer to Warren's.

128. I consulted the following printed exams in the Harvard University Archives: "Harvard University Examinations, 1911–1912, June 1912," "Architecture 1c," HUC 7911, box 278; "Harvard University Examinations, 1913–1914," "Fine Arts 5a (Architecture 1c)," HUC 7913, box 278.

129. Kimball, "Architecture at the Turn of the Century," p. 3.

130. Boyd, "Notes and Comments," p. 589.

131. See Warren's June 1912 exam, "Harvard University Examinations, 1911–1912, June 1912."

132. H. Langford Warren, "Architecture in New England," in *Picturesque and Architectural New England,* vol. 1, Boston: D. H. Hurd, 1899, pp. 9–45; Warren, "Architecture: Renaissance and Modern," in Buckley, *The Fine Arts,* pp. 228–232.

133. "Lantern Slides Log Book 1, Architecture Department," unpublished bound book, first entries from 1901, Visual Resources, Gund Hall, Harvard University.

134. Warren, "Architecture in New England," p. 9.

135. The house was designed and built between 1884 and 1886 in Washington, D.C. See Jeffrey Karl Ochsner, *H. H. Richardson: Complete Architectural Works,* Cambridge, Mass.: MIT Press, paperback ed., 1984, pp. 344–349.

136. Henry Adams, *The Education of Henry Adams,* 2 vols., New York: Time, 1964 (originally published 1918).

137. Writing about Boston's elite in *The Urban Establishment,* Frederic Cople

Jaher concluded, "Patrician optimists accepted the dominant values of their era, attained success, and believed in America." More despairing individuals, Jaher added, sequestered themselves in the past, p. 124.

138. H. L. Warren, untitled transcription of comments about a paper presented by Ralph Adams Cram, *American Architect and Building News*, vol. 54, no. 1096 (Dec. 26, 1896), pp. 109–110.

139. Kimball, "Architecture at the Turn of the Century," p. 4.

140. Warren, "The Department of Architecture," p. 140.

141. "A College Chapel" by Rhodes Robinson, *Architectural Quarterly of Harvard University*, vol. 1, no. 3 (Sept. 1912).

142. "Department of Architecture. Records of Meetings, 1902–1917."

143. Ibid., Dec. 15, 1915. "A Social Service Group" by Howard H. Barton.

144. Warren's involvement with the journal is not noted in it, but his role was recognized by Kenneth J. Conant, s.v. "H. Langford Warren," in *Dictionary of American Biography*, vol. 9, supplement 1, New York: Scribner's Sons, 1944.

145. Howard Moise, "Brunelleschi and His Influence on the Development of Renaissance Architecture," *Architectural Quarterly of Harvard University*, vol. 1, no. 2 (June 1912), pp. 45–57.

146. Kenneth John Conant, "Raphael as Architect," *Architectural Quarterly of Harvard University*, vol. 2, no. 3 (Mar. 1914); Sidney Fiske Kimball, "Thomas Jefferson as Architect: Monticello and Shadwell," *Architectural Quarterly of Harvard University*, vol. 2, no. 4 (June 1914).

147. Kenneth J. Conant, "Three Vanished Harvard Buildings," *Harvard Illustrated Magazine*, vol. 15 (June 1914), pp. 486–489. Conant explicitly acknowledges the assistance he received from Warren.

148. George Harold Edgell, "The Development of the Architectural Background in the Painting of the Umbrian Renaissance," Ph.D. dissertation, Harvard University, 1913. Harvard University Archives, HU90.946.

149. Ibid., p. 8.

150. Dorothy May Anderson, *Women, Design, and the Cambridge School*, West Lafayette, Ind.: PDA Publishers, 1980.

151. Shillaber, *Massachusetts Institute of Technology, School of Architecture and Planning*, p. 34.

152. Ibid., p. 50.

Chapter 4. The Society of Arts and Crafts (pp. 84–101)

1. Recently the contribution of the Society of Arts and Crafts, Boston, to the broader movement has been considered in some depth, although it is still not widely recognized. The most important publication on the Society is Marilee Boyd Meyer, consulting curator, *Inspiring Reform: Boston's Arts and Crafts Movement*, Wellesley, Mass.: Davis Museum and Cultural Center, Wellesley College,

1997. See also Wendy Kaplan, ed., *"The Art That Is Life": The Arts and Crafts Movement in America, 1875–1920*, Boston: Bulfinch Press, 1998 (reprint of Museum of Fine Arts exhibition catalogue, 1987); Eileen Boris, *Art and Labor: Ruskin, Morris, and the Craftsman Ideal in America*, Philadelphia: Temple University Press, 1986; and Beverly Kay Brandt, " 'Mutually Helpful Relations': Architects, Craftsmen, and the Society of Arts and Crafts, Boston, 1897–1917," Ph.D. dissertation, Boston University, 1985.

2. Peter Stansky, *Redesigning the World: William Morris, the 1880s, and the Arts and Crafts*, Palo Alto, Calif.: Society for the Promotion of Science and Scholarship, 1996 (originally published by Princeton University Press, 1985).

3. See Doreen Bolger Burke et al., *In Pursuit of Beauty: Americans and the Aesthetic Movement*, New York: Metropolitan Museum of Art and Rizzoli, 1986.

4. James F. O'Gorman, *Living Architecture: A Biography of H. H. Richardson*, New York: Simon and Schuster, 1997, pp. 137–139.

5. Mary Alice Molloy, "Richardson's Web: A Client's Assessment of the Architect's Home and Studio," *Journal of the Society of Architectural Historians*, vol. 54, no. 1 (Mar. 1995), pp. 8–23.

6. On Evans, see Ann Clifford, "John Evans (1847–1923) and Architectural Sculpture in Boston," M.A. thesis, Tufts University, 1992. For Davenport, see Burke et al., *In Pursuit of Beauty*, p. 418.

7. See Susan J. Montgomery, "The Potter's Art in Boston: Individuality and Expression," in Meyer, *Inspiring Reform*, pp. 58–69.

8. Trevor J. Fairbrother, "Painting in Boston, 1870–1930," in *The Bostonians: Painters of an Elegant Age, 1870–1930*, exhibition catalogue, Boston: Museum of Fine Arts, 1986, p. 33.

9. Edward S. Cooke, Jr., "Talking or Working: The Conundrum of Moral Aesthetics in Boston's Arts and Crafts Movement," in Meyer, *Inspiring Reform*, pp. 20–23. Norton also is discussed in Craig Hugh Smyth and Peter M. Lukehart, eds., *The Early Years of Art History in the United States: Notes and Essays on Departments, Teaching, and Scholars*, Princeton, N.J.: Princeton University, Department of Art and Archaeology, 1993. See essays by Agnes Mongan, "Harvard and the Fogg," pp. 47–50, and Sybil Gordon Kantor, "The Beginnings of Art History at Harvard and the 'Fogg Method,' " pp. 161–174.

10. Fairbrother, "Painting in Boston," p. 33. See also Wendy Kaplan, "Spreading the Crafts: The Role of the Schools," pp. 298–307, in Kaplan, *"The Art That Is Life."*

11. *Prize Competition Instituted by the Art Department of the Twentieth Century Club, Boston Massachusetts*, pamphlet filed with the Boston/New England Artist Archives, Fine Arts Department, Boston Public Library. Other members of the committee were Edwin J. Lewis, Jr., William Ordway Partridge, Irene Weir, and Lucia True Ames.

12. Warren later delivered a lecture before the Committee on the Utilization

of the Museums of Art by Schools and Colleges. This lecture was published as "What May the Schools Do to Advance the Appreciation of Art?" in 1908 in the *New England Magazine;* it was reissued under the same title and published by the Boston Museum of Fine Arts in 1924. In the lecture, Warren encouraged teaching children to appreciate beauty in nature through drawing instruction. He believed that museums were most effective in educating their teachers.

13. These catalogues are available in the Fine Arts Department of the Boston Public Library. For example, see *Catalogue of the First Annual Exhibition of the Boston Architectural Club*, Boston: Boston Architectural Club, 1890.

14. See letters written in April of 1906 by the Reverend James Reed at the Swedenborgian School of Religion Archives, Newton, Mass., box 72.9, R255, "Ragatz-Reed," folder marked "Reed, James." One of the letters is written to the Reverend Samuel M. Warren, Herbert's father.

15. Papers of the Society of Arts and Crafts, Boston, Archives of American Art–Smithsonian Institution, microfilm reel 319, frames 704–707; reel 322, frames 165, 177, 210 (hereafter cited as SACB Archives, AAA/SI reel: frame). See also May R. Spain, *The Society of Arts and Crafts, 1897–1924*, Boston and New York: Society of Arts and Crafts, 1924 (available on microfilm, SACB Archives, AAA/SI 319: 492–510).

16. SACB Archives, AAA/SI 319: 705.

17. The architect-advisers were Charles Cummings, A. W. Longfellow, Jr., C. Howard Walker, and R. Clipston Sturgis, SACB Archives, AAA/SI 322: 165.

18. A tribute to Warren after his death, published by the Society of Arts and Crafts, notes that Warren served as chairman of the meetings held in 1897 when the Society was organized, SACB Archives, AAA/SI 319: 26.

19. "Show Next Year Perhaps. Advisability of an Arts and Crafts Exhibition in 1898," *Boston Herald*, Apr. 16, 1897, SACB Archives, AAA/SI 322: 217. Also "Favor Annual Exhibits. First Steps Toward an Arts and Crafts Organization Taken at an Enthusiastic Meeting," *Boston Daily Globe*, Apr. 16, 1897, SACB Archives, AAA/SI 322: 216.

20. "Favor Annual Exhibits."

21. "Arts and Crafts in 1898. Meeting of Those Interested in Proposed Exhibition," *Boston Herald*, Apr. 30, 1897, and "The Arts and Crafts," *Boston Advertiser*, Apr. 30, 1897, SACB Archives, AAA/SI 322: 224.

22. "Encouraging Applied Art. Permanent Society Formed, with Many Members," *Boston Herald*, May 14, 1897, SACB Archives, AAA/SI 322: 225.

23. Robert Judson Clark, ed., *The Arts and Crafts Movement in America, 1876–1916*, Princeton, N.J.: Princeton University Press, 1992 (reprint of Art Museum, Princeton University, and The Art Institute of Chicago, exhibition catalog, 1972), p. xiv. The Minneapolis Chalk and Chisel Club was formed in 1895, the Deerfield Society in 1896, and the Chicago Arts and Crafts Society in October of 1897.

24. Spain, *The Society of Arts and Crafts*, p. 10.

25. Ibid., pp. 11–12.

26. Henry Adams, *The Education of Henry Adams*, vol. 1, New York: Time, 1964 (originally published 1918), p. 59.

27. Spain, *The Society of Arts and Crafts*, p. 12.

28. *Exhibition of the Society of Arts and Crafts*, Boston, 1899, SACB Archives, AAA/SI 319: 735; also SACB Archives, AAA/SI 322: 228.

29. SACB Archives, AAA/SI 319: 26.

30. For more about the dominance of architects in the Society, see Beverly K. Brandt, "The Essential Link: Boston Architects and the Society of Arts and Crafts," *Tiller*, vol. 2, no. 1 (Sept.–Oct. 1983).

31. "The Fine Arts. Another Arts and Crafts Exhibition to Be Held," *Boston Transcript*, Jan. 14, 1899, SACB Archives, AAA/SI 322: 228.

32. *Exhibition of the Society of Arts and Crafts*, SACB Archives, AAA/SI 319: 751–752.

33. Spain, *The Society of Arts and Crafts*, p. 14. "Exhibition of the Society of Arts and Crafts," SACB Archives, AAA/SI 319: 740–746.

34. Newspaper clipping, SACB Archives, AAA/SI 322: 245.

35. "Admission Today 10 Cents. Society of Arts and Crafts Puts Its Exhibition Within Reach of People With Small Incomes, for One Day," unattributed newspaper clipping, SACB Archives, AAA/SI 322: 245.

36. "Arts and Crafts Exhibit Will Be Kept Open Until the 22d of the Month," unattributed newspaper clipping, SACB Archives, AAA/SI 322: 246. It was scheduled to run from Apr. 4 to 15, 1899, and was extended until Apr. 22.

37. *Exhibition of the Society of Arts and Crafts*, SACB Archives, AAA/SI 319: 733–734. Warren repeated this same quote in "What May the Schools Do," p. 16. Stansky, in *Redesigning the World*, pp. 70–72, compares Morris with Arthur H. Mackmurdo, who was more positive about the role of machinery in artistic production.

38. *Exhibition of the Society of Arts and Crafts*, SACB Archives, AAA/SI 319: 734.

39. *Catalogue of the Architectural Exhibition, Boston Architectural Club and Boston Society of Architects*, Boston, 1899.

40. Ibid., entries 301 and 302.

41. The sculpture was from residences in Troy, N.Y., the Scripps mortuary chapel in Detroit, and the National Church of the Holy City in Washington, D.C. Evans is identified as the carver in "Report of the National Committee on House of Worship in Washington City, D.C.," May 5, 1896, filed at the Swedenborgian School of Religion Archives, Newton, Mass., box 66.753/W1.02, folder labeled "Washington, D.C., Society—1909."

42. *Catalogue of the Architectural Exhibition, Boston Architectural Club*, Boston, 1902. Cairns is listed for entries 39 ("Study for Pediment, State House,

Boston; Charles Brigham, architect") and 303 ("Six Models for stone carving, Theological Church, Cambridge, Mass.; Warren, Smith, & Biscoe, Architects").

43. Spain, *The Society of Arts and Crafts*, p. 15.

44. Ibid., p. 16.

45. *Handicraft*, vol. 1, no. 3 (June 1902), ii.

46. H. Langford Warren, "The Qualities of Carving," *Handicraft*, vol. 1, no. 9 (Dec. 1902), pp. 193–224.

47. H. Langford Warren, "Our Work and Prospects," *Handicraft*, vol. 2, no. 9 (Jan. 1903), p. 185.

48. Ibid., p. 186.

49. Ibid., p. 187.

50. Elenita C. Chickering, *Arthur J. Stone*, Boston: Boston Athenaeum, 1981, p. 7, n. 15.

51. "A Loving Cup Given to President Eliot, of Harvard University," *Handicraft*, vol. 2, no. 12 (Mar. 1904), pp. 258–260.

52. The cup was exhibited in the 1907 exhibition of the Society of Arts and Crafts as "designed by H. Langford Warren, executed by Arthur J. Stone, Gardner," SACB Archives, AAA/SI 320: 81.

53. Letter from Warren to Frederic Allen Whiting, Sept. 3, 1903, SACB Archives, AAA/SI 300: 388–392. The Sept. 3, 1903, visit by the Warrens to Chipping Campden also is noted in the visitors' book for the Guild of Handicraft, collection of the Guild of Handicraft Trust, Chipping Campden. See W. Scott Braznell, "The Influence of C. R. Ashbee in His Guild of Handicraft on American Silver, Other Metalwork, and Jewelry," in *The Substance of Style: Perspectives on the American Arts and Crafts Movement*, Bert Denker, ed., Winterthur, Del.: Henry Francis du Pont Winterthur Museum, 1996, p. 32, n. 9.

54. Beverly K. Brandt, " 'All Workmen, Artists, and Lovers of Art': The Organizational Structure of the Society of Arts and Crafts, Boston," p. 40, and Jeannine Falino, "Circles of Influence: Metalsmithing in New England," pp. 74–75, in Meyer, *Inspiring Reform*.

55. Letter from Warren to Whiting, Sept. 3, 1903, SACB Archives, AAA/SI 300: 391.

56. Spain, *The Society of Arts and Crafts*, p. 17.

57. Letter from Warren to Arthur Astor Carey, Nov. 12, 1903, SACB Archives, AAA/SI 300: 416–417.

58. Letter from Warren to Mary Ware Dennett, Nov. 12, 1903, SACB Archives, AAA/SI 300: 418.

59. Spain, *The Society of Arts and Crafts*, p. 17.

60. Letter from Carey to Warren, no date, SACB Archives, AAA/SI 300: 419.

61. Arthur Astor Carey, *Nervous Prostration and Its Spiritual Cause*, Boston: n.p., 1904. He also published *New Nerves for Old*, Boston: n.p., 1914, and *The Scout Law in Practice*, Boston: n.p., 1915.

62. For more on Dennett, see Constance M. Chen, *"The Sex Side of Life":
Mary Ware Dennett's Pioneering Battle for Birth Control and Sex Education*, New
York: New Press, 1996. In 1912, divorced from her husband, she moved to New
York City, where she became a leading activist on behalf of women's rights and
birth control.

63. Letter from Whiting to Warren, Apr. 2, 1904, SACB Archives, AAA/SI
300: 423.

64. Spain, *The Society of Arts and Crafts*, p. 19.

65. Letter from Ashbee to Whiting, July 22, 1904, SACB Archives, AAA/SI
300: 427; letter from Ashbee to Whiting, Dec. 2, 1904, SACB Archives, AAA/SI
300: 441.

66. Louisiana Purchase Exposition—Department of Art Papers, Archives of
American Art/Smithsonian Institution, reel 1734: frame 285 (hereafter cited as
Louisiana Purchase papers, AAA/SI reel: frame).

67. Untitled typescript, Louisiana Purchase papers, AAA/SI 1734: 626. Apparently written by Ives, the announcement states that the Department of Art was
planning a broader display than those established by former international expositions. This display would make "no distinction between what has been commonly considered as 'fine art' and that which has been termed 'industrial art.' "

68. In a letter from Ives to Robert D. Andrews, May 16, 1903, Ives noted that
Warren had agreed to serve on the Advisory Committee, Louisiana Purchase
papers, AAA/SI 1734: 921.

69. For advisers to the New York Committee on the Applied Arts, see Louisiana Purchase papers, AAA/SI 1753: 485. Other architects who advised the New
York Committee included H. J. Hardenberg, John Galen Howard, and George
B. Post. See *Universal Exposition of 1904: The Division of Exhibits*, St. Louis:
n.p., 1904, p. 11.

70. For the committee members, see typed list, Louisiana Purchase papers,
AAA/SI 1734: 860.

71. *Universal Exposition of 1904: The Division of Exhibits*, p. 11. Architecture
was Group XII.

72. *Universal Exposition, St. Louis, 1904: Illustrations of Selected Works in the
Various National Sections of the Department of Art*, St. Louis: Louisiana Purchase
Exposition Company, 1904, p. xxxi and p. xxxv.

73. Spain, *The Society of Arts and Crafts*, pp. 17–18.

74. *Universal Exposition, St. Louis, 1904: Illustrations*, p. xxxv.

75. Halsey C. Ives, "Art," in *Universal Exposition of 1904: The Division of
Exhibits*, p. 9.

76. "Foreword, Department B., Art," *Official Catalogue of Exhibitors. Universal Exposition. St. Louis, USA, 1904*, rev. ed., St. Louis: Official Catalogue
Company, 1904, p. 17.

77. Beverly K. Brandt, " 'Worthy and Carefully Selected': American Arts and

Crafts at the Louisiana Purchase Exposition, 1904," *Archives of American Art Journal*, vol. 28, no. 1 (1988), pp. 2–16. Brandt writes, n. 62, that aside from Native American craftsmen, who were admitted by special invitation, of 172 craftsmen remaining, 80 were members of the Society of Arts and Crafts, Boston.

78. *Official Catalogue of Exhibitors*, under "United States—Applied Arts. Group 14. Original Objects of Art Workmanship," p. 75.

79. Letter from Warren to Ives, June 19, 1904, Louisiana Purchase papers, AAA/SI 1741: 918–919.

80. Spain, *The Society of Arts and Crafts*, p. 21.

81. "Records of the Committee on Exhibitions, Feb. 14, 1906," SACB Archives, AAA/SI 316: 55.

82. *Exhibition of the Society of Arts and Crafts Together with a Loan Collection of Applied Art*, Copley and Allston Halls, Boston, Feb. 5–26, 1907, SACB Archives, AAA/SI 320: 49.

83. Ibid., SACB Archives, AAA/SI 320: 79 and 81. The cup is illustrated in *Handicraft*, vol. 2, no. 12 (Mar. 1904), p. 259.

84. *Exhibition of the Society of Arts and Crafts*, SACB Archives, AAA/SI 320: 84–88.

85. Ibid., SACB Archives, AAA/SI 320: 85.

86. Ibid., SACB Archives, AAA/SI 320: 106.

87. Ibid.

88. Ibid., SACB Archives, AAA/SI 320: 112 ff.

89. On the influence of Japanese woodblock prints on Dow and other New England printmakers, see David Acton, "The Flourish of Color Relief Printmaking in New England," in Meyer, *Inspiring Reform*, pp. 152–162. Cram's firm designed the Japanese Garden Court for the Museum of Fine Arts in Boston in 1909. See Douglass Shand-Tucci, *Built in Boston: City and Suburb, 1800–1950*, Amherst, Mass.: University of Massachusetts Press, 1979 (reprint 1988), pp. 164–165.

90. See Montgomery, "The Potter's Art in Boston."

91. SACB Archives, AAA/SI 316: 579. Others elected were Arthur W. Dow, first vice president; Mrs. Madeline Yale Wynne, second vice president; Frederic Allen Whiting, secretary and treasurer; and Elizabeth Pitfield, Helen Plumb, and Henry C. Mercer on the executive committee.

92. See also Spain, *The Society of Arts and Crafts*, pp. 22–23.

93. *The Society of Arts and Crafts Thirteenth Annual Report*, Boston, 1910, p. 2, SACB Archives, AAA/SI 318: 681.

94. *The Annual Report of the Society of Arts and Crafts*, Boston, 1912, p. 6, SACB Archives, AAA/SI 318: 763.

95. *The Annual Report of the Society of Arts and Crafts, Boston, Massachusetts, for the Year 1916*, Boston, 1917, p. 5, SACB Archives, AAA/SI 319: 002.

96. Spain, *The Society of Arts and Crafts*, pp. 25–26.

97. "List of Books in the Library of the Society," published in *The Annual Report of the Society of Arts and Crafts, Boston, Massachusetts, for the Year 1917*, Boston, 1918, pp. 20–23, SACB Archives, AAA/SI 319: 34–35.

98. The collection included *Art and Its Producers, The Arts and Crafts of Today*, and *Hopes and Fears for Art*, all by Morris; *The Bases of Design* and *Line and Form* by Walter Crane; *Stained Glass Work* by C. W. Whall; *Woodcarving, Design and Workmanship* by George Jack; *Composition, Part I* by Arthur W. Dow; and *A Theory of Pure Design* by Denman W. Ross.

99. "Notable Wood Carving. Mr. Kirchmayer's 'Coronation of the Virgin' at the Arts and Crafts Gallery," *Boston Transcript*, Jan. 16, 1913, SACB Archives, AAA/SI 322: 314.

100. Feb. 13, 1913, Council minutes, SACB Archives, AAA/SI 316: 129; and Oct. 23, 1913, Council minutes, SACB Archives, AAA/SI 316: 135.

101. These thoughts were expressed by Warren in a speech at a Society of Arts and Crafts dinner, Apr. 23, 1912, SACB Archives, AAA/SI 300: 706–707.

102. When the Society was approached by the publisher of *House Beautiful* in October of 1914, Warren appointed a committee to study the possibility of running a regular page. He served on it along with the salesroom manager, Henry P. Macomber, and Frederick P. Cabot, Alexander W. Longfellow, and F. S. Kershaw. See Council minutes in SACB Archives, AAA/SI 316: 147, and *The Annual Report of the Society of Arts and Crafts, Boston, Massachusetts, for the Year 1914*, Boston, 1915, p. 6, SACB Archives, AAA/SI 318: 866.

103. On the 1916 exhibition, see *The Annual Report of the Society of Arts and Crafts, Boston, Massachusetts, for the Year 1916*, Boston, 1917, p. 12, SACB Archives, AAA/SI 319: 006 and AAA/SI 320: 132. On the 1917 exhibition, see newspaper clippings in SACB Archives, AAA/SI 322: 341–341 and 352.

104. See "The Fine Arts. The Joint Exhibition. Retrospective Room of Boston Society of Architects a Feature—Architecture and the Allied Arts," *Boston Transcript*, Nov. 6, 1917, SACB Archives, AAA/SI 322: 352. The exhibit included a model of the Norfolk County Tuberculosis Hospital (Olympus Specialty Hospital), Braintree, Mass., and a general view and details of Jordan Hospital, Plymouth, Mass.

105. See "The Fine Arts: Arts and Crafts Activities," *Boston Transcript*, Sept. 29, 1917, SACB Archives, AAA/SI 322: 352.

106. Letter from Ashbee to Whiting, Apr. 2, 1910, SACB Archives, AAA/SI 300: 628.

Chapter 5. An Architectural Practice (pp. 102–149)

1. For studies of these architects and their work, see William Morgan, *The Almighty Wall: The Architecture of Henry Vaughan*, New York and Cambridge, Mass.: Architectural History Foundation and MIT Press, 1983; Douglass Shand-

Tucci, *Boston Bohemia, 1881–1900. Ralph Adams Cram: Life and Architecture*, Amherst, Mass.: University of Massachusetts Press, 1995; Shand-Tucci, *Built in Boston: City and Suburb, 1800–1950*, Amherst, Mass.: University of Massachusetts Press, 1978 (reprint 1988); and Margaret Henderson Floyd, *Architecture after Richardson: Regionalism before Modernism—Longfellow, Alden, and Harlow in Boston and Pittsburgh*, Chicago and London: University of Chicago Press in association with the Pittsburgh History and Landmarks Foundation, 1994.

2. Walter C. Kidney, *The Architecture of Choice: Eclecticism in America, 1880–1930*, New York: Braziller, 1974; Richard W. Longstreth, "Academic Eclecticism in American Architecture," *Winterthur Portfolio*, vol. 17 (spring 1982), pp. 55–82.

3. Richard Guy Wilson has written about the role of the period's revival architecture and its relationship to Arts and Crafts ideology, recognizing the diversity and inconsistencies of the work associated with the movement. See Wilson, "American Arts and Crafts Architecture: Radical though Dedicated to the Cause Conservative," in *"The Art That Is Life": The Arts and Crafts Movement in America, 1875–1920,* ed. Wendy Kaplan, Boston: Bulfinch Press, 1998 (reprint of Museum of Fine Arts exhibition catalogue, 1987), pp. 100–131.

4. See Peter Davey, *Arts and Crafts Architecture*, London: Phaidon, 1995.

5. Both Warren and Bacon identify themselves as members of this firm in the 1894 Boston directory. In the 1895 directory, they no longer list themselves as members of the firm.

6. See carbon copy of "Data for Who's Who in Architecture, 1925," prepared by F. Patterson Smith, in which he reports that he began working for Warren in 1896. The form is in the collection of Richard Smith Joslin of Cambridge, Mass. The 1896 Boston directory also records that Smith was working at 9 Park Street.

7. The partnership of Smith and Biscoe is recorded in the 1899 Boston directory.

8. The partnership of Warren, Smith, and Biscoe was announced in the *American Architect and Building News*, vol. 68, no. 1274 (May 26, 1900), p. x, under "Architects' Removals, Etc." It also was listed in entries for Smith and Warren in the 1900 Boston directory. Their new offices were located at 110 Boylston Street, and from 1902 through 1904, they worked at 120 Boylston Street.

9. The move is recorded in the 1905 Boston directory.

10. Biscoe's departure for Denver is noted in the 1906 Boston directory.

11. My understanding of Smith's character and knowledge about his family comes from his grandson, Richard Smith Joslin of Cambridge, Mass.

12. Longfellow's model tenement block was designed in 1889 and built on Harrison Avenue in Boston. See Floyd, *Architecture after Richardson*, p. 377. See also Amy Elizabeth Johnson, "The Boston Cooperative Building Company: Tenement House Reform in Boston, 1871–1914," M.A. thesis, Tufts University, 1998. On Norton's activities, see Cynthia R. Zaitzevsky, "Housing Boston's Poor: The

First Philanthropic Experiments," *Journal of the Society of Architectural Historians,* vol. 42, no. 2 (May 1983), pp. 157–167.

13. Ralph Adams Cram, *English Country Churches: One Hundred Views Selected by Ralph Adams Cram, Architect,* Boston: Bates & Guild, 1898; C. Howard Walker, *Parish Churches of England,* Boston: Rogers and Manson, 1915.

14. Two other important churches produced by Warren's firm were the chapel for the Troy Orphan Asylum, 1900–1902, and the Episcopalian Church of the Epiphany in Winchester, Mass., begun in 1904. From the beginning, a chapel was planned for the Troy Orphan Asylum, as shown in the plan and rendering published in the *American Architect and Building News,* vol. 32, no. 798 (Apr. 11, 1891). A revised plan for the chapel was published in the *American Architect,* vol. 69, no. 1285 (Aug. 11, 1900), along with an elevation, section, perspective drawing, and details. See also the *American Architect,* vol. 78, no. 1409 (Dec. 27, 1902). On the Church of the Epiphany, see the *American Architect,* vol. 86, no. 1509 (Nov. 26, 1904); *Brickbuilder,* vol. 14, no. 11 (Nov. 1905); *Architectural Review,* vol. 12, no. 10 (Oct. 1905), pp. 284–285; and *Church Militant,* vol. 8 (Nov. 1905), pp. 6, 7, and 13.

Other church designs produced by Warren and his firms include Cliftondale, Mass., Congregational Church, 1892, published in the *Boston Real Estate Record and Building News,* Feb. 25, 1893; Craigsville, Va., Presbyterian Church, 1902, published in the *American Architect and Building News,* vol. 78, no. 1407 (Dec. 13, 1902); competition design for the Foundry Methodist Episcopal Church, Washington, D.C., 1902, published in the *Brickbuilder,* vol. 12, no. 1 (Jan. 1903); Glens Falls, N.Y., Methodist Episcopal Church, 1907–1908; and Church of the Advent (Episcopalian) chancel, Cincinnati, 1908.

15. Morgan, *The Almighty Wall,* pp. 88–100.

16. Shand-Tucci, *Boston Bohemia,* pp. 111–112, and p. 477, n. 49. The illustration ran in the *American Architect,* vol. 31, no. 785 (Jan. 10, 1891).

17. Shand-Tucci, *Boston Bohemia,* pp. 131–132.

18. The history and architecture of the building are described in Sue A. Kohler and Jeffrey R. Carson, *Sixteenth Street Architecture,* vol. 1, Washington, D.C.: Commission of Fine Arts, 1978, pp. 194–231. When I visited the Church of the Holy City in July of 1998, the Reverend Jonathan Mitchell, newly appointed as minister, was not able to locate many of the sources cited in this entry. I am therefore relying to some extent on the *Sixteenth Street* entry for its documentation of the church's archival material. The papers that I did examine were randomly stored, and many of the records have been damaged by heat.

19. Ibid., p. 205, and illustrated on p. 206.

20. Ibid., p. 197.

21. One of the members of the building committee was Warren's uncle, E. Burgess Warren of Lake George, N.Y., ibid., p. 231.

22. Ibid., p. 200. Articles and sketches of the church appeared in the *Wash-*

ington Evening Star, Dec. 8, 1894, and May 2, 1896; and the *Washington Post,* May 3, 1896.

23. See C. Howard Walker, typed lecture notes for "History of Architecture" by H. Langford Warren, Special Collections, Loeb Library, Harvard University, Rare NA200.W252, vol. 2, pp. 177–178. See also Kenneth John Conant, "Notes Taken in Fine Arts 4a," 1914–1915, p. 97, Harvard University Archives, HUC 8914.328.4, box 846.

24. Illustrated in Kohler and Carson, *Sixteenth Street,* p. 198. The Reverend Mitchell located this elevation for me; it has suffered from water damage since it was photographed for the authors of *Sixteenth Street.*

25. An illustration of the Epiphany Church as designed with a tower carrying a spire was published in the *American Architect and Building News,* Nov. 26, 1904.

26. Kohler and Carson note that the north entrance crockets recall those at Ely Cathedral, *Sixteenth Street,* p. 208, for example.

27. The photographs showing the inscription are in the collection of Richard Smith Joslin of Cambridge, Mass. The inscription was already painted over and not evident in the photographs of the interior of the church published in Kohler and Carson, *Sixteenth Street.*

28. Payment to Evans & Co. is noted in the "Report of the National Committee on House of Worship in Washington City, D.C., May 5, 1896," Swedenborgian School of Religion Archives, Newton, Mass., box 66.753, W1.02, "Washington, D.C., Society—1909," p. 21.

29. May R. Spain, *The Society of Arts and Crafts, 1897–1924,* Boston and New York: Society of Arts and Crafts, 1924, p. 10 (available on microfilm, SACB Archives, AAA/SI 319: 492–510).

30. The windows are described and attributions provided in *The Stained Glass Windows of the Church of the Holy City, Swedenborgian National Church,* an undated pamphlet prepared by the church. It was shown to me by Lance Kasparian of Salem, Mass. Windows by Ford and Brooks are located in the chancel and were installed over a number of years, between 1895 and 1912; Ford and Brooks also produced a tripartite window in the north transept, from 1895. Kasparian notes that in 1895, a Ford and Brooks window also was installed at Memorial Hall on the Harvard University campus. In the south wall of the church nave, a window by Donald MacDonald was installed in 1895. MacDonald designed and made many of the windows at Memorial Hall.

Membership in, and exhibition with, the Society of Arts and Crafts is documented for these artisans in Karen Evans Ulehla, ed., *The Society of Arts and Crafts, Boston, Exhibition Record, 1897–1927,* Boston: Boston Public Library, 1981.

31. Payment to L. Haberstroh and Son is noted in the "Report of the National Committee" from 1896. On the firm's association with the Society of Arts and Crafts, see Ulehla, *The Society of Arts and Crafts.*

32. See Sally Zimmerman, "Church of the New Jerusalem/Swedenborgian Chapel," Landmark Designation Study Report for the Cambridge, Mass., Historical Commission, Feb. 4, 1999. Later that year, the city of Cambridge granted landmark status to the church.

33. *Catalogue of the Architectural Exhibition, Boston Architectural Club and Boston Society of Architects,* Boston, 1899, nos. 299 and 300; "Exhibition of the Boston Architectural Club," *American Architect and Building News,* vol. 64, no. 1224 (June 10, 1899), p. 83; *American Architect,* vol. 65, no. 1231 (July 29, 1899); *Architectural Review,* vol. 8, no. 3 (Mar. 1901), plates 17 and 18; *Catalogue of the Architectural Exhibition, Boston Architectural Club,* Boston, 1902, nos. 327 and 328; *Official Catalogue of Exhibitors. Universal Exposition. St. Louis, U.S.A., 1904,* rev. ed., St. Louis: Official Catalogue Company, 1904, p. 69, exhibits 2581–2583; *Architectural Review,* vol. 12, no. 10 (Oct. 1905), p. 250.

34. H. Langford Warren, "The Year's Architecture," in *Catalogue of the Architectural Exhibition,* 1899, p. 18.

35. See *Catalogue of the Architectural Exhibition,* 1899, no. 298; the watercolor of the church is illustrated on p. 75.

36. "Specification for a Chapel for the New Church Theological School at Cambridge, Mass.," Warren, Smith, and Biscoe, Architects, Boston, Society for the Preservation of New England Antiquities Archives, Boston, Mass., "Architecture—Building accounts, bills, etc.," box 1, folder 16C, p. 15.

37. H. Langford Warren, "On the Use of Color in Architectural Design," *American Architect and Building News,* vol. 42, no. 931 (Oct. 28, 1893), p. 47, reprint of a paper read at the World's Congress of Architects, Chicago.

38. For the attribution of Cairns to the sculpture, see "One of the Prettiest Churches. Swedenborgian Society of Cambridge Holds First Service in Its New Chapel," *Boston Sunday Globe,* November 1901 [date is cut off], clipping filed at the Swedenborgian School of Religion Archives, Newton, Mass., box 66.74441, C1.22, "Cambridge, Ma., Society," folder titled "Cambridge Society, Constitution and Bylaws, General Historical Material." See also *Catalogue of the Architectural Exhibition,* 1902, no. 303, under Hugh Cairns, "Six Models for Stone Carving, Theological Church, Cambridge, Mass.; Warren, Smith, and Biscoe, Architects." On Cairns as a founding member of the Society of Arts and Crafts, see Spain, *The Society of Arts and Crafts,* p. 10.

39. See "Payments on Acct. of Chapel Building," a summary sheet of payments, Society for the Preservation of New England Antiquities Archives, "Architecture—Building accounts, bills, etc.," box 1, folder 16A, as well as a payment receipt from the firm of Irving and Casson in the same folder.

40. The purchase of the tiles from Mercer is not documented, but the patterns are recognizable as his.

41. Payment to Cairns for "carving angels" is recorded in "Payments on Acct. of Chapel Building" and in an architect's receipt.

42. "Payments on Acct. of Chapel Building" and an architect's receipt. The

payment sheet and another receipt also show that the source for the iron electric light fixtures was R. Hollings & Co., an established lighting firm located in Boston. Clearly an artisan was involved in crafting the fixtures, but I have not been able to identify the individual, who may have been associated with the Society of Arts and Crafts.

43. "One of the Prettiest Churches." The article reports, "The windows of cathedral glass were made from the special design of Prof. Warren and are very rare."

44. I would like to thank Lance Kasparian, who is researching the career of MacDonald, for helping me understand the significance of this glass. He wrote a memo to me about it on Oct. 25, 1999. According to Kasparian, the grisaille glass represents an entirely different approach for MacDonald and indicates the role that Warren played as designer.

45. See Walker, typed lecture notes for "History of Architecture," vol. 2, p. 85.

46. See letter from William McGeorge, Jr., to Ralph P. Barnard, July 19, 1911; letter from William McGeorge, Jr., to Ralph Barnard, Aug. 8, 1911, folder marked "Sunday School. From Job Barnard's Archives," Church of the Holy City archives.

47. Letter from Paul J. Pelz to Job Barnard, Aug. 31, 1911, folder marked "Sunday School. From Job Barnard's Archives." Pelz had worked as the supervising architect associated with Warren on the church, so he could not have been considered an impartial judge. Nonetheless, his opinion appears to have satisfied the critics on the building committee.

48. Kohler and Carson, *Sixteenth Street,* p. 205.

49. The stairhall is compared to a lady chapel in ibid., p. 209.

50. For example, see the James A. Noyes house, Cambridge, Mass., 1893–1894, in Floyd, *Architecture after Richardson,* pp. 117–119.

51. See Warren's typed tribute to McKim written for Harvard University in 1909, Harvard University Archives, UAV 322.7, subseries III, box 3. The tribute was published as "Remarks of Professor H. Langford Warren of Harvard" in Alfred Hoyt Granger's *Charles Follen McKim: A Study of His Life and Work,* Boston and New York: Houghton Mifflin, 1913, pp. 120–123.

On the Harvard Memorial Fence, see Bainbridge Bunting, *Harvard: An Architectural History,* completed and edited by Margaret Henderson Floyd, Cambridge, Mass.: Belknap Press of Harvard University Press, 1985, p. 82, and illustration 246 on p. 280.

52. H. Langford Warren, "Architecture in New England," in *Picturesque and Architectural New England,* vol. 1, Boston: D. H. Hurd, 1899, p. 20, and illustration on opposite page.

53. Ibid., pp. 43–44.

54. A line drawing, elevations, and plans of Concord, N.H., City Hall appeared in the *American Architect and Building News,* vol. 77, no. 1387 (July 26, 1902). A photograph, elevation, and plans were published in the *Brickbuilder,*

vol. 13, no. 11 (Nov. 1904), and the illustration was reproduced in *Architectural Review,* vol. 12, no. 1 (Jan. 1905).

Other municipal projects included Billerica, Mass., Town Hall, 1894, Warren and Bacon, published in the *American Architect,* vol. 45, no. 978 (Sept. 22, 1894), and vol. 53, no. 1080 (Sept. 5, 1896); Claremont, N.H., Town Hall, by Warren, published in the *American Architect,* vol. 49, no. 1023 (Aug. 3, 1895); and a design for a municipal building for New York City, Warren with Alexander S. Jenney, published in the *American Architect,* international and imperial editions, vol. 52, no. 1063 (May 9, 1896); letter from Warren crediting Jenney, *American Architect,* vol. 52, no. 1064 (May 16, 1896).

55. See the plans in the *Brickbuilder,* vol. 13, no. 11.

56. H. Langford Warren, "The Influence of France Upon American Architecture," *American Architect and Building News,* vol. 66, no. 1248 (Nov. 25, 1899), pp. 67–68, reprint of a paper read at the thirty-third annual convention of the American Institute of Architects, Pittsburgh, Nov. 14, 1899.

57. Ralph Adams Cram, *My Life in Architecture,* Boston: Little, Brown, 1936, pp. 37–38.

58. See "Sleep, Elliott, and King: Concerning Their Work in Concord City Hall and Elsewhere," *American Architect and Building News,* vol. 83, no. 1471 (Mar. 5, 1904), advertiser's trade supplement, p. i.

59. H. Langford Warren, "Recent Domestic Architecture in England," *Architectural Review,* vol. 9, no. 1 (Jan. 1904), p. 5.

60. Ibid., pp. 5–12.

61. Warren, "The Influence of France," p. 68.

62. Joy Wheeler Dow, *American Renaissance,* New York: William T. Comstock, 1904.

63. Warren, "The Year's Architecture," p. 17.

64. Warren, "Recent Domestic Architecture in England," p. 12.

65. "House of Everett D. Chadwick, Esq., Winchester, Mass." appeared in *American Architect,* vol. 105, no. 1985 (Jan. 7, 1914); it also appeared in the *Architectural Review,* new series, vol. 3, no. 2 (Feb. 1914), pp. 30–31. Plans for the house are at the archives of the Society for the Preservation of New England Antiquities, Boston.

66. For more about this house, see Maureen Meister, "Chadwick House Built of Concrete," *Winchester (Mass.) Star,* July 7, 1994, p. 4A.

67. See Linda F. Dyke, "Henry Mercer's Fonthill: An Arts & Crafts House in the 'Red House' Tradition," *Arts and Crafts Quarterly Magazine,* vol. 7, no. 2 (Aug. 1994), pp. 12–17. See also Cleota Reed, *Henry Chapman Mercer and the Moravian Pottery and Tile Works,* Philadelphia: University of Pennsylvania Press, 1987.

68. Upham's Boston house was located at 233 Bay State Road, and it has been demolished.

69. H. Langford Warren, "Architecture: Renaissance and Modern," in *The*

Fine Arts: A Course of University Lessons on Sculpture, Painting, Architecture, and Decoration, in Both Their Principles and History, ed. Edmund Buckley, Chicago: International Art Association, 1900, pp. 228–229.

70. Gardner lent objects to the Society of Arts and Crafts for exhibition, and she routinely received Harvard's fine-arts students at Fenway Court. See SACB Archives, AAA/SI 319: 752. A Harvard exam for Fine Arts 9 asks students to discuss one of Gardner's paintings. See "Final Exams for 1912–1913," Harvard University Archives, HUC 7912, box 278, p. 92.

71. In 1906, Warren's firm designed extensive additions to Richard Bond's library, Gore Hall, dating from 1838. A rendering of the enlarged library as well as a photograph of it are in the collection of Richard Smith Joslin, Cambridge, Mass. Photographs of it are preserved at the Harvard University Archives, HUV 48. In 1912, Warren and Smith were responsible for interior renovations to the old Fogg Museum, designed by Richard Morris Hunt in 1893. Photographs of interiors of the old Fogg building, presumably taken for Warren after the completion of the work, are in the Joslin collection.

72. The Knapp buildings are discussed and illustrated in Shand-Tucci, *Boston Bohemia*, pp. 403–410. Cram traveled to Japan in 1898 after working on the Knapp house. See also Ralph Adams Cram, *Impressions of Japanese Architecture and the Allied Arts,* New York: Baker and Taylor, 1905.

73. See Floyd, *Architecture after Richardson*, pp. 120–121, 361–371.

74. Ibid., pp. 120–121.

75. I would like to thank William Floyd for sharing with me the photographs that he and his late wife Margaret took of the demolished Carey Cage. Because of their efforts, the brackets were saved and taken to Richardson's Robert Treat Paine house in Waltham, Mass.

76. See Bunting, *Harvard*, p. 116, which says the lodge was built of the same concrete and brick combination. I have not found any further confirmation in the Harvard archives, but Bunting is probably reliable, as the lodge lasted into the early 1960s.

77. Ira N. Hollis, "Origin of the Harvard Stadium," *Harvard Engineering Journal*, vol. 3, no. 2 (June 1904), p. 100.

78. H. Langford Warren, "Ancient Stadia and Circuses," *Harvard Engineering Journal*, vol. 3, no. 2 (June 1904), pp. 145–152.

79. See Heather Makechnie, "History of Proctor Academy," *Proctor Alumni Directory*, White Plains, N.Y.: Bernard C. Harris, 1988, p. vii.

80. Cary House burned in April of 1977.

81. The best documentation of the firm's work for the campus is the *Proctor Academy Catalogue,* 1909–1910, preserved in the Proctor Academy admissions office. Photographs of the buildings, taken for Warren and Smith, are in the collection of Richard Smith Joslin, Cambridge, Mass.

82. The early campus plan is published in *Proctor Academy Bulletin*, vol. 2 (Apr. 1918).

83. For example, see Mary H. Northend, *Remodeled Farmhouses*, Boston: Little, Brown, 1915.

84. Both the campus plan and photographs of Flowers Hall taken for Warren and Smith are in the collection of Richard Smith Joslin, Cambridge, Mass.

85. The plans and elevations for this work are still owned by the Winchester Country Club. The date for this project, while not appearing on the plans, is derived from a letter to club members, dated Jan. 18, 1916, and signed by the board of directors and club president John Abbott. He describes the renovation work that is about to begin on the barn, mentioning the new assembly room and locker rooms.

86. Henry Smith Chapman, *History of Winchester, Massachusetts*, vol. 1, Winchester, Mass.: Town of Winchester, 1975 (originally published 1936), pp. 342–343.

87. Cruft Laboratory is mentioned but not analyzed in Bunting's *Harvard*, and no architects are attributed to it. The files on the building at the Harvard archives also reveal a lack of interest by recent scholars.

88. The master plan is discussed in Bunting, *Harvard*, p. 151.

89. At the Harvard archives, I consulted correspondence filed under UAV.246.238 and under UAV.299.7.

90. Guido Goldman, *A History of the Germanic Museum at Harvard University*, Cambridge, Mass.: Minda de Gunzburg Center for European Studies, Harvard University, 1989. This book, while a valuable history of the building, unfortunately has no footnotes. For basic sources on this building, see Bunting, *Harvard*, pp. 306–307, nn. 20–22.

91. "Germanic Museum Begun," *Boston Transcript*, June 8, 1912, Harvard University Archives, HUB.1421.2.

92. Francke published Warren's design in 1908 in a *Handbook of the Germanic Museum*, noted in Goldman, *A History of the Germanic Museum*, p. 24.

93. Goldman, *A History of the Germanic Museum*, p. 26.

94. Bestelmeyer's conceptual drawings are preserved in the Harvard University Archives, UAI.15.25 pf.

95. Goldman, *A History of the Germanic Museum*, p. 34.

96. Ibid., p. 35.

97. "Scaffolding Comes Down and Discloses a Thoroughly German Building," *Boston Sunday Herald*, Sept. 17, 1916, Harvard University Archives, HUB.1421.2.

98. "The Fine Arts. Arts and Crafts Activities," *Boston Transcript*, Sept. 29, 1917, in SACB Archives, AAA/SI 322: 352.

99. See letters written by Arthur Shurtleff, Frederick Law Olmsted, Jr., and Warren, Harvard University Archives, UAV.322.7, subseries III, box 3.

100. Ibid., letter from Warren to Sturgis, June 28, 1915.

101. Untitled lead editorial, *Architectural Review*, vol. 3, no. 7 (Oct. 1915), p. 89.

Chapter 6. Final Years (pp. 150–157)

1. Warren was secretary of the Boston Society of Architects between 1891 and 1895 and director of the American Institute of Architects between 1893 and 1896. See "Recent Deaths. Professor H. Langford Warren," *Boston Transcript*, June 27, 1917; and [James Sturgis Pray], "Faculty of Architecture. Minute on the Life and Services of Dean Herbert Langford Warren," *Harvard University Gazette*, Dec. 1, 1917, pp. 45–46, Harvard University Archives, HUG 1875.80. He participated in several American Institute of Architects committees and was chairman of its Committee on Education. As chairman, he wrote the "Report of the Committee on Education of the American Institute of Architects," *American Architect and Building News*, vol. 66, no. 1250 (Dec. 9, 1899), pp. 84–85; and "Report of the Committee on Education, AIA," *American Architect*, vol. 87, no. 1520 (Feb. 11, 1905), pp. 47–49. Warren was a trustee of the American Academy in Rome and a member of the Archaeological Institute of America. See [Pray], "Minute on the Life," p. 46.

2. Letters from Herbert Langford Warren to Harold Broadfield Warren dated Aug. 1, 1914, and Aug. 17, 1914, owned by Elizabeth Warren Stoutamire of Tallahassee, Fla.

3. Ibid.

4. See Morton Prince, "Herbert Langford Warren," obituary, *Journal of the American Institute of Architects*, vol. 5, no. 7 (July 1917), pp. 353–355. See also Prince's letter to the editor, " 'A Patriot Through and Through,' " *Boston Transcript*, June 30, 1917.

5. H. Langford Warren, "The English Tradition," letter to the *Nation*, vol. 100, no. 2600 (Apr. 29, 1916), pp. 468–469.

6. See the *Atlantic Monthly*, vol. 118 (July 1916). His views are discussed in John H. Thompson, *Reformers and War: American Progressive Publicists and the First World War*, Cambridge: Cambridge University Press, 1987, p. 166.

7. Charles W. Eliot, "Prepare to Enter the War, Dr. Eliot's Message," *New York Times*, Mar. 12, 1916. "Civilization" was a key word in both France and Britain, writes Hew Strachan in *The First World War*, vol. 1, *To Arms*, Oxford: Oxford University Press, 2001, p. 1125.

8. "Demand U.S. Aid Allies' Cause," *Boston Globe*, Jan. 31, 1916; "Brand of Cain on Germany for *Lusitania*—Prof. Josiah Royce," *Boston Herald*, Jan. 31, 1916; "Demands We Back Allies," *New York Times*, Jan. 31, 1916. Josiah Royce, of Harvard's philosophy department, was identified as the meeting's most stirring speaker. Also see Prince's obituary, "Herbert Langford Warren," p. 354.

9. Prince, "Herbert Langford Warren." See also "Hope Only for Teuton Defeat. Voiced in Address to Allied Peoples," *Boston Globe*, Apr. 17, 1916; "500 Americans Assure Allies of Sympathy," *Boston Herald*, Apr. 17, 1916; "500 Americans Send 'Address' to Allies," *New York Times*, Apr. 17, 1916.

10. "The French Reply to the American Address," *New York Times*, Aug. 17, 1916.

11. Charles Franklin Thwing, *The American Colleges and Universities in the Great War, 1914–1919: A History*, New York: Macmillan, 1920, pp. 14–18. Thwing was among the signers of the "Address of the Five Hundred."

12. "Eliot Says We Must Help Allies Win War," *New York Times*, June 23, 1916.

13. Charles W. Eliot, "American Ideals and the Issues of the War," *New York Times*, July 27, 1916.

14. Letter from Herbert Langford Warren to Harold Broadfield Warren, dated Sept. 13, 1916, owned by Elizabeth Warren Stoutamire of Tallahassee, Fla.

15. Advertisement, *New York Times*, Feb. 12, 1917.

16. For a discussion of the broader context of American intellectuals of this period, see David M. Kennedy's chapter, "The War for the American Mind," in *Over Here: The First World War and American Society*, New York: Oxford University Press, 1980, pp. 45–92.

17. [Pray], "Minute on the Life."

18. Ralph Adams Cram, letter to the editor, "Masters in Architecture—Langford Warren, Henry Vaughan," *Boston Evening Transcript*, July 2, 1917.

19. Guido Goldman, *A History of the Germanic Museum at Harvard University*, Cambridge, Mass.: Minda de Gunzburg Center for European Studies, Harvard University, 1989, pp. 42–43.

20. Winifred B. Warren, "My Father and My Mother," written after 1969, unpublished manuscript, original copy owned by her niece, Elizabeth Warren Stoutamire of Tallahassee, Fla.

21. "Recent Deaths. Professor H. Langford Warren." The cause of his death is given by Kenneth J. Conant in *Dictionary of American Biography*, vol. 11, supplement 1, New York: Charles Scribner's Sons, 1944, s.v. "Herbert Langford Warren." Tributes by Pray and others noted that Warren was a fellow of the American Institute of Architects and of the American Academy of Arts and Sciences. In 1902 Harvard awarded him an honorary degree of Master of Arts.

22. R. Clipston Sturgis, "Herbert Langford Warren," obituary, *Journal of the American Institute of Architects*, vol. 5, no. 7 (July 1917), p. 353.

23. Prince, "Herbert Langford Warren."

24. [Pray], "Minute on the Life," p. 46.

25. Goldman, *A History of the Germanic Museum*, p. 44.

26. Fiske Kimball, introduction to H. Langford Warren, *The Foundations of Classic Architecture*, New York: Macmillan, 1919, p. xiv.

27. See George H. Edgell, "The Schools of Architecture and Landscape Architecture," in Samuel Eliot Morison, *The Development of Harvard University Since the Inauguration of President Eliot, 1869–1929*, Cambridge, Mass.: Harvard University Press, 1930, pp. 443–450.

28. Warren, *Foundations of Classic Architecture*. Also published after Warren's death was Morris Hicky Morgan's translation of *Vitruvius: The Ten Books of Architecture*, Cambridge, Mass.: Harvard University Press, 1926. Its illustrations and designs were prepared under Warren's direction.

29. "Boston Godparents of Bell," *Boston Transcript*, Oct. 27, 1923. Cram was designated a "godparent" at the bell's christening, along with Francesca Copley Greene, whose father Henry Copley Greene had made arrangements for the bell the previous summer. See also "Church Bell as Memorial," *Boston Transcript*, July 29, 1922.

30. Edward R. Bosley, *Greene and Greene*, London: Phaidon Press, 2000, pp. 18–19. See also Barbara Ann Francis, "The Boston Roots of Greene and Greene," M.A. thesis, Tufts University, 1987, pp. 30–36.

31. Biscoe's buildings and projects include the Municipal Center, Denver, published in the *Architectural Record*, vol. 19, no. 5 (May 1906); Denver Public Library, published in the *Western Architect*, vol. 20, no. 5 (May 1914); and Memorial Stadium, Colorado Springs, published in the *American Architect*, vol. 108, no. 2080 (Nov. 3, 1915).

32. See the commercial and apartment block in Waban, Mass., published in the *American Architect and Building News*, vol. 54, no. 1088 (Oct. 31, 1896); "Baker Street Primary School-House, West Roxbury, Mass.," published in the *American Architect and Building News*, vol. 63, no. 1209 (Feb. 25, 1899).

33. On Smith and Little, see Edward S. Cooke, Jr., "Talking or Working: The Conundrum of Moral Aesthetics in Boston's Arts and Crafts Movement," in Marilee Boyd Meyer, consulting curator, *Inspiring Reform: Boston's Arts and Crafts Movement*, Wellesley, Mass.: Davis Museum and Cultural Center, Wellesley College, 1997, p. 25. Cooke notes that these men became noted regionalist designers. On Shaw, see "Thomas Shaw of Concord, Prominent Architect, 86," *Boston Herald*, Feb. 19, 1965, and Harvard University Archives, UAIII15.75.10. His firm was Perry, Shaw, Hepburn, and Dean. Shaw was recognized for his design work at Brown University, including Wriston Quadrangle.

34. Conant, *Dictionary of American Biography*, s.v. "Herbert Langford Warren," p. 699.

35. Kenneth John Conant, *Carolingian and Romanesque Architecture, 800–1200*, Hammondsworth, England: Penguin Books, 2d ed., 1966 (1st ed. 1959), p. 11. Conant added that his greatest debt was to Arthur Kingsley Porter.

36. Fiske Kimball and George H. Edgell, *A History of Architecture*, New York and London: Harper, 1918.

37. Cram, "Masters in Architecture."

Index